BLOOD ON THE ALTAR

Confessions

of a

Jehovah's

Witness

Minister

DAVID A. REED

PB **Prometheus Books**

59 John Glenn Drive
Amherst, New York 14228-2197

Published 1996 by Prometheus Books

00 99 98 97 96   5 4 3 2 1

Library of Congress Cataloging-in-Publication Data

Reed, David A.
    Blood on the altar : confessions of a Jehova's Witness minister / David
A. Reed.
        p.   cm.
    Includes bibliographical references and index.
    ISBN 1–57392–059–2 (alk. paper)
    1. Jehovah's Witness—Controversial literature. 2. Blood—Transfusion—Religious aspects—Jehova's Witness—Controversial literature.
3. Reed, David A. I. Title.
BX8526.5.R373   1996

289.9'2—dc20   95–13435
                                                                                CIP

Printed in the United States of America on acid-free paper

Contents

Preface and Acknowledgments

"They built high places for Baal in the Valley of Ben Hinnom to sacrifice their sons and daughters . . . though I never commanded, nor did it enter my mind, that they should do such a detestable thing. . . ."
Jeremiah 32:35 New International Version

Child sacrifice was never God's idea, the prophet Jeremiah quoted the Almighty as saying. He never commanded it, nor did it even enter his mind for worshipers to do such a horrible thing. Yet the ugly practice arose among professedly religious people in Old Testament times. Self-appointed spokesmen for the Deity commanded that a child be consigned to the flames, and faithful followers obeyed.

How far we have come in the twenty-five centuries since Jeremiah's day!

Or have we? It was the late 1970s when Rev. Jim Jones told some nine hundred People's Temple followers in Jonestown, Guyana, that it was time to die by drinking a cyanide-laced soft drink, and they obediently killed their children before ingesting the poisoned beverage themselves. Those bloated bodies spread out under the tropical sun drew TV cameras just as they drew flies. Reporters at the scene wore masks but still complained of the stench. Night after night the evening news ruined our suppers with the sight of whole families, face down on the ground with arms over each other's shoulders, lying where they had fallen after drinking from the deadly communion cup. It was the early 1990s when David Koresh ordered his Branch Davidians to remain in-

7

side Waco's Ranch Apocalypse as it burned to the ground, and they obediently sacrificed their children's lives along with their own.

My own story is a confession of complicity in another cult's conspiracy to commit child sacrifice—a burden that haunts my mind to this day. We caused the deaths of more children (and more adults, too) than Waco and Jonestown combined, but we never made the same headlines. Our victims died quietly, one at a time.

Like millions of other Americans, I watched as Waco burned. But, unlike most others, I knew why the cultists remained inside with their children. I had been in similar circumstances myself.

"There are men, women, and children in there!" voices on the TV exclaimed in anguish. "Why don't they come out? Why don't they send their kids out? How can they watch their children die?"

I *knew* why. More than that—I *understood* why they didn't come out. I sympathized with them. I knew how they felt. There was a time when I had felt like that, a time when I wouldn't have come out either. And there was a time when I would have watched my child die. Like the Branch Davidians, I would have thought I was doing God's will.

For years I carried in my wallet, along with my driver's license and credit cards, a "no blood" card, a miniature legal document declaring my refusal to accept a blood transfusion. All loyal Jehovah's Witnesses (which I often abbreviate as JWs) carry such a card and furnish their children with a similar ID. If I had been rendered unconscious by an automobile accident during my years as a JW, emergency medical personnel responding to the scene would have found my card and would have been warned not to give me blood, even if I were bleeding to death. Happily, as matters turned out, my thirteen years as a Witness passed without any life-threatening accidents or health problems. Some of my friends were not so fortunate.

A former school friend—I'll call him Jack—was in his forties when car trouble forced him to the side of an Ohio highway one night in 1979. Short and thin, with thick curly hair, he was a deep thinker prone to sharing riddles, puzzles, and intellectual ironies. I can picture Jack reciting some sardonic soliloquy as he bent over to open the trunk of his car, only to be cut short by a drunk driver running into him from behind. The driver must have been doing forty in the breakdown lane when his front end met Jack's rear bumper like the opposing blades of a pair of scissors, nearly snipping off my friend's legs at the knees.

"No blood!" was all that the doctors heard from Jack's mouth when conscious, from the card in his pocket, from passengers who had been with him in the car, and from family and friends streaming into the hospital. Keeping his integrity was more important than remaining alive, and Jack kept his to the death. Hundreds of Jehovah's Witnesses showed up at his funeral to show their support for the stand he had taken, faithful to the end.

Jack and others who had refused blood transfusions came to mind as I watched Waco updates on the TV in the family room of my home, where I spend most of my time writing. The upper floors of our front-to-back-split level were empty, as my wife, Penni, was off teaching school and our eleven-year-old, Kyle, was a pupil in her class. Thank God Kyle came after Penni and I left the Witnesses! I, too, could have watched one, or both, of them bleed to death. The thought wrenched my gut and brought tears to my eyes as I watched Waco burn.

Soon it became clear that the entire cult compound was engulfed in flames and that it was burning to the ground, with no mass exodus of the occupants. Voices of TV reporters began reciting numbers, trying to come up with a tentative death toll. How many children? How many women? How many men? How many people had died? It would take weeks before experts would complete the grisly task of separating charred bones and teeth to arrive at a final count of eighty-one victims.

But I already knew that the number would be small in comparison to my former brothers and sisters in the faith who had died obediently as Jehovah's Witnesses. The only reason we escaped the notoriety of the Branch Davidians was that our deaths occurred privately, one at a time, and in different locations. My friend Jack's story made the local newspaper, but most JW stories involving blood loss appear on paper only in confidential patient files, scribbled in the attending physician's cryptic script. Police officers don't file reports when hemorrhaging occurs on the operating table or results from stomach ulcers or complications of pregnancy. Published obituaries simply list "a brief illness" or "a long illness" as the cause of death.

My thoughts, as I watched Waco burn, were intensely personal: a mishmash of pain, guilt, and the relief of knowing that my family and I were now out of danger, but with this the lingering self-doubt arising from past deception that haunted me like a ghost. At the same time I felt deep concern for the millions of people who were being led on at that very moment, unaware of any similarity between Jehovah's Witnesses and the deadly scenario in Texas unfolding on their TV screens. Unlike the deaths at Waco and Jonestown, the sect I belonged to has no final published death toll; no one seems to notice, but the dying among Jehovah's Witnesses continues without letup.

Before I give the wrong impression, however, I should hasten to add that Jehovah's Witnesses are far from lifeless automatons marching zombie-style toward a precipice of death. Their story is often one of triumph, not tragedy. Witnesses in Hitler's Germany stood firmly against the Nazi regime, while most other religious groups backed down or compromised. Their zeal in spreading their faith is rarely matched. And my thirteen years among them were mostly happy years, especially those spent joined in marriage to Penni, who came to me from her Witness parents with the beauty of a Farrah Fawcett and the wisdom of a Mother Teresa. Many of my fondest memories are of friends I left behind in that organization, who taught me the meaning of courage, compassion, and dedication. I have no axe to grind; Jehovah's Witnesses treated me well, even honoring and elevating me as a public speaker, an elder, and a presiding overseer—until I began knowingly breaking the rules. I credit Jehovah's Witnesses with helping me as a young man to return to faith in God; I thank them for teaching me much of what I know about the Bible, particularly the Old Testament; and I commend them for guiding me in building a strong marriage.

The faraway reality of JWs dying for lack of blood does not intrude on the average Witness's *joie de vivre* any more than Dachau or Auschwitz spoiled the parties and nightlife of National Socialist Berlin. But how will history judge the Watchtower movement as a whole? Hopefully historians will have all the facts at their disposal, rather than the misconceptions that fill the minds of many today. Because I have seen the sect from the inside as an active member for thirteen years, and have since then had another thirteen years away from it to reflect on what I saw happening, I feel an obligation to supply some of those facts, both from personal experience and from extensive research. The story about the ongoing tragedy among Jehovah's Witnesses is a tale that must be told. Although putting it all together may be as distasteful for me as sorting through the charred body parts remaining from the Waco fire, I have a duty to do so as an act of penance for my own share of responsibility.

In order to explain adequately why millions of members today are willing to forego the benefits of blood transfusions, it will be necessary to look back in time nearly a century and a half to the religious musings of a precocious Pennsylvania teenager, a young man whose worshipful bent led him from managing his father's clothing store to starting his own religion. I had to learn about him and his colorful successors, because the process of breaking free from the controlling mindset of the sect involved unearthing enough of its history to undermine its claim to authority over my life.

In contrast to the Waco and Jonestown cults that sprang up like poisonous plants and then died like weeds at the end of a season, the Watchtower movement has deep roots. After germinating in the same fertile soil of American religious ferment, it developed a tall but twisted trunk and spread gnarled branches far and wide—growing strong and sturdy before producing its first crop of bitter fruit. Even now, the poison apples are concealed behind such lush foliage that most onlookers admire the old tree's vibrant growth and dismiss any suggestion that it could be a first cousin to the deadly plants of Waco and Jonestown. My job in this book will involve pulling back the leaf-cover to expose the rotten wood and peeling back layers of outer bark in order to reveal infestation and disease.

While David Koresh and Jim Jones were quick both to claim life-and-death authority over their followers and to use that authority to the fullest extent, the concentration of awesome power in the hands of Watchtower leaders has taken place gradually; it is only in relatively recent decades that they have begun demanding the lives of followers, a small percentage each year, again like a tree growing to maturity before producing an annual crop of bitter fruit. I will trace the organizational development that resulted in such totalitarian control today, and I will examine closely how religiously inclined but freedom-loving people can be drawn—by the hundreds of thousands every year—into that deadly stranglehold through massive recruitment efforts.

The story is my story—my family and friends, my thirteen years of exclusive devotion to the sect; but it is also the story of thirteen million people attending Jehovah's Witness meetings today and additional tens of millions of their impacted family members and friends. It is a story stretching over several generations and affecting many people.

Unfortunately, some of those to whom I owe the greatest debt of gratitude for providing information that has gone into this book cannot be thanked here. Public acknowledgment of high-ranking Jehovah's Witnesses at the Watchtower Society's Brooklyn headquarters or in its hierarchy of traveling overseers would cause immeasurable personal harm to these individuals and their wives. Having been in the organization's full-time service for many decades as "unpaid volunteers," they are too old to enter the secular job market, but not yet eligible for Social Security benefits. If their role in the underground network of secret dissenters were exposed, they would face trial before a judicial committee and expulsion from the only support network available to them.

Rank-and-file JWs who helped by providing current internal documents and verbal updates on the sect's latest "new truths" are ordinary working people who do not depend on the organization financially, but thanking them here would result in their facing similar trials before ecclesiastical courts, with the punishment of being severed from the fellowship of those very loved ones for whose sake they play the role of loyal Witnesses.

I ask readers not to judge those in the categories named above who feel compelled at this time to remain closet freethinkers rather than openly speak their minds and face the consequences. If the Old Testament prophet Elisha could make allowance for the miraculously healed Naaman to accompany Syria's king to Rimmon's idol temple, and if Jesus could let Nicodemus visit him secretly at night, we can certainly find room in our hearts for those who feel compelled—usually out of unselfish love for another—to lead a double life as Jehovah's Witnesses.

Ex-Witnesses to whom I am indebted would fill another book. I hesitate to start listing them for fear of the inevitable inadvertent omissions. Ten years ago Gordon Bryden kindly gave me the rare, old Watchtower books that formed the initial nucleus of my research library—primary source materials essential for accuracy and documentation. Former Watchtower headquarters worker Preston Walter provided considerable information on the real estate comprising the Brooklyn complex. Former Brooklyn Bethel workers Joan Cetnar and her late husband, Bill, by hosting their annual Witnesses Now for Jesus convention, provided a support network that helped sustain me and the many prior researchers on whose work I built.

Outside the ex-Witness network, or rather overlapping it to a large extent, are the broader countercult community and the nurturing fellowships of Christian believers who underwrite and support much of the work that is done to reach cultists and to heal hurting escapees. George Mather placed himself in my path so as to feed me liberating information on two occasions years before I left the Watchtower, and then, when I finally emerged, took me under his wing to introduce me to the late Dr. Walter Martin's Christian Research Institute and to show me practical methods for outreach that I still find useful today. Bob Hinckley went out of his way to welcome Penni and me into a supportive fellowship that allowed us to get our spiritual bearings and to refocus our religious priorities, and he and his church family at First Baptist in Abington, Massachusetts, have continued to provide essential support for my efforts at research and outreach.

Literally hundreds of correspondents over the years have sent me JW literature and directed my attention to relevant points contained within it, as well as newspaper clippings and other valuable information. Persons not yet named whose published works proved most helpful include Angel Arellano, James Bales, Darek Barefoot, Peter Barnes, Jerry Bergman, James Beverly, Royce Bilusack, Heather and Gary Botting, Robert Bowman, Leonard Chretien, John Francis Coffey, Marley Cole, Robert Countess, Gordon Duggar, Homer Duncan, Jean Eason, John Farkas, Craig Fox, Raymond Franz, Leroy and Diane Gholson, Kurt Goedelman, Edmond Gruss, Doug Harris, Barbara Grizutti Harrison, Steven Hassan, Joe Hewitt, Anthony Hoekema, David Horowitz, LaToya Jackson, Carl Olof Jonsson, Herbert Kern, Wilbur Lingle, A. H. Macmillan, Duane Magnani, Ralph Miller, Wayne Monbleau, Robert Morey, Alex Nova, George Orwell, Carolyn Pemberton, James Penton, Kevin Quick, Ken Raines, Casey Sabella, William Schnell, Latayne Scott, Margaret Singer, James Sire, Fritz Springmeier, Chandler Sterling, F. W. Thomas, James Walker, Randall Watters, David Weeks, Timothy White, Gerald Wright, and Pat Zarpentine. This present volume was made possible in a very immediate sense by the enthusiastic interest of Prometheus Books and my agent, Julian Bach, who brought us together. And it was made more readable through the editorial efforts of Eugene O'Connor.

Finally, but first in importance, I thank my wife, Penni, who has been my closest friend and supporter ever since our 1971 Kingdom Hall wedding. Her insight and honesty contributed to this project from beginning to end, starting with her courageous refusal to be intimidated by arrogant male hierarchs and culminating in her critical review of manuscript drafts.

My apologies, also, are extended here for any errors I have accidentally allowed to remain in the text; they are my fault entirely. Those named above or in the text certainly share none of the blame for my mistakes or my conclusions with which they may disagree. Lastly, I offer my sincere thanks in advance to readers who will be so kind as to bring needed corrections to my attention.

The information in this book is true. However, to protect the privacy of those individuals, aside from my family, who played a role in my personal history, I have changed their names, physical characteristics, and other identifying references. Actual names are used for historical figures and prominent Jehovah's Witnesses who are public figures, but local elders and others who impacted on my life are disguised.

1

Jehovah's Witnesses: Harmless or Deadly?

It is difficult to imagine the frustration of a doctor who wants to help but who is forced to watch a Jehovah's Witness patient bleed to death. A three-page article by Dr. Elisabeth Rosenthal in the August 1988 issue of Discover *magazine (pp. 28–31) related her feelings and observations as she watched her JW patient, a Ms. Peyton, die from loss of blood. The patient welcomed every treatment except the one that would save her.*

Most people view Jehovah's Witnesses as a nuisance—they ring the doorbell when you're bathing the baby or when the family is just sitting down to Sunday dinner, and they keep coming back year after year even though you've made it abundantly clear to them that you have no interest whatsoever in their religion. Their summer conventions fill baseball stadiums and generally receive good press as stadium workers comment on their cleanliness and efficiency. Policemen praise them as law-abiding and confess that crowd control is effortless as masses of Jehovah's Witnesses function as one person. They break neither the Ten Commandments nor the city's traffic laws. The only complaints come from shopkeepers, who find it unprofitable and unbelievable that thousands of people can come to town for the weekend without breaking a ten-dollar bill.

New converts baptized at Witness conventions often have amazing stories to tell of changes the sect has accomplished in their lives. A bank robber has turned himself in, served time for his crime, and is now baptized as a model citizen. A former drug dealer now sells *Watch-*

tower magazines instead. A prostitute has cleaned up her life and become a happy housewife.

Some older folks recall that President Eisenhower's mother was a Jehovah's Witness. Novelist Mickey Spillane, known for his Mike Hammer novels, answered a knock at the door in 1950 and was baptized into the sect the following year; to my knowledge, he remains a member as of this writing. Michael Jackson made headlines when he formally quit the sect in 1987; his sister LaToya's 1991 autobiography quotes *Watchtower* articles, and explains that her posing nude for *Playboy* and Michael's grabbing his crotch in music videos were "to get back at the religion" that had shaped their childhood.

People who know a bit about JW beliefs label them as unorthodox, perhaps even cultic; but hardly anyone puts them in the same class with the sect that brought infamy to Waco, Texas. Witnesses reject the doctrine of the Trinity and instead see only the Father ("Jehovah") as God. Jesus, to them, was a human incarnation of Michael the Archangel—the first angel God created. The "holy spirit" (JWs avoid capitalizing either word) is neither God nor a person at all, but is a mere force God uses to accomplish things. They reject traditional concepts of heaven and hell, believing instead that death equals total annihilation, with bodily resurrection to eternal life on an earth restored to paradise the hope God offers to obedient humans. The sect is ruled by a Governing Body of a dozen men, more or less (it varies), most of whom serve on the interlocking boards of directors of several Watchtower corporations—collective successors to entrepreneur Charles Taze Russell, who began publishing *Zion's Watch Tower* magazine in 1879.

Witnesses' rejection of Christmas and Easter as "pagan holidays" raises eyebrows, and their refusal to salute the flag or to serve in the military raises some people's blood pressure. Few outsiders, however, know that JWs are forbidden to run for public office or even to vote; or that members who question the leaders can be put on trial and punished—factors that should raise red flags in thinking people's minds.

"The Waco cult was deadly" is the typical response made by people asked to compare the two, "while Jehovah's Witnesses are merely unorthodox and annoying."

Why is it not generally known that JW leaders at Watchtower headquarters in Brooklyn, New York, have led many more people to an early death than the eighty-seven Branch Davidians who died at Waco? The problem is largely a matter of perception and of media coverage. When many die together at one time, people notice and headlines are made. But when one or two die here and there at different times, it can easily escape public notice—even when the individual deaths add up to a much greater catastrophe.

Compare the common perception of air travel. When a commercial airliner crashes, the death toll easily exceeds a hundred, and the story is reported on the evening news. As a result, many people view air travel as dangerous. The possibility of dying is much more likely to cross a person's mind when boarding a plane than when climbing into a car. However, the facts are at variance with this common misconception. In actuality, highway deaths far outnumber those due to plane crashes. But, while air disasters receive prime-time coverage on network TV, auto accidents seldom get beyond the front pages of local newspapers. That is because they rarely involve more than a few people at a time.

Watchtower leaders have never grabbed the headlines commanded by David Koresh or Jim Jones. The closest founder C. T. Russell came was when major newspapers in the Northeast followed his wife's prolonged battle in divorce court over alimony. (More about that later.) Russell's immediate successor as president of the Watchtower Society, fiery attorney Joseph F. Rutherford, made the front page with a twenty-year prison sentence for sedition during the First World War—more about that, too, in a later chapter—but the succeeding leaders down to and including present-day chief, Milton Henschel, have all avoided the notoriety attached to Russell and Rutherford; in fact, they have largely escaped public notice altogether, their names seldom appearing in print but for a corporate appointment or an obituary. If Koresh and Jones were perceived as superheroes by their followers and as supervillains by the public, Watchtower presidents since the 1940s would fit the comic book character of mild-manned Clark Kent, bland administrators rather than charismatic leaders. And they have ruled over Jehovah's Witnesses through a multi-level hierarchy of bland bureaucrats like themselves, all lacking the luster people expect in a cult leader.

The dying outside Waco began on February 28, 1993, when an armed force of more than a hundred agents from the Bureau of Alcohol, Tobacco and Firearms (ATF) raided the Branch Davidians' compound. A warrant had been obtained to search the premises for illegal automatic weapons, but the raiders walked into an ambush, leaving four of their number dead and fifteen wounded. Although the total killed or injured among the cult members could not then be determined, six deaths were later attributed to the February raid. Fifty days later, on April 19, the dying resumed when an assault by FBI-manned armored tanks culminated in a fire at the compound. Some of those inside shot themselves or others, while the remainder were killed by smoke and flames. The final death toll stood at eighty-seven sect members and four ATF agents.

In a manner much less spectacular, Jehovah's Witnesses have been dying one at a time, refusing vaccinations for themselves and their children between 1931 and 1952, refusing organ transplants between 1967 and 1980, and refusing blood transfusions and certain blood fractions since the mid-1940s, all in obedience to new interpretations of Old Testament dietary laws. As will be detailed in a later chapter, vaccinations and transfusions were seen as violating Moses' command to remove and dispose of blood from kosher meat, and transplanted organs were human flesh. Therefore, to "partake" of them would be not kosher but cannibalism.

No one seems to have kept statistics on the number of JW deaths. But with the steady accumulation of a man dying here, a child there, a woman in another place, an infant somewhere else—for roughly fifty years—the JW death toll is substantial.

Ironically, perhaps the largest single published report is found in one of the sect's own recent publications. Photos of handsome boys and beautiful smiling girls—"Youths Who Put God First"—brightened the cover, of the May 22, 1994, *Awake!* magazine, making it an easy issue to place in the hands of householders answering the door to Jehovah's Witnesses. (*Awake!* features general interest articles and is often used to front for the more doctrinal *Watchtower* when JWs offer the pair of magazines at the door.) Only upon opening the magazine did readers discover that the appealing photos were of kids who had died in obedience to the Watchtower Society's ban on blood transfusions.

Posed together in a group portrait in the cover's foreground are three extremely photogenic youngsters. Fifteen-year-old Adrian Yeatts died September 13, 1993, the magazine explains, after the Supreme Court of Newfoundland, Canada, declared him a "mature minor" capable of determining his own fate, and rejected the Child Welfare Department's request for court-ordered transfusions. Twelve-year-old Lenae Martinez died in California on September 22, 1993, after the Valley Children's Hospital ethics committee ruled her a "mature minor" and decided not to seek a court order. Canadian twelve-year-old Lisa Kosack died (no date given), after holding off transfusion therapy by threatening that she "would fight and kick the IV pole down and rip out the IV no matter how much it would hurt, and poke holes in the blood."[1]

Did the Watchtower Society actually summon Adrian, Lenae, and Lisa for a group photo session in morbid anticipation of their martyrdom? Evidently not, since each is shown in the identical pose in separate photos with different backgrounds on pages 3, 9, and 12 of the magazine. The group portrait was produced, no doubt, in the photo-composition lab at the sect's sprawling Brooklyn headquarters. Individual photos of twenty-three other attractive youths fill the background on *Awake!*'s cover. These other youngsters are neither named nor discussed, but the clear implication is that they, too, all died refusing blood products.

Featured articles on "Youths Who Put God First" filled the first fifteen pages—nearly half of the May 22 *Awake!* More than a third of this space was devoted to handsome, dimple-cheeked Adrian. The story related pleasant anecdotes from his early childhood and revealed him to be a sensitive, intelligent, lovable boy anyone would be proud to have as a son. At age eleven Adrian rescued three orphaned raccoon babies he found alongside the highway and escorted them to a safe home at an animal shelter. The kindness and respect he showed for a mentally challenged girl in his class at school—the butt of other children's jokes—endeared him to the girl's mother. Adrian was fourteen when doctors found a fast-growing tumor in his stomach. A series of autopsies revealed a large lymphoma in his abdomen, plus evidence of leukemia in his bone marrow. Oncologist Dr. Lawrence Jardine at the Dr. Charles A. Janeway Child Health Centre in St. John's, Newfoundland, prescribed aggressive chemotherapy accompanied by blood transfusions. When it became clear that Adrian, at his parents' urging, would accept the chemotherapy but refuse the transfusions, child welfare workers went to court seeking protective custody. Watchtower lawyers produced a strongly worded signed affidavit from the teenager: "The way that I feel is that if I'm given any blood that will be like raping me, molesting my body. I don't want my body if that happens. I can't live with that. I don't want any treatment if blood is going to be used, even a possibility of it. I'll resist use of blood." On July 19, 1993, Justice Robert Wells of the Supreme Court of Newfoundland ruled the boy to be "a mature minor whose wish to receive medical treatment without blood or blood products is to be respected." With only weeks to live, the brave young man fulfilled a few wishes. He visited the Watchtower branch office at Georgetown, Ontario. He went to a Blue Jays baseball game and had his picture taken with part of the team. On September 12, a handful of Jehovah's Witnesses held a special service in the hospital's physiotherapy room and baptized Adrian in one of its steel tanks, thus officially inducting him into membership, and he died the next day.

Why did young Adrian take this course? The *Awake!* article mentioned that he "felt that his biblical hope of eternal life would be threatened" if he agreed to a transfusion.[2] Like other JW children he had been taught that death on a hospital bed was to be chosen over "an even graver risk, the risk of losing God's approval by agreeing to a misuse of blood." Adrian's parents no doubt followed the organization's instructions to "review these matters with their children" and to "hold practice sessions in which each youth faces questions that might be posed by a judge or a hospital official."[3] In other words, Adrian had been thoroughly indoctrinated.

Virtually all JW youngsters receive this training to one extent or another, but not all end up in circumstances that require them to go through with it. How many actually do? The caption on page 2 accompanying *Awake!*'s cover photo states that "thousands of youths died for putting God first" in "former times" and adds that "they are still doing it, only today the drama is played out in hospitals and courtrooms, with blood transfusions the issue."[4] Nowhere, however, does the article specify exactly which "former times" are being referred to. Nor are any statistics provided on whether the number of JW youths dying "today" over blood transfusions similarly run into the thousands.

Most hospitals and courts nowadays grant adult JWs the freedom to refuse blood products even when it means certain death for them. The adult simply signs a form releasing the hospital and its staff from liability. On the other hand, when the patients are babies or young children, physicians secure court orders almost automatically. Their motivation in doing so is twofold: a desire to save the child's life, of course, and concern over liability should death or permanent disability result from lack of blood. An article in the November 18, 1995, *Houston Chronicle* bears out that this latter concern is justified. It reports the outcome of a malpractice lawsuit brought against a surgeon and his anesthesiologist after they performed heart surgery without blood on a two-year-old boy at the request of his parents. When the boy died, the JW parents sued. In this case a jury trial cleared the doctors of responsibility, but such an outcome is not always guaranteed.

A battle continues to rage, however, as the Watchtower Society attempts to persuade medical and legal authorities to view JW kids in the twelve-through-seventeen-year-old range as "mature minors" who should be allowed to die.

Courts are caught in a dilemma when faced with ailing youngsters determined to resist blood therapy with whatever strength they can muster. Some teenagers and preteens are simply repeating well-rehearsed arguments drilled into them at congregation meetings and during role playing at family study practice sessions. Others have become persuaded in their own minds that it would be wrong or immoral for them to accept blood products. All know that they face disgrace before their peers, loss of parental approval, and disciplinary action from the organization if they accept the forbidden blood products.

Some doctors hesitate to force blood products on such youngsters for fear that the resulting emotional stress might offset the medical advantages. While they do not want to see their patients deprived of needed blood, they hesitate to force a treatment that would leave youngsters feeling violated, polluted, guilt-ridden, and lacking the will to live.

Why are parents willing to sacrifice beloved children on the altar of organizational doctrine? Little meets the eye when outsiders puzzle over the unnatural actions of Witnesses in the hospital or the courtroom. Specially trained JW elders serving on "Hospital Liaison Committees" quickly step in to make the organization's voice heard alongside patients and their families. These elders appeal to the broader issues of patients' rights and personal conscience, but they make no mention of secret Watchtower judicial committees that enforce blood transfusion rulings on sect members. Doctors and judges are largely unaware of the intense indoctrination Witnesses undergo on a daily basis, and the punishment they face if not obedient to their leaders.

When confronted with objections against his healing a man who was ill on the Sabbath, Jesus knew that his opponents took a much gentler view of religious restrictions when their own vital interests were at stake. So, he asked the Pharisees, "Who of you, if his son or bull falls into a well, will not immediately pull him out on the sabbath day?" (Luke 14:5 JW *New World Translation*) The parallel question to JW parents would be, "Who of you, if his son is bleeding to death, will not immediately give him a transfusion?" Yet, Witness parents in case after case have shown themselves willing to sacrifice the lives of their offspring, as well as their own.

Actually, Jehovah's Witnesses will take blood—that is, they will accept certain blood components, and they will accept whole blood if it is administered in a certain way. This surprising aspect of their beliefs is detailed in an article in the November 27, 1981, *Journal of the American Medical Association* prepared by the Watchtower Society to set forth the JW view, and reprinted in the *Awake!* magazine of June 22, 1982 (pp. 25–27). This *Awake!* article explains that JWs must *refuse* the following forms or components of blood:

- plasma
- red blood cells
- white blood cells
- platelets
- whole blood from another person
- whole blood from the patient himself, if removed from circulation, even briefly.

At the same time, it states that JWs may accept these forms or components of blood:

- albumin
- Rh immune globulins
- hemophiliac preparations (Factors VIII and IX)
- whole blood from the patient himself if in uninterrupted circulation through tubes that take it outside the body and return it again, such as in a heart-lung machine.

No biblical verses are cited to back up these arbitrary distinctions; they stand as evidence that the prohibitions derive solely from the personal whims of Watchtower Society leaders. These leaders allow blood to leave a Witness's body, pass through a heart-lung machine, and enter the patient's body again, but they do not allow a JW to receive an "autologous transfusion" of his or her own blood drawn and stored during the weeks and months before a scheduled operation. They allow a JW hemophiliac to take repeatedly the Factor VIII blood fraction needed to keep from bleeding to death, but they do not allow an accident victim to take the different components he or she needs to keep from bleeding to death.

Actually, only a small percentage of "blood transfusions" nowadays involve whole blood. Blood banks routinely separate blood into its various components and doctors transfuse only the components needed—red cells for a patient with anemia, platelets for one with leukemia or undergoing cancer chemotherapy, plasma with clotting factors for a patient with liver disease, and so on. Whole blood is generally administered to persons who are hemorrhaging rapidly and therefore need all components.

Jehovah's Witnesses' favorite argument defending their stand to outsiders is this: "Refusing blood protects us from AIDS; that shows that we are right." People who don't know that Witnesses do take certain blood fractions are often thrown off guard by this argument. However, JWs themselves can and do get AIDS from contaminated blood products. Although rejecting "transfusions of whole blood, red cells, white cells, platelets, or blood plasma," the Watchtower Society, as listed above, does permit its followers to receive such blood products as Factor VIII (for hemophiliacs), Rh immune globulin (for pregnant women with Rh incompatibility), albumin (for shock), and various blood serums (antitoxins) to fight disease, according to the booklet *How Can Blood Save Your Life?*[5] The Society nonetheless acknowledges that Witnesses taking such blood products face "health risks involved in an injection made from others' blood."[6] So, just like the rest of the population, Jehovah's Witnesses run the risk of getting AIDS from polluted blood. In fact, because the hemophiliac preparation is made from blood fractions drawn from many donors and combined in the laboratory, JWs who take Factor VIII run a higher risk of infection than recipients of whole blood. (Improved screening of donors in recent years has largely eliminated such problems with the blood supply, but JWs ignore this and still offer the same argument.)

Like other medical procedures, blood transfusions do carry with them a certain amount of risk. Even the surgeon's knife, while saving many, occasionally slips and causes someone to die. But when Jehovah's Witnesses bring up medical rather than religious objections to such treatment, this is a red herring—an attempt to win the argument by causing a diversion. The real reason JWs refuse blood is that the Watchtower Society tells them transfusions are against God's law, and the Society is viewed as God's spokesman on earth. (Why the leadership chooses to offer that interpretation is anyone's guess. The "law" against vaccination and the "law" against transplants were later dropped. Retaining the ban on blood may be a case of holding a tiger by the tail: how can they let go after so many have died?)

During the same month that the above-mentioned *Awake!* magazine presented details on blood components, *The Watchtower* also included the following brief item:

> Would it be wrong for a Christian, under medical treatment, to allow leeches to be applied to him to draw off some blood?
>
> It would not be contrary to God's Word to permit the medical withdrawal and disposal of some blood. But to do this through the use of leeches would conflict with what the Bible says. . . .
>
> However, though leeches parasitically feed on blood in their nat-

ural state at present, it would not be proper for a Christian to permit leeches to draw his blood. (Proverbs 30:15) Even where this was used for medical reasons and the leeches would later be disposed of, the use of leeches would involve deliberately feeding blood to these creatures. That would conflict with the Bible's indication that blood, being sacred and representing life, should be disposed of if it is removed from a body.[7]

Yes, leeches suck blood, but don't let them suck *yours*! To non-Witnesses, of course, the idea that it is wrong for leeches or mosquitoes to eat blood, and that their habits will someday be reformed, makes about as much sense as teaching celibacy to a tomcat. These creatures are merely doing what they are designed to do.

Several years earlier, *The Watchtower* featured a lengthy discussion pointing out that it would be "a violation" of the same Old Testament laws for a Witness to permit a veterinarian to give a blood transfusion to a pet or other animal.[8] (The owner would be sinning, not the pet.) This article also prohibited the use of commercial fertilizer containing the blood of animals. And, although a canine might kill a small animal and eat it, including its blood, *The Watchtower* warned that Jehovah's Witnesses must not feed their pet any dog food containing blood. If "the label of a container of dog food" does not list blood as an ingredient, the dog owner might still "put his conscience to rest by making reasonable inquiry" of the manufacturer, it suggested.

Equally absurd are some of the arguments the Watchtower Society has used against blood transfusions. JWs have been taught, for example, that "The poisons that produce the impulse to commit suicide, murder, or steal are in the blood," and that "moral insanity, sexual perversions, repression, inferiority complexes, petty crimes—these often follow in the wake of blood transfusion"; yet blood banks "obtain blood for transfusion from criminals who are known to have such characteristics."[9] As living proof of such a personality transplant, and hence the inadvisability of accepting a transfusion, the July 8, 1969, issue of *Awake!* says this:

> For forty years Robert Khoury was known as an honest man. Then he was given a blood transfusion after a fall. "I learned the donor was a thief," Khoury told police. "When I recovered I found I had a terrible desire to steal." And steal he did. He confessed to stealing £10,000 in six robberies in three months. Khoury threatened to sue the doctor who arranged the transfusion, if he receives a severe sentence for his thievery.[10]

This nonsense about receiving a personality transplant through a blood transfusion, carefully checking the ingredients of dog food, and not feeding blood to leeches, all helps to demonstrate that JWs are simply taking whatever the Watchtower Society hands out in the way of instructions. The notion that the JW ban on transfusions comes from the Bible is no more valid than the idea that these teachings on leeches and dog food are divinely inspired; all derive from the creative imagination of the men at the sect's Brooklyn headquarters offices. I am embarrassed to admit acquiescence and even complicity in teaching such ideas. Rather than see it as evidence of my own stupidity—after all, I won a National Merit Scholarship and acceptance to Harvard—I now see it as testimony to the power of cult mind control.

While we are troubled when we hear or read about the mass deaths at Waco or Jonestown, we manage somehow to dismiss these incidents with the thought that the world has always had its share of kooks and lunatics. When a hundred or a thousand of them assemble together to perform their lunacy in unison, they grab world attention for a brief time but are soon forgotten. Jehovah's Witnesses, however, deserve closer scrutiny because, although their people are just as committed as the followers of Jones and Koresh, they are not huddled together in a small group in some far-off cult compound. There are more than twelve million people attending JW meetings, and they are living in our neighborhoods, shopping in our stores, sending their kids to school with our kids, working alongside us at our jobs, and quietly going about their business in our midst—like a time bomb waiting to go off, as the evidence will reveal.

How many, altogether, have followed Watchtower commands to their deaths? American Red Cross figures published in 1980 indicated that one hundred people per thousand, or 10 percent, need blood in some form every year. With today's Watchtower organization drawing more than twelve million people worldwide to its meetings, nearly five million of these being active Witnesses and the rest children and new converts in the process of joining, 10 percent would mean that between 500,000 and 1,200,000 among them "need" blood in some form every year, yet refuse treatment. (The lower figure represents 10 percent of the fully committed, active Witnesses, while the higher figure is based on the same percentage of those attending meetings but not yet fully committed, so the number *obeying* Watchtower instructions would lie somewhere between the two.)

How many of those needing blood would actually die without it? Again, few statistics are available. A chart published in the February

1993 issue of *The American Journal of Medicine* shows that studies based on 1,404 operations—mostly cardiovascular surgery and hip replacement—performed on Jehovah's Witnesses without blood transfusions reveal that 1.4 percent of the patients died due to lack of blood as a primary or contributing cause of death. Extrapolating that figure to the entire membership, if 1.4 percent die in cases where a JW "needs" blood, and 10 percent of the five million active Witnesses and twelve million attending JW Kingdom Halls "need" blood each year, that 1.4 percent death rate would mean that between seven thousand and 16,800 die by refusing blood each year.

However, that 1.4 percent death rate in scheduled routine surgery suggests a much higher figure in cases of uncontrolled hemorrhaging due to childbirth complications, automobile and industrial accidents, and other common causes of extreme blood loss. But even if blood products were critical in only 1 percent of the cases where a JW "needs" blood, and 10 percent of the five million active Witnesses and twelve million attending JW Kingdom Halls "needed" blood each year, a 1 percent death rate would mean that between five thousand and twelve thousand die by refusing blood every year.

The November 8, 1960, issue of *Awake!* magazine quoted Dr. Bruce Chown, a Canadian laboratory director, as stating, "I would hazard the guess that not 5 percent—no, not 1 percent—of transfusions so given [to women] have been life saving."[11] Well, if we give them the benefit of the doubt and assume that the death rate is not 1 percent but as low as one-tenth of 1 percent, that would mean between five hundred and twelve hundred JW deaths annually. And even if we very conservatively estimate that only one in ten thousand who "needs" blood would actually die without it, that would still mean between fifty and one hundred twenty needless deaths each year—a tragedy on the magnitude of Waco, Texas, repeated among Jehovah's Witnesses on an annual basis, year after year after year. Again, that is based on very conservative estimates. The actual figure is likely much higher.

The Witnesses themselves, who obviously are in the best position to keep track of these deaths, are unwilling to publish their figures for equally obvious reasons. But certain statements they have made to defend their position indirectly testify to the size of the problem. For example, after citing a case in which a California court respected a Japanese Witness's decision to die rather than accept blood, and two other cases in which courts ordered transfusions, *Awake!* magazine of September 22, 1992, added that "There are numerous other cases pending in appeals courts and new ones arising daily."[12] If the JWs are to be taken at their word, the admission that new cases are arising daily points to *at least* 365 such cases every year, perhaps many times that number.

Ever since the Watchtower Society banned blood transfusions for its followers in the mid-1940s, JWs have scrambled to keep watch at patients' bedsides and to remove children through hospital windows—all with the aim of blocking blood transfusions. At first, except for the occasional organized distribution of booklets to doctors, the Watchtower Society usually left parents, spouses, and JW patients themselves to carry the burden of defending their stand before doctors and judges. However, that situation has changed.

The November 22, 1993, *Awake!* magazine revealed a major new offensive spearheaded from Watchtower headquarters. It says that JWs "are being assisted to obey Jehovah's perfect law on abstaining from blood. . . ."[13] Committees of specially trained JW elders now enter directly into hospitals and courtrooms to intervene on the Witness patients' behalf. These Hospital Liaison Committees are armed with persuasive literature—medical, legal, and sociological. Their basic tool is a 260-page loose-leaf Watchtower handbook titled *Family Care and Medical Management for Jehovah's Witnesses*, updated constantly with new information on blood substitutes, alternative treatments, and patients' rights, plus evidence that JWs are good parents.

One aim, of course, is to stop judges from declaring JW children wards of the state for the purpose of giving them needed blood, and to stop doctors from seeking such court orders. Adult JW compliance with the blood ban is also enforced by the watchful elders.

The same November 22 *Awake!* article, titled "Jehovah's Witnesses and the Medical Profession Cooperate," gives the impression that transfusions are really unnecessary, and that "informed" doctors can secure "the healthy recovery of the patient" through alternative treatments. The article presents recombinant erythropoietin (EPO) as a wonder drug eliminating the need for blood transfusions by stimulating the body's production of new blood cells. But long-time JWs may recall *Awake!* speaking excitedly about "artificial blood,"[14] which was later found ineffective and its use abandoned.[15] *Awake!* boasts that more than thirty "bloodless medical and surgery centers" have been set up worldwide and that a growing list of over thirty thousand physicians are "willing to cooperate," which means—when nonblood alternatives won't do the job—they are willing to let the JW die.

An article titled "Blood Transfusions Overrated?" in the October 15, 1993, *Watchtower* quoted a doctor favorable to JWs, to the effect that significant costs and possible side effects make blood transfusions not worth the price. But the same doctor admitted that forgoing transfusions added "0.5 percent to 1.5 percent mortality to the overall operative risk."[16] That averages out to 1 percent or one out of a hundred JWs dying for refusing blood in routine operations. That number seems small, but, as calculated above, a 1 percent death rate translates into thousands of deaths annually. *The Watchtower* concluded that "Any medical risk of refusing blood is probably less than the risks involved in accepting blood transfusions," but it cited no statistics to support this claim. Why? Because statistics already in the Society's files show refusing blood to be many times more dangerous than the risk of side effects from taking it. The November 22, 1993, *Awake!* article discussed above quoted from an academic paper, "Blood, Sin, and Death: Jehovah's Witnesses and the American Patients' Rights Movement," by Dr. Charles H. Baron, professor of law at the Boston College Law School, presented at the recent University of Paris Colloquium "Sang et Droit" (Blood and Law). And that same paper, in a portion *Awake!* chose not to quote, reported that side effects of transfusions caused "one death for every 13,000 bottles of blood transfused"—much better odds than the one out of a hundred JWs dying from refusing blood in routine surgery!

The Watchtower Society has banned blood transfusions for its members for some fifty years now; so, although lower memberships in earlier years would yield lower death tolls for those years, the total number of deaths attributable to this policy must be staggering. Yet, as mentioned earlier, the ban on blood is not the Watchtower's only deadly doctrine. At various times Witnesses have been taught to avoid vaccination and organ transplants such as kidney replacement. These policies, no doubt, added to the total number of persons dying in obedience to the sect's teachings.

Amazingly, little of this is public knowledge, and even the normally alert investigative news media have virtually tripped over the story without noticing it. When CBS's "60 Minutes" program of December 19, 1992, devoted a segment to Jehovah's Witnesses, its focus was on child custody cases in which religion is an issue. The report pointed out the unfairness of situations where the Watchtower Society freely provides expert legal assistance to the JW party, while the mate who is a nonmember faces out-of-pocket expenses totaling thousands of dollars. "Sixty Minutes" appeared to fault the First Amendment's religious freedom guarantees for allowing the JW lifestyle to be imposed on children, but scarcely a word was mentioned about the literal skeletons pouring out of the Watchtower's closet.

❦   ❦   ❦

Virtually every day the news media report to us the death toll from at least one military clash, storm, fire, earthquake, accident, or other cause of multiple fatalities, but such figures take on more meaning when actual names and faces replace mere numbers. Then we can more readily identify with the loss. The same was true when the news media began interviewing family members of the Waco victims. When parents, brothers, sisters, and other relatives of those who died began sharing their photos and their fond memories, the depth, and not simply the scope, of this tragedy came to be felt.

So, as we examine the history of the organization that teaches Jehovah's Witnesses what forms of medical treatment they may or may not accept, it seems appropriate to consider a number of real life examples of what this is all about.

I could relate some of these from my own experience, but it seems more appropriate to focus primarily on cases that are a matter of public record, cases reported fairly recently in major newspapers, magazines, and books that can be looked up and verified through the facilities of any town library. These real-life examples are highlighted and presented throughout this book to illustrate the nature of the problem and scope of the Jehovah's Witness tragedy, which is indeed far worse than any cult-related tragedies that have grabbed world headlines in recent years. Some similar cases have made national headlines, while others are noted only in the news or obituary columns of small town newspapers. Still others—the overwhelming majority—are never documented in print beyond physicians' notes in confidential patient records. The focus here is primarily on cases that are a matter of public record, cases reported fairly recently in the print media.

The Watchtower Society has, of course, in its secret files at Brooklyn headquarters collections of names and stories from around the world detailing deaths due to its medical policies, but there is no other central collection agency for such data. Our inquiry to the World Health Organization was directed to its Global Blood Safety Initiative office in Geneva, Switzerland, which, in turn, responded to the effect that no information is available. Even facts and figures for the United States are lacking, according to an official response from the National Center for Health Statistics maintained at Hyattsville, Maryland, by the U.S. Department of Health and Human Services.

The actual cases documented here primarily involve Americans and are taken mainly from reports found in major American newspapers and wire services. Since U.S. Witnesses account for only about 20 percent, or one-fifth, of the JW population worldwide, it would be reasonable to project that each such death reported in this country could be accompanied by four additional heartrending stories from other parts of the world.

Mexico and Brazil, each with more than a million attending Jehovah's Witness Kingdom Halls, certainly have their share of deaths. And so do Argentina, France, Germany, Italy, Nigeria, Zaire, Zambia, the Philippines, and Japan, since Watchtower followers number roughly in the quarter-million to half-million range in each of those countries. The lack of cases reported here from any of these nations certainly cannot be taken to mean that the more than nine million people attending Kingdom Halls outside the United States are not refusing blood and dying at the same rate as their American counterparts. Most certainly they are, and the headlines and human interest columns of newspapers printed in the Japanese, Spanish, Portuguese, and various African languages just as certainly carry their share of hospital dramas and JW obituaries.

It should be stressed again that most adult Witnesses who refuse blood products in life-or-death situations die quietly in hospitals without attracting outside attention. Well in advance of a scheduled operation or procedure, they seek out a cooperative physician who will not fight them on the issue. Only cases involving police accident reports, court intervention on behalf of a child, or other legal controversies are likely to come to the attention of the press and to be reported in major newspapers. When JWs sign legal waivers and doctors agree to exclude blood from the operating room or the treatment schedule, the role this plays in the resulting death usually escapes public notice.

Multiplying the overall tragedy, in addition to the Jehovah's Witnesses who die in this manner, there are untold numbers who just barely make it through an operation or who survive an accident, but with permanent damage due to loss of blood. Some suffer irreversible brain damage. Others lose limbs or lose the full use of them. Less dramatic than actual deaths, these cases go largely unreported. Yet there are victims everywhere. There was a JW in my local Massachusetts congregation whose stiff fingers testified to an incident involving blood loss years earlier.

So, as the various cases are encountered throughout the book, it should be kept in mind that these are only a small sampling of the overall picture. They represent just the tiny visible tip of a gigantic hidden iceberg—a mammoth tragedy of vast proportions.

NOTES

1. *Awake!* May 22, 1994, p. 13.
2. Ibid., p. 5.
3. *The Watchtower,* June 15, 1991, p. 15.
4. *Awake!* May 22, 1994, p. 2.
5. *How Can Blood Save Your Life?* (Brooklyn, N.Y.: Watchtower Society, 1990), p. 4.
6. *The Watchtower,* June 1, 1990, pp. 30–36.
7. *The Watchtower,* June 15, 1992, p. 31.
8. *The Watchtower,* February 15, 1964, p. 127–28.
9. *The Watchtower,* September 1, 1961, p. 564.
10. *Awake!* July 8, 1969, p. 30.
11. *Awake!* November 8, 1960, p. 22, brackets in original.
12. *Awake!* September 22, 1992, p. 12.
13. *Awake!* November 22, 1993, p. 27.
14. *Awake!* August 8, 1980, p. 29–30.
15. *The Watchtower,* April 15, 1986, p. 21.
16. *The Watchtower,* October 15, 1993, p. 32.

2

Charles Taze Russell:
Announcer of Christ's Invisible Return

"New mother who rejected blood transfusions dies at thirty." This heading in the December 7, 1990, Buffalo News *introduced a front-page article on Joanne Mangione, a thirty-year-old Jehovah's Witness who died at 3:30 P.M. on December 6, 1990, two days after Sister's Hospital in Buffalo, New York, agreed not to give her blood transfusions. The published report states that the hospital had gone to New York State Supreme Court on Tuesday, December 4, requesting an order to administer blood against the patient's wishes. But when Mrs. Mangione's attorneys said they would not hold the hospital responsible for complications resulting from lack of blood, hospital officials agreed to hold back the transfusions. The woman was mother of a three-year-old child and a new baby whose birth by Caesarean section on November 28 had led to complications.*

The designation *Jehovah's Witnesses* is a relatively new one that the sect assumed in 1931. Prior to that its members referred to themselves as Bible Students, or International Bible Students, while outside observers often called them Russellites, after the Watchtower organization's founder, Charles Taze Russell. Members, however, have been taught that their founder was not actually Russell, but rather God (Jehovah) himself. Hence, they believe they should bear God's name rather than Russell's.

What is the oldest religion on the face of the earth? Judaism? Paganism? Animism? No, it's Jehovah's Witnesses! At least, that is the answer JWs themselves will readily offer. And they really believe it to be true. Members of the Watchtower sect are accustomed to answering every sort of objection or challenge as they knock on doors and encounter people of other faiths. They are used to Roman Catholics telling them, "My church goes all the way back to the Apostle Peter, and yours just got started a hundred years ago; so, why should I listen to you?" JWs are accustomed to defending themselves against the charge that they belong to one of the "new religions," as cults are sometimes called in polite circles. Their official response is found in their 1959 book *Jehovah's Witnesses in the Divine Purpose*, in a chapter titled "A People with the Most Ancient History." It declares that "Jehovah's witnesses are the most ancient religious group of worshipers of the true God, the people whose history runs farther back than any religious denomination of Christendom, or even of Jewry."[1] In fact, it adds impressively, "Jehovah's witnesses have a history almost six thousand years long, beginning while the first man, Adam, was still alive," and then it explains that Adam's son Abel was "the first of an unbroken line of Witnesses," and that "Jesus' disciples were all Jehovah's witnesses [*sic*] too."[2] (The lower-case "w" is intentional, to show that the expression is a descriptive term rather than a denominational name—a usage typical of Watchtower publications from the 1940s and 1950s.)

It is obvious to outsiders, of course, that the sect has simply appropriated to itself all the characters named in the Bible as faithful servants of God. By such extrapolation, and based on a fundamentalist reading of scripture, the denomination is able to stretch its history back to the beginnings of the human family—at least in the eyes of the faithful who feel obligated to believe whatever the leadership says. A comparison could be drawn with the Mormon practice of tracing ancestral roots and inducting long-dead ancestors into church membership through proxy baptism; Mormons may believe that famous historical figures who predated Mormonism by centuries have now joined their church, but outsiders simply brush aside such claims as ludicrous. Similarly, outside observers dismiss this Jehovah's Witness rhetoric and instead reckon the birth of the sect as coinciding with the publication of the first issue of *Zion's Watch Tower* in July 1879.

It came into being as one of several Adventist denominations that trace their lineage back to the Millerite movement of the early 1800s. Although some of those have since developed other denominational distinctions, Adventists originally differed from mainline Protestants only in the matter of expecting the imminent return of Christ, perhaps at a certain specified time. William Miller was a Baptist lay preacher who studied eschatology and chronology and reached the conclusion that Christ would return in 1843 or 1844. When Miller began publicly preaching this exciting prophetic message in 1816, he caused quite a stir. Lay people and even clergy began listening to him—both Baptists and those of other denominations. Estimates indicate that perhaps fifty thousand believers put aside the ordinary affairs of life with full confidence that Christ would come on the day Miller appointed. While these whole-souled converts to his chronology prepared to be raptured away to heaven, countless numbers of other people kept looking nervously at the calendar, too skeptical to join but at the same time unable simply to dismiss the matter. "What if the Millerites are right?" was the thought that troubled more people than would care to admit it.

Well, Miller was proven wrong. The anticipated commotion in the heavens, with angels blowing trumpets to announce the end of the world, did not occur, nor did Christ return in March 1843. No problem! There must have been a minor miscalculation. Miller refigured the date and found that it should have been March 1844, not 1843. ("I am fully convinced that sometime between March 21, 1843, and March 21, 1844, according to the Jewish mode of computation of time, Christ will come."[3] The same scenario was repeated. Once more, believers gathered in eager expectation; once more, anxiety troubled many who believed enough to worry but not enough to join. Again, tension rose as the day approached, and, again, Miller was proven wrong.

Once more, he recalculated, this time settling on October of the same year. Now skeptics were more confident and believers were subject to more ridicule. Only those who were fully convinced would take a public stand again and risk becoming three-time losers. Alas, that October 1844 date passed as uneventfully as had the other two. After what became known as the "Disappointment of 1844" Miller's following fell apart. By the time Miller died in 1849, most of those who had been inspired by his prophecies had returned to their respective churches and their normal, everyday routine. Other disappointed followers, however, kept the movement alive, although in fragmented form. Under the leadership of various preachers they coalesced into several sects, including the Advent Christian Church, the Life and Advent Union, the Seventh-day Adventists, and various Second Adventist groups—one of which later spawned the breakaway Watchtower movement.

We may not be surprised to learn that Jehovah's Witnesses share common roots with the Branch Davidians of Waco, Texas. Both trace their origins to nineteenth-century Adventism. This is how the lineage of the martyred followers of David Koresh goes: In 1935 the Seventh-day Adventist Church expelled a Bulgarian immigrant named Victor

Houteff, who had begun teaching his own views on certain passages of the Revelation or Apocalypse, the last book of the Bible. Houteff and a small group of followers established themselves near Waco. After first referring to their tiny new sect as The Shepherd's Rod, Houteff and his people in 1942 incorporated and renamed themselves Davidian Seventh-Day Adventists (after King David).

Houteff died in 1955, and in 1961 his wife, Florence, officially disbanded the sect. Some diehard followers, however, refused to abandon Houteff's vision and clung together in small groups. One of these independent little cells, under the leadership of west Texas businessman Benjamin Roden, took over the property outside Waco. Roden died in 1978, leaving behind his wife, Lois, and his son George. And it was at the Waco compound, in 1987, that Vernon Howell, alias David Koresh, engaged in a violent shootout with George Roden, winning for himself the leadership of the Branch Davidians.

The Jehovah's Witnesses descend from a different, but closely related, branch of Adventism. When the Civil War ended in 1865, former Millerites were already promoting new dates for the Second Coming. George Storrs of Brooklyn, New York, who published the *Bible Examiner* and was instrumental in forming the Life and Advent Union, pointed confidently to the year 1870, while a group headed by Nelson H. Barbour of Rochester, New York, looked to 1873 or 1874, and published their hopeful calculations in Barbour's periodical titled *Herald of the Morning*. Besides being an Adventist, Storrs was also a "conditionalist"; he interpreted Scripture to mean that men do not have immortal souls, but that one can go to heaven and live forever only on the *condition* of receiving from God the gift of everlasting life. In the 1850s George Storrs had published a book titled *The Watch Tower* (and subtitled *Or, Man in Death; and the Hope for a Future Life*). The teachings of Adventist leaders Barbour and Storrs would later be adopted, with some modifications, by a newcomer to the religious scene, teenager Charles Taze Russell. In fact, young Russell would even appropriate the very title of Storrs's book for a magazine that would eventually be delivered to the doorstep of nearly everyone on the planet.*

Born on February 16, 1852, in Pittsburgh, Pennsylvania, Charles was raised in the church of his parents, Joseph L. and Eliza Birney Russell. Of Scottish-Irish (Ulster Protestant) descent, they saw to it that their son received the Presbyterian catechism. Eliza hoped that her son

---

*The original spelling of the magazine was *Watch Tower*. In 1931, it was changed to *Watchtower*.

would grow up to pursue the ministry, but she died young, before she could see her dream come true. Joseph, the owner of a men's clothing business, sent the boy to public school and supplemented his education by hiring private tutors. At the age of fourteen, however, Charles was put to work in the haberdashery. Soon the boy was helping to manage the business, and within a year he was traveling to Philadelphia as his father's representative to make wholesale purchases. Shortly after that he entered into full partnership with his father. As the store expanded, Russell and son accumulated considerable wealth. In the meantime, the two transferred their membership to a local Congregational church.

Charles had witnessed the Civil War as a pre-adolescent, with the battle lines drawn at times inside his home state, prompting the thoughtful youngster to ponder questions of life and death, injustice and the social order. He was eleven years old when the battle of Gettysburg raged, a day's horseback ride from his home, leaving some forty-five thousand men dead or wounded. It was at the age of sixteen that Russell became a member of the Congregational church, but at this time (1868), he found himself losing faith. He had been seven years old when Charles Darwin published *The Origin of Species,* so the bookish lad soon encountered the Darwinian evolutionary theory. Now he found himself beginning to doubt not only church creeds and doctrines, but also God and the Bible itself. While at this crossroad Russell unexpectedly visited a small group of Second Adventists in Allegheny, Pennsylvania. Their preacher, Jonas Wendell, put his thinking back on a religious track and restored his faith:

> Seemingly by accident, one evening I dropped into a dusty, dingy hall, where I had heard religious services were held, to see if the handful who met there had anything more sensible to offer than the creeds of the great churches. There, for the first time, I heard something of the views of Second Adventists, the preacher being Mr. Jonas Wendell, long since deceased.[4]

Russell continued his biblical studies with the guidance and help of various Adventist laymen and clergy, notably George Stetson, pastor of the Advent Christian Church in Edinboro, Pennsylvania, and the *Bible Examiner*'s publisher, George Storrs. Russell acknowledged this later in life:

> Thus I confess indebtedness to Adventists. . . . And here I should and
> do gratefully mention assistance rendered by Brothers Geo. Stetson
> and Geo. Storrs, the latter the editor of *The Bible Examiner,* both now
> deceased. The study of the Word of God with these dear brethren
> led, step by step, into greener pastures. . . .[5]

Russell met locally on a regular basis with a small circle of friends to
discuss the Bible, and this informal study group came to regard him as
their leader or pastor, in spite of his being barely past his teens.

Another turning point occurred in January 1876. Russell encountered a small Adventist group that had recently broken free from the
recurring pattern of predicting a date for Christ's return. The members
of this group received their instruction and encouragement from the
magazine titled *Herald of the Morning,* published in Rochester, New
York, by Dr. Barbour. The twenty-three-year-old Russell received a
copy and immediately recognized something new and different about
Barbour's teachings: his belief that Christ had, in fact, returned in 1874
as the group had predicted—only invisibly! This concept presented in
the *Herald* captured Russell's attention. It was totally different from
everything he had been accustomed to hearing from other Adventist
sources, as well as from the teaching of the mainline churches.

Was the invisible return idea mere wishful thinking, born of a stub-
born refusal to admit the error of failed chronological calculations? Or,
was it solidly founded on something in Scripture that Russell had
missed all those years—something the rest of the Christian world had
also missed for centuries? Russell was fascinated; he examined carefully the arguments Barbour was able to put forward in support of his
assertions. The 1874 date was nothing new, of course; it was arrived at
by the same sort of calculations Miller and others had used. The concept of Christ's invisible return, however, was the novelty in Barbour's
teaching, and this is how it came about: A reader of the *Herald* by the
name of B. W. Keith had discovered a peculiar rendering of the Greek
word *parousia* (usually rendered "coming") in an obscure Bible translation and had called this to Barbour's attention. This enabled Barbour
to come up with a biblical basis for reinterpreting the Second Coming
as an invisible event. The book *Jehovah's Witnesses in the Divine Purpose,*
mentioned earlier, tells it this way:

> It seems that one of Barbour's group had come into possession of
> Benjamin Wilson's *Diaglott* translation of the "New Testament." He
> noticed, at Matthew 24:27, 37, 39, that the word rendered "coming"

in the King James Version is translated "presence" in the *Diaglott*. This was the clue that had led Barbour's group to advocate, in addition to their time calculations, an invisible presence of Christ.[6]

This rendering of the Greek *parousia* as "presence" instead of the traditional "coming" was the work of Benjamin Wilson, a newspaper editor in Geneva, Illinois. He included it in his Greek/English interlinear translation of the New Testament titled *The Emphatic Diaglott*, which he published in 1864. Regarding Wilson's religious affiliations the Jehovah's Witness *Awake!* magazine's predecessor, *Consolation*, says:

> Mr. Wilson was reportedly a Christadelphian. Christadelphians believe the organized churches are apostate, do not believe in the "trinity," do not believe in the "inherent immortality of the soul" or in "eternal torment," but hold that eternal death is the punishment awaiting the wicked. Though free from these basic errors, they are in bondage to religion. . . .[7]

According to other sources, however, Benjamin Wilson was a personal friend of John Thomas, who had founded the Christadelphians, but was not himself a member of Thomas's group; rather, be belonged to the "Church of God (Faith of Abraham)," a tiny denomination still claiming a small number of members today.[8]

In any case, Barbour used Wilson's translation of *parousia* to turn what would have been "the disappointment of 1874" into a cause for rejoicing instead. This new interpretation of Christ's return as an invisible presence meant that Barbour's prophecies had not failed, that his followers' faith had not been misplaced, and that they were indeed living in a special time in human history, a time Christians had been eagerly anticipating for centuries.

This idea completely captivated young Charles Taze Russell. In the summer of 1876 he paid Barbour's travel expenses so that the two could meet in Philadelphia and discuss it further. It was then that Russell learned the details of the magazine publisher's financial difficulties. The story of an invisible Second Coming had failed to capture the imagination of the reading public—not even the nation's Adventist readers. Lacking subscribers and financial supporters, the *Herald of the Morning* was doing poorly. Russell's retail business, on the other hand, was doing extraordinarily well. The solution was obvious, and the two men struck a deal. Russell became the *Herald*'s financial backer and, as a reward, he also became one of its assistant editors. This meant that he would break into print as a religious writer with articles published over his byline and his name listed in the magazine's masthead. Russell also affiliated his small Allegheny Bible study group with Barbour's fellowship.

In 1877 Russell published a pamphlet titled *The Object and Manner of Our Lord's Return*, which presents Christ as returning invisibly at the Second Coming in a spiritual body.[9] At this time Russell also helped Barbour complete and publish *Three Worlds, or Plan of Redemption*, a work setting forth teachings on chronology, eschatology, and prophecy. The title page bears both men's names, but Barbour's appears first and in larger type. The text is written in the first person singular, and Barbour refers to himself as "the writer" in a preface signed by him alone. Thus it appears Russell's contribution was again largely financial, making publication possible. This explains, perhaps, the trinitarian theology espoused in *Three Worlds*, which attacks Christadelphians for reducing the Holy Spirit to an impersonal principle or element of power like electricity—the same view of the Holy Spirit held by Jehovah's Witnesses today. Russell apparently had no qualms about trinitarianism at this time, at least not publicly; it was not until July 1882 that he would renounce the doctrine of the Trinity in his own writings.

One of the tenets of Barbour's fellowship, which Russell, too, apparently believed, was that Christ's invisible return in 1874 was to be followed in the spring of 1878 by the Rapture, when "the living saints would be suddenly and miraculously caught away bodily" to be with the Lord in heaven.[10] When this failed to happen, it could not be explained away as having taken place invisibly. Barbour, Russell, and all their associates were still standing upon the earth, in the flesh, plainly visible. Russell was greatly disappointed. Barbour responded to the failure of his predictions by reinterpreting Scripture and recalculating dates. Soon Barbour announced that these efforts had shed for him new light on the Rapture, the significance of Christ's death on the cross, and other doctrines. Russell, however, disputed some of the new ideas and ended up rejecting them outright. He also used his influence with the group—especially those who had been with him before affiliating with Barbour—and persuaded other members to oppose Barbour's new interpretations. Finally, Russell, as he himself explained, "withdrew entirely from the *Herald of the Morning* and from further fellowship with Mr. B." and decided "that I should start another journal in which the standard of the cross should be lifted high."[11] Titling his new magazine *Zion's Watch Tower and Herald of Christ's Presence*, Russell published the first issue in July 1879. When he resigned his assistant editorship at the

Herald of the Morning, Russell evidently took with him a copy of the mailing list, because the initial circulation of his new publication consisted primarily of Barbour's readers, and Russell devoted considerable space to refuting his former mentor on points of disagreement.

Some readers may find it ironic that JW publications paint Russell as a hero for following this course of action, in view of the fact that a Watchtower headquarters worker today following a parallel course—rejecting the organization's "new light" on one subject or another and leaving the sect to start his own opposing magazine—would be harshly condemned as an apostate and an enemy of God. Yet, instead of "waiting on Jehovah," as a JW who has problems accepting new teachings would be advised today, Russell rejected Barbour's doctrinal revisions, spoke out against them, and persuaded others to join him in leaving Barbour's organization to start his own.

Now Charles Russell no longer wanted even to consider himself an Adventist, nor a Millerite. Still, however, he saw Miller and other Adventist leaders as instruments of God who had been divinely used in fulfilling prophecy. In 1881, the *Watch Tower*'s third year of publication, Russell wrote, "For the sake of many new readers of the *WATCH TOWER*, it may not be amiss to give a general review of the steps of faith by which the Lord has been leading us as a people, during the last seven years, and in a general sense during the preceding thirty-five years."[12] To whom was Russell referring by "us as a people"? If we count backward seven years from 1881, that takes us to 1874, and another thirty-five years before brings us to 1839. So, when he spoke of "us as a people" during the years since 1839, Russell could not have been limiting his remarks to the Watchtower movement he began in 1879; rather, in saying "us" he must have included the Millerites and Adventists.

Similarly, Russell wrote of "the advance of the knowledge of truth for ten years past," and added, "Looking back to 1871, we see that many of our company were what are known as Second Adventists."[13] Moreover, he wrote concerning Jesus' parable of the ten virgins:

> While we are neither "Millerites" nor "Adventists," yet we believe that this much of this parable met its fulfillment in 1843 and 1844, when William Miller and others, Bible in hand, walked out by faith on its statements, expecting Jesus at that time. . . . A brother, Barbour of Rochester, was, we believe, the chosen vessel of God through whom the "Midnight Cry" issued to the sleeping virgins of Christ, announcing a discrepancy of thirty years in some of Miller's calculations . . . and the Bridegroom due in that morning in 1874. . . .

> If these movements were of God, and if Bros. Miller and Barbour were his instruments, then that "Midnight Cry," based on the prophetic and other statements and evidences, was correct, and the "Bridegroom came" in 1874. We believe that Midnight Cry was of God. . . .[14]

Obviously, Russell continued to view Miller and Barbour as instruments chosen by God to lead His people. Although Jehovah's Witnesses today think of Russell as the *first* in a succession of leaders, earlier Watchtower publications present Russell as the *successor* of Nelson H. Barbour: "Pastor Russell took the place of Mr. Barbour who became unfaithful and upon whom was fulfilled the prophecies of Matt. 24:48–51 [the evil servant] and Zech. 11:15–17 [the foolish shepherd]."[15]

In sharp contrast to this, Jehovah's Witnesses today do not consider themselves to be an Adventist offshoot, or their founder Charles Taze Russell to be a successor to previous Adventist leaders. In fact, they generally don't even speak of Russell as a former Adventist, even though he studied under the tutelage of Adventist clergy for some ten years (1869–1879). The recent JW history, *Jehovah's Witnesses—Proclaimers of God's Kingdom*, relates sufficient information about Russell's involvement with Adventist clergy and churches to demonstrate that he *was* an Adventist, but it fails to draw that conclusion. It merely states that "Charles Taze Russell and a small group of associates in and around Allegheny, Pennsylvania, formed a class for Bible study in 1870"[16] and presents this as the beginning of the history of JW meetings. However, this omits the fact, obvious from discussion of the same time period in earlier chapters,[17] that Russell and his friends were meeting as *Adventists* rather than as Jehovah's Witnesses or as independent "Bible Students." Russell did not break from the established Adventist sects to form his own until the middle of 1879, when he began publishing *Zion's Watch Tower*, and, even then, his new splinter group repudiated the Adventist *name* without really departing from the tradition.

Unbelievably, some Watchtower publications today discuss the Adventists and the Millerites without the slightest acknowledgment of any connection with their own history. For example, the October 22, 1989, *Awake!* magazine does refer to the Seventh-day Adventists as "the largest of some 200 Adventist denominations" and adds that "the Adventists stem from Baptist lay minister William Miller's movement of the early 1840s."[18] But this same article goes on to discuss the beginnings of Jehovah's Witnesses without any hint that they share the same ancestors. Nor does it contain any admission that the Witnesses also stem from the Millerites and are therefore closely related to the Seventh-day Adventists. Rather than acknowledge a connection, similarity, or relationship with other groups, the Watchtower Society seems intent on portraying Jehovah's Witnesses as the only "true followers of Christ," totally separate from "Christendom's religions."[19]

Watchtower leaders actually redefine the word Christendom, so as to exclude their group from the company of other denominations. Since the Witnesses are a sect claiming to follow Christ, they are automatically a part of the nominally Christian world, hence a part of Christendom according to standard dictionary definitions. The sect, however, recasts the word to include all other nominally Christian groups, but not itself. In order for the organization to secure from its followers the intense commitment that it demands of them, it is essential that they see the Watchtower organization as God's only representative in a satanic world of counterfeit "Christian" churches.

There is little mention in current Witness literature of the personal life of the sect's founder. *Proclaimers* relates briefly: "In 1879, Charles Taze Russell married Maria Frances Ackley . . . in November 1897 she left him . . . she was awarded, in 1908, a judgment, not of absolute divorce, but of divorce from bed and board, with alimony."[20] Even less information is available on Maria's background, except that she graduated from high school and received some college training at the Pittsburgh Curry Normal School, with the intention of becoming an elementary school teacher. Hence she had considerably more education than her husband.

The breakup was a messy one, the more than ten years of separation filled with bitter charges and countercharges circulated first by word of mouth among their friends and co-religionists, then by accusations in letters and privately published tracts circulated among Russellite congregations, and finally in the columns of secular newspapers and in the pages of the *Watch Tower* itself—a major scandal by turn-of-the-century standards.

Maria's formal charges against her husband involved money matters and emotional mistreatment, but her testimony in court also accused him of improper relationships with young women who had been servants or guests in their home, a large one with many rooms (and bedrooms). Maria testified that her husband had described himself as "like a jellyfish floating around," who was "embracing all who would respond." Russell emphatically denied making such a remark. She claimed to have discovered him in their household servant Emily's bedroom with the door locked. Russell explained that he entered her room in the morning "to see her and prescribe medicine" because she complained of being sick, and that he locked the door "less than a minute, probably not half a minute" because noise from the plumbing was making it difficult to hear her.[21] Maria told of his having his ward Rose Ball sit on his lap and kiss him; Charles explained that Rose came to live with them at the age of eleven or thirteen, and that he was merely expressing fatherly affection. On another occasion, Maria found him sitting by Rose's bed, holding her hand; he explained that he was taking her pulse.

It appears to me that certain enemies of the Watchtower organization have occasionally been too eager to believe and to repeat every charge made against the Society's first president. At the same time, it appears that writers of the JW *Proclaimers* book have, on their part, been too eager to lay the blame for their divorce entirely at his wife's feet. It is difficult to find a truly unbiased account, since those contemporaries who had enough interest to write about the matter usually had strong feelings about it as well, and the same could be said of most modern commentators. Considering the two strong-willed personalities that were involved, and the eccentric bent of each, I have little doubt that there was enough blame to go around, with both parties sharing responsibility for the marriage's failure.

To say that it was a peculiar marriage would be an understatement. After twenty-seven years—the first eighteen of which they spent living together—both parties testified freely that there was no sexual relationship whatsoever between them, that they never had a sexual relationship, and that thus they had never consummated the marriage. A major issue in the divorce proceedings was Maria's contention that Charles was depriving her of the pleasure of sex, countered by Charles's insistence that Maria had always shared his preference for celibacy. Charles wrote (referring to himself in the third person):

> Mrs. Russell's bill of complaint admitted that there had been no cohabitation between herself and her husband, and her attorney attempted to make out of this fact she was deprived of one of the chief pleasures of life. The Court would not permit this. The fact is that the matter was in Mrs. Russell's own control. She did understand that her husband preferred to live a celibate life, but she agreed and expressed the same as her preference.[22]

Yes, the whole matter was aired in the pages of the *Watch Tower* at great length, as well as in secular newspapers. Russell used his religious magazine to state his case, to respond to his wife's charges, and to produce letter upon letter from loyal friends and followers defending their mentor and testifying to his upright moral character. The July 15, 1906, issue, devoted largely to the editor's personal defense, carried the subtitle, "A Confidential Explanation by the Editor of His Peculiar Trials—The Wide Spreading of Untruth Makes Necessary This Statement of the Truth." Russell expressed his desire for copies to circulate only among regular subscribers, adding immediately to this subtitle in smaller print, "It is requested that this issue be not loaned or otherwise publicly circulated."[23] It was just as true in 1906, of course, as it is today that controversy sells newspapers, and scandal sells more newspapers than controversy. So, as savvy a publicist as Russell was, he must have known that a special *Watch Tower* issue on sex, slanderous allegations, and all sorts of other nasty mischief would circulate far more widely among the reading public than any regular issue analyzing Bible verses and picking apart the Greek words in ancient religious manuscripts.

Much of the conflict in the Russell home evidently centered around the office. Maria and Charles were married the same year that Charles resigned as assistant editor of Nelson Barbour's *Herald of the Morning* and started publishing *Zion's Watch Tower and Herald of Christ's Presence*. Maria evidently regarded it as *their* magazine rather than just her husband's. She wrote articles of her own as well as helping to edit his. When he tried to edit hers in turn, arguments ensued—or so Russell claimed. In fact, he blamed the entire divorce suit on these questions of editorial judgment:

> I must presume therefore that the motive back of this suit is revenge;
> to have an opportunity of defaming me and scandalizing the truth, as
> a retaliation for my refusal to permit her all the liberties she desired
> in the columns of ZION'S WATCH TOWER.[24]

The judge granted Maria's petition for divorce and alimony, citing Charles for arrogant domination that no woman should have to bear. There was no ruling on whether or not Charles had actually had intercourse with other women as sometimes implied—but never actually stated—in Maria's court testimony. Considering the intensity of the battle between Charles and Maria, it seems reasonable to assume that she would have actually charged him with adultery if there had been even the flimsiest grounds for doing so. Instead, her charges of impropriety went no farther than alleged flirtation, and the case rested more heavily on accusations of neglect and mistreatment—such as Charles opening and reading her mail. Did he really get away with adultery unobserved? Perhaps, but a more likely scenario was that the total absence of sex in the relationship where he had the greatest opportunity—his marriage—was reflected in the absence of sex in his friendship with other women. It would appear that he never went beyond holding hands or a peck on the cheek with members of the opposite sex. In any case, it is an interesting fact that Russell's marital problems would have disqualified him from serving even as a local elder in a JW congregation today.

Ironically, Maria Russell played a major role in elevating her husband, in the eyes of their co-religionists, to the position of God's representative to the modern world. Several years after he began publishing the *Watch Tower,* Russell came to see himself as God's spokesman and channel of communication. He spoke of "the truths I present as God's mouthpiece."[25] Perhaps he felt it would seem too presumptuous to make the initial announcement of this "fact" himself; in any case, Russell used Maria to make known to the world his appointment to this position. It was during the mid-1890s, according to *Jehovah's Witnesses—Proclaimers of God's Kingdom*, that "Brother Russell's wife publicly expressed the idea that Russell himself was the faithful and wise servant."[26]

This position or title Russell took upon himself—"the faithful and wise servant," used sometimes with and sometimes without capitalization—is a reference to Matthew 24:45–47 in the King James Bible:

> Who then is a faithful and wise servant, whom his lord hath made ruler over his household, to give them meat in due season? Blessed is that servant, whom his lord when he cometh shall find so doing. Verily I say unto you, That he shall make him ruler over all his goods.

Bible commentators outside the Watchtower organization generally interpret the passage as a parable Jesus spoke to encourage each of his followers individually to be a faithful and wise servant rather than an evil slave. Jesus continues by saying,

> But and if that evil servant shall say in his heart, My lord delayeth his coming; And shall begin to smite his fellow servants, and to eat and drink with the drunken; The lord of that servant shall come in a day when he looketh not for him, and in an hour that he is not aware of, And shall cut him asunder, and appoint him his portion with the hypocrites: there shall be weeping and gnashing of teeth. (Matt. 24:48–51)

The account is immediately preceded and followed by similar parables contrasting the outcome for those who are waiting watchfully when Christ returns with that for those neglectful of his Second Coming.

Russell, however, succeeded in converting this admonition to be a faithful rather than an evil servant into a personal appointment as *the* Faithful and Wise Servant—God's spokesman to humankind. A few months after Russell's death, the magazine he founded confirmed, "*The Watch Tower* unhesitatingly proclaims brother Russell as 'that faithful and wise servant.' "[27]

The key to understanding Jehovah's Witnesses is found in this one doctrine: the alleged appointment of *the* "faithful and wise servant." JW leaders today claim to have inherited the position by virtue of being Russell's successors, and hence God's appointed mouthpieces to humankind. I cannot emphasize enough the importance of this one piece of information. Efforts to understand the sect doctrinally or sociologically—and to debate with members on their beliefs and practices—are doomed to failure when this point is not understood. Once they accept this doctrine, new JWs no longer require other teachings to be based on the Bible or even to be logical; all that is required is for the teaching to come through God's channel of communication. If the Faithful and Wise Servant teaches it, it *must* be true. More will be said on this in a later chapter.

The very first issue of *Zion's Watch Tower and Herald of Christ's Presence* quoted from Matthew 24 and declared the magazine's purpose to be "to give the 'meat in due season' to the 'household of faith.' "[28] From 1881 through 1895, the magazine taught that the "Servant" was "the whole body of Christ"—that is, the church collectively.[29]

Then the new teaching was introduced gradually, first through Maria Russell, suggesting that God was supplying the church "through *one* particular servant—'that servant.' "[30] "The view that she voiced concerning the identity of the 'faithful servant' came to be generally held by the Bible Students for some thirty years," says the *Proclaimers* book,[31] adding, "Brother Russell did not reject their view, but he personally avoided making such an application of the text" to himself. Elsewhere, JW publications have acknowledged that Russell did apply the verses in Matthew to himself. According to the anonymous biography of Pastor Russell printed in the 1925 edition of his *Studies in the Scriptures*, "His [Russell's] modesty and humility precluded him from openly claiming this title, but he admitted as much in private conversation."[32] Very openly, however, in an article titled "That Servant" in the *Watch Tower* of March 1, 1896, Russell himself wrote:

This lesson, from Matthew's account (Matt. 24:42–51), was treated in our issue of April, 1 '95. We have no further comment to make except upon one point: "that [special] servant." In our examination of this text we seem to have treated the term "that servant" as though the Spirit had erred in saying "that servant" when it meant servants (plural), and we applied it to *all true* servants of God. Since then we have been met from various quarters with objections to so general an application, and the suggestion that it would be wrong to allow modesty or any other consideration, good or bad, to warp our judgment in the exposition of the inspired Word; to which proposition we agree.

... [T]he food will be dispensed through a steward to "fellow servants" and the "household" in general. (Brackets and emphasis in original)[33]

So, from 1896 onward, the official teaching was that Russell himself was the "faithful and wise servant" appointed by God as the one and only divine spokesman to modern man.

This teaching served the organization well. It invested its leader with virtually papal authority in spiritual affairs. Even in administrative and other matters, who could question God's faithful and wise servant? In any other organization the question would arise as to succession: Who could possibly replace God's final messenger to humankind? By definition, Russell was to have no successor. That was not a problem, however, since Russell's calculations called for the world to end and for God's Kingdom to take over earth's affairs by October 4 or 5, 1914. (More on this in chapters 3 and 10.) Even if he were to die before that, a caretaker committee could hold things together until the end, and his will so provided. As matters turned out, however, the year 1914 passed but the world remained. Russell interpreted the World War that began in August of that year as the beginning of global destruction. Confident that the world could last only a few more months, he set out on a cross-country speaking tour in the autumn of 1916. Though ill and weak, he persisted. When Russell preached his last sermon in Los Angeles, he was too weak to stand, and so he delivered his sermon sitting down. After his train left Los Angeles on the return trip to Brooklyn, he became weaker. The official biography printed in the 1925 edition of his *Studies in the Scriptures* describes Russell's final hours this way:

Seven hours before his death, addressing his traveling companion, Brother Menta Sturgeon, he said: "Make me a Roman toga." Using the bed sheets, Brother Sturgeon made a toga, which Brother Russell put on himself. He stood erect for a moment, and then lying down on the couch in his Pullman drawing room, closed his eyes. . . .[34]

Charles Taze Russell died on October 31, 1916, and was buried north of Pittsburgh, after which a massive stone pyramid was erected next to his grave, as he had instructed. That Pennsylvania pyramid and its connection with the Egyptian pyramids Russell studied will be explained in the next chapter, along with a look at the religious movement he started. But the chapter on Russell himself cannot close here, because his followers were convinced that he was still running the organization from the invisible realm.

The Finished Mystery, published in 1917 as the "Posthumous Work of Pastor Russell," asserts that the Watchtower organization is under the controlling influence of Russell's departed spirit, according to Revelation 8:3: "This verse shows that, though Pastor Russell has passed beyond the veil, he is still managing every feature of the Harvest work."[35] It adds that "we hold that he supervises, by the Lord's arrangement, the work yet to be done."[36] The same claim that Russell was still directing the organization from beyond the grave is also reflected in the November 1, 1917, *Watch Tower* magazine: "Hence our dear Pastor, now in glory, is without doubt, manifesting a keen interest in the harvest work, and is permitted by the Lord to exercise some strong influence thereupon."[37]

Presented as the seventh volume of Russell's *Studies in the Scriptures, The Finished Mystery* was actually written by Russell's close associates George H. Fisher and Clayton J. Woodworth, and was published under the direction of Russell's successor, Joseph F. Rutherford. The Society's second president soon found himself under siege from both inside and outside the organization. Needing all the help he could get, Rutherford let Pastor Russell's departed spirit continue running the organization "by the Lord's arrangement" from Russell's new heavenly home on the star Alcyone in the Pleiades star cluster, deep within the constellation Taurus—as will be detailed in the next two chapters—until finally repudiating this belief as "foolish" in 1934.

During his lifetime Russell had traveled more than a million miles and preached more than thirty thousand sermons. He had authored works totaling some fifty thousand printed pages, and nearly twenty million copies of his books and booklets had been sold. Yet, Jehovah's Witnesses today look back at his legacy with mixed feelings. The May 1, 1989, *Watchtower* puts it this way:

In the early part of our 20th century prior to 1919, the Bible Students, as Jehovah's Witnesses were then known, had to be released from a form of spiritual captivity to the ideas and practices of false religion. . . . Some were exalting creatures, indulging in a personality cult that focused on Charles T. Russell, the first president of the Watch Tower Bible and Tract Society[38]

NOTES

1. *Jehovah's Witnesses in the Divine Purpose* (Brooklyn, N.Y.: Watchtower Society, 1959), p. 8.
2. Ibid., pp. 8–9.
3. *Awake!* March 22, 1993, p. 3.
4. *Zion's Watch Tower,* July 15, 1906, p. 3821 Society Reprints.
5. Ibid.
6. *Jehovah's Witnesses in the Divine Purpose,* p. 18.
7. *Consolation,* November 8, 1944, p. 26.
8. See M. James Penton, *Apocalypse Delayed* (Toronto: University of Toronto Press, 1985), p. 17. See also the *History Newsletter* of the Church of God General Conference (Oregon, Ill.), October 5, 1985, and Paul M. Hatch, "Benjamin F. Wilson and the 'Emphatic Diaglott,' " *The Restitution Herald,* June 15, 1964, reprinted in the Christadelphian publication *Ecclesia.*
9. During the 1970s and 1980s Jehovah's Witnesses claimed that Russell published this in 1873, apparently so that they could say he promoted the invisible return doctrine before encountering it through Nelson Barbour. In the *1975 Yearbook of Jehovah's Witnesses* (p. 36), they say that "in 1873 twenty-one-year-old C. T. Russell wrote and published at his own expense a booklet entitled 'The Object and Manner of the [sic] Lord's Return.' " The *Watch Tower Publications Index 1930–1985,* p. 916, also assigns it to 1873. Interestingly, however, the *Watch Tower Publications Index 1930–1960* (p. 306) gives the date as 1877, and the sect's most recent history, *Jehovah's Witnesses—Proclaimers of God's Kingdom,* published in 1993, returns to the 1877 date (p. 47). I found this latter acknowledgment personally gratifying since, in my book *Jehovah's Witness Literature: A Critical Guide to Watchtower Publications,* which I completed some months before the JWs released their *Proclaimers,* book, I argued in favor of the 1877 date—pointing out that the only extant copy I had seen bore the 1877 date over the heading "Rochester, N.Y.: Office of Herald of the Morning" and made reference on page 51 to the *Emphatic Diaglott*'s rendering of *parousia* as Christ's "presence," a piece of information which, JWs acknowledged, Russell learned through Barbour in 1876.
10. *Zion's Watch Tower,* July 15, 1906, p. 3823 Society Reprints.
11. Ibid.
12. *Zion's Watch Tower,* November 1881, p. 288 Society Reprints.
13. *Zion's Watch Tower,* February 1881, p. 188 Society Reprints.
14. *Zion's Watch Tower,* November 1881, pp. 288–89 Society Reprints.
15. *The Finished Mystery,* vol. 7 of *Studies in the Scriptures* (Brooklyn, N.Y.: Watchtower Society, 1917 ed.).
16. *Jehovah's Witnesses—Proclaimers of God's Kingdom,* pp. 236–37.

17. Ibid., pp. 43–48, 120–22, 132–35.

18. *Awake!* October 22, 1989, pp. 17–21.

19. *Mankind's Search for God* (Brooklyn, N.Y.: Watchtower Society, 1990), p. 346.

20. *Proclaimers*, p. 645.

21. *The Watch Tower*, pp. 3815–16 Society Reprints.

22. *Zion's Watch Tower*, July 15, 1906, p. 3815 Society Reprints.

23. Ibid., p. 3808.

24. Ibid., p. 3815.

25. Ibid., p. 3821.

26. *Jehovah's Witnesses—Proclaimers of God's Kingdom*, p. 143. A footnote on the same page adds: "Sadly, it was only a short time after this that she parted from him because of her own desire for personal prominence."

27. *The Watch Tower*, March 1, 1917, p. 6049 Society Reprints.

28. Society Reprints, p. 3.

29. *Zion's Watch Tower*, November 1881, p. 291 Society Reprints.

30. Her letter can be found in the Society Reprints of the *Watch Tower*, July 15, 1906, p. 3811, under the heading "An Open Letter to the Church by Mrs. Russell, Published in *Zion's Watch Tower*, June, 1894."

31. *Jehovah's Witnesses—Proclaimers of God's Kingdom*, p. 143.

32. Charles Russell, *Studies in the Scriptures* , vol. 1, p. 7.

33. Charles Russell, "That Servant," *Zion's Watch Tower*, March 1, 1896, p. 1946 Society Reprints.

34. Russell, *Studies in the Scriptures*, p. 20.

35. *The Finished Mystery*, p. 144.

36. Ibid., p. 256.

37. *The Watch Tower*, November 1, 1917, p. 6161 Society Reprints.

38. *The Watchtower*, May 1, 1989, p. 4.

3

The Watchtower Movement
Departs from Mainstream Beliefs

"Life flowed out of him ounce by ounce" for four days, a Cox News Service report printed in various papers on July 8, 1989, said concerning twenty-four-year-old Jehovah's Witness John Truong. Under the heading "New citizen dies exercising his freedom of religion," it stated that he had been taken to Bethesda Memorial Hospital in Boynton Beach, Florida, on June 26, the victim of a motor vehicle accident on Interstate 95.

Near death, Truong finally agreed to take blood four days later, but the three units pumped into him within fifteen minutes came too late to save the young electrician, according to family members quoted in the report.

The Watchtower movement actually came into being in July 1879, when Charles Taze Russell consummated his break with Nelson H. Barbour's *Herald of the Morning* by printing the first issue of his own competing magazine, *Zion's Watch Tower*. Although Russell had published his pamphlet titled *The Object and Manner of Our Lord's Return* in 1877, and his name appeared under Barbour's on the title page of the book *The Three Worlds* that same year, he was still primarily a men's clothing retailer dabbling in religious writing, and still a member in good standing of an Adventist religious organization. It was not until *Zion's Watch Tower* first appeared that Russell became a religious leader in his own right and that his following became something more than a subgroup of Barbour's.

After the break with Barbour occurred, it took a while for Russell to redirect his attention—to start looking forward instead of back at the movement he was breaking away from. The *Watch Tower* and *Herald of the Morning*, in agreement on most major doctrines, competed for reader loyalty and warred against each other over personalities and other issues. Russell's immediate break was not with Adventism, but with the man N. H. Barbour and his editorial control.

As the new magazine publisher began to direct his attention outward, beyond the confines of the Adventist community, it was not immediately clear where he was headed. He welcomed subscribers of every persuasion. Some of these were church members and even clergy who did not yet sense the young editor's growing hostility toward mainstream Christianity. The first issue of *Zion's Watch Tower* even featured a short article signed, "By a Lutheran Minister." Russell traveled about, speaking from the pulpits of Protestant churches as well as to gatherings of his own followers. In 1879, the year of his marriage, Russell organized some thirty study groups or congregations scattered from Ohio to the New England coast. Each local *class* or *ecclesia*, as the groups were called, came to recognize him as "Pastor," although he was unable to maintain a truly pastoral relationship with such a widely scattered flock.

Proclaimers comments that "Brother Russell encouraged a full and free discussion of the study material"[1] in these gatherings. If this is true—and evidence does indicate that those early meetings were freewheeling in comparison with today's rigidly controlled Kingdom Hall services—it is a marked contrast with the instructions JWs receive today to "avoid independent thinking . . . questioning the counsel that is provided by God's visible organization" and to "fight against independent thinking."[2]

Russell formed Zion's Watch Tower Tract Society on February 16, 1881, with an associate, W. H. Conley, as president, and himself as secretary and treasurer. At this stage Russell did not have many volunteers to distribute his literature as Jehovah's Witnesses do today, so he hired the services of hundreds of young men and paid them to do the job. In 1884 Russell legally incorporated Zion's Watch Tower Tract Society in Pennsylvania, with himself as president. In 1886 he published *The Divine Plan of the Ages*, his first book in the *Millennial Dawn* series that would later be renamed *Studies in the Scriptures*. Between 1887 and 1898 he used his own privately owned Tower Publishing Company to produce these books, and in 1898 he transferred the assets of the Tower Publishing Company by donation to the Society.

The local study groups or congregations of Russell's followers usually met in private homes or in donated or rented commercial space, but in 1890 a group of Bible Students built their own meeting place at **Mount Lookout, West Virginia.** "It was known as the 'New Light'

Church because those who associated there felt that as a result of reading Watch Tower publications, they had new light on the Bible," according to the *Proclaimers* book.[3]

The possibility of forming a new denomination was a topic Russell brought up more than once in the pages of his periodical during 1883, but each time he concluded that it was inappropriate—not simply for pragmatic reasons, but because he was philosophically opposed. He wrote that "a visible organization, and the adopting of some particular name" should be rejected as appealing only to the worldly, natural man, while believers should be content to belong only to Christ's "perfect organization, invisible to the world."[4] Russell maintained that through his publishing and public speaking campaigns "no earthly organization is attempted" or needed, since "we are as one—all united to the one head and following the leadings of his Word and Spirit."[5]

Interestingly, the *Proclaimers* account quotes Russell (without citing its source) as writing: "We felt greatly grieved at the error of the Second Adventists, who were expecting Christ in the flesh, and teaching that the world and all in it except Second Adventists would be burned up."[6] The *Proclaimers* book's anonymous writers apparently saw no problem with pointing the finger at the Adventists for embracing such a belief, despite the similar belief of Jehovah's Witnesses today that everyone in the world except Jehovah's Witnesses will be destroyed.

TRINITARIANISM

Russell and his associates started out on their own as Adventists who held to a conditionalist* version of redemption and who carried dispensationalism† to the extreme of setting specific dates for the invisible return of Christ and the Rapture. Now Russell began leading his followers farther away from the mainstream churches by openly rejecting the doctrine of the Trinity in 1882. Prior to this he had not publicly opposed Nelson H. Barbour's trinitarianism, but willingly signed on as co-author of the latter's book, which took a slap at the Christadelphians for deviating from orthodoxy in this regard, as mentioned earlier. In fact, when Russell broke away to start his own magazine, he

---

*Conditionalists see immortality as something to be gained by meeting certain conditions (such as having faith or performing works), not as an inherent feature of the soul or spirit.

†Dispensationalism is the school of thought that sees God as sectioning off epochs of time ("dispensations") for dealing with humankind under different arrangements.

took with him the *Herald of the Morning*'s other assistant editor, John H. Paton, whom Russell knew to be a trinitarian. The topical index to the Society's seven-volume *Watch Tower* Reprints (1879–1919) lists under "Trinity," among many negative references such as "theory absurd," one solitary reference that says, "true," referring readers to an article titled "God Is Love," beginning on page 9 of the Reprints, and signed by "J. H. P." In it Paton writes:

> No theologian need attempt an *explanation* of the Divine Sonship of our Lord. "But it pleased the Father that in Christ should all fullness dwell,"—"All fullness of the Godhead bodily." . . . "The Word was with God and the Word was God." . . . He of whom it was said, "Let *all* the angels of God worship him," [that must include Michael,] and "Thy throne, O God, is forever and ever." . . . (Brackets and emphasis in original)

The bracketed expression, "that must include Michael," directly contradicts the *Watch Tower*'s later (and current) teaching that Jesus *is* Michael, not God but rather a being created by God, an angel.*

Articles signed "J. H. P." continued to appear regularly, and Paton's name (sometimes spelled Patton) was put at the top of the list of "Regular Contributors" on the masthead of the *Watch Tower* from its first issue through that of July/August 1881, after which the list was dropped. In the July/August 1881 issue Russell inserted, instead of the regular contributors list, this disclaimer:

> The Editor recognizes a responsibility to the Master, relative to what shall appear in these columns, which he can not and does not cast aside; yet he should not be understood as endorsing every *expression* of correspondents, or of articles selected from other periodicals. (Emphasis in original)

In that same issue, under the subheading "Godhead," there appeared a lengthy quote from "H. V. Reed in the *Restitution*" which was presented as authoritative. In it he spoke against "the word trinity . . . the heathen dogma of the *God society*, or *trinity*," which he declared to be "contrary alike to sound reason and the Scriptures of truth" (em-

---

*The JW argument is that Scripture names only one archangel—Michael—at Jude 9, and that 1 Thess. 4:16 says the Lord will descend from heaven "with an archangel's voice." Hence Jesus must be Michael. Watchtower authority fills the gap for those who do not find this logically compelling.

phasis in original).[7] A year later Russell himself finally penned a lengthy article expounding his theology. He wasted no time stating his position clearly in the opening words:

> Our readers are aware that while we believe in Jehovah and Jesus and the holy Spirit, we reject as totally unscriptural, the teaching that these are *three* Gods in *one person*, or as some put it, *one* God in *three persons*. The doctrine of the Trinity had its rise in the third century, and has a close resemblance to the heathen doctrines prevalent at that time, particularly Hindooism. (Emphasis in original)[8]

Russell laid out a system of theology essentially the same as that followed by Jehovah's Witnesses today. They believe that Yahweh, the God revealed to the Jews in the Old Testament, is the only true God; that believers must refer to God and address him in prayer as "Jehovah," even though publications of the sect acknowledge this to be a mistaken rendering of the Hebrew Tetragrammaton (YHWH); that Jesus Christ is merely an alias for Michael the archangel, the first angel God created, who therefore became like a firstborn son to him; that Christ is "a god" but is not God; and that "holy spirit" is an impersonal force that God uses to get things accomplished.

THE GREAT PYRAMID

Occasionally the Jehovah's Witness magazine The Watchtower *reports the death of a Witness refusing blood as an example for others to follow. Thus the issue of September 1, 1971, reports on page 531 concerning "a thirteen-year-old girl in Berlin," whose mother refused to let doctors administer transfusions to treat the girl's leukemia. "I would rather die faithful to Jehovah," The* Watchtower *quotes the girl as saying, and then adds, "This girl did die."*

✍   ✍   ✍

Another aspect of Russell's teachings that helped separate him and his followers from the more traditional churches was his fixation with the pyramids of Egypt, in particular the Great Pyramid of Giza. Russell promoted pyramid teachings throughout his life, and even after his death through a pyramid-shaped monument he had erected near his grave in the Watch Tower Society's cemetery. This pyramid still stands in the northern suburbs of Pittsburgh, Pennsylvania, where it serves as a tourist attraction as well as a mute testimony to the religious roots of Jehovah's Witnesses.

The name "WATCH TOWER BIBLE AND TRACT SOCIETY" is engraved in large capital letters on the pyramid's side, just below the wreathed cross and crown symbol used by the Society for many years. Russell's own headstone stands nearby, bearing his portrait and an inscription identifying him as "The Laodicean Messenger," a reference to the belief that he was "the messenger of the congregation in Laodicea" (Rev. 3:14 *Emphatic Diaglott*); that is, God's spokesman to Christians during the Laodicean period or final phase of church history in this interpretation, which views the seven churches named in Revelation, chapter 2, as seven historical periods.

Tourists from all over the world come to have their picture taken next to the Watch Tower Pyramid, according to the locals who watch such comings and goings with curious interest. Breakaway groups of Bible Students, who look to Russell's works but who reject the Watchtower organization and its more recent teachings, still attach importance to both Russell and his pyramid. Not many years ago a cemetery worker reported to an acquaintance of mine that some of these Bible Students maintain their custom of gathering at Russell's graveside on the anniversary of his death, which, coincidentally, is also Halloween. Mostly wrinkled old folk, they hold hands in a large circle around the pyramid and sing hymns peculiar to their group—truly a surprising sight that onlookers could easily mistake for some eerie Halloween celebration.

Most Jehovah's Witnesses today have no idea of the extent to which the Watchtower organization based many of its teachings on the Great Pyramid of Egypt for some fifty years, under the presidencies of both Russell and Rutherford. The *Watch Tower* of June 1, 1910, under the heading "Our Visit to the Pyramid," describes Russell's visit, with over a dozen other representatives of the Society, to Egypt for the second time (the first had occurred in 1892):

> Since we visited it eighteen years ago several of the casing stones have been found at the base of the Pyramid by the removal of the rubbish which had covered them for centuries. . . . The Brothers Edgar, of Scotland, visited the Pyramid last year to go over the measurements of its passageways. . . .
>
> We went all over the structure again—not, however, with the view of taking measurements, for these, we believe, have already been taken more accurately than instruments then at our command would permit. We merely reviewed this Great Witness to the Lord of hosts and recalled to mind its testimony, which we have already pre-

sented . . . in the last chapter of the third volume of STUDIES IN THE SCRIPTURES. . . .[9]

This book, *Studies in the Scriptures*, the first edition of which was published by the Society in 1891, features diagrams of Pyramid chambers and passageways, along with calculations based on their measurements. Such measurements were interpreted as prophetic. The tenth chapter of *Studies*, titled in capital letters "THE TESTIMONY OF GOD'S STONE WITNESS AND PROPHET, THE GREAT PYRAMID IN EGYPT," says:

> . . . The Great Pyramid . . . seems in a remarkable manner to teach, in harmony with all the prophets, an outline of the plan of God, past, present and future. . . .
> The Great Pyramid, however, proves to be a storehouse of important truth—scientific, historic and prophetic—and its testimony is found to be in perfect accord with the Bible, expressing the prominent features of its truths in beautiful and fitting symbols. . . .
> It is conjectured that Melchizedek, though not himself an Egyptian, used Egyptian labor for the construction of the Great Pyramid. And to some extent the traditions of Egypt support such a theory. [10]

Prominently featured facing the title page of the book *Thy Kingdom Come*, volume 3 of *Studies in the Scriptures*, is an illustration captioned "Vertical Section of the Great Pyramid of Jeezeh [*sic*]," showing such internal passages of the Egyptian monument as the King's Chamber, the Queen's Chamber, the Grand Gallery, and the Grotto—all of which are interpreted as prophetic. The following excerpt from the 1903 edition of this book shows how Russell manipulated measurements from within the Great Pyramid to arrive at prophetic dates:

> So, then, if we measure backward down the "First Ascending Passage" to its junction with the "Entrance Passage," we shall have a fixed date to mark upon the downward passage. This measure is 1,542 inches, and indicates the year B.C. 1542, as the date at that point. Then measuring down the "Entrance Passage" from that point, to find the distance to the entrance of the "Pit," representing the great trouble and destruction with which this age is to close, when evil will be overthrown from power, we find it to be 3,416 inches, symbolizing 3,416 years from the above date, B.C. 1542. This calculation shows A.D. 1874 as marking the beginning of the period of trouble; for 1,542 years B.C. plus 1,874 years A.D. equals 3,416 years. Thus the Pyramid witnesses that the close of 1874 was the

chronological beginning of the time of trouble such as was not since there was a nation—no, nor ever shall be afterward.[11]

In the 1908 edition of *Studies in the Scriptures*, after he decided to change the dates, Russell and his friends at Watchtower headquarters stretched the Great Pyramid forty-one inches to obtain the following results:

So, then, if we measure backward down the "First Ascending Passage" to its junction with the "Entrance Passage," we shall have a fixed date to mark upon the downward passage. This measure is 1,542 inches, and indicates the year B.C. 1542, as the date at that point. Then measuring down the "Entrance Passage" from that point, to find the distance to the entrance of the "Pit," representing the great trouble and destruction with which this age is to close, when evil will be overthrown from power, we find it to be 3,457 inches, symbolizing 3,457 years from the above date, B.C. 1542. This calculation shows A.D. 1915 as marking the beginning of the period of trouble; for 1,542 years B.C. plus 1,915 years A.D. equals 3,457 years. Thus the Pyramid witnesses that the close of 1914 will be the beginning of the time of trouble such as was not since there was a nation—no, nor ever shall be afterward.[12]

Stretching the Great Pyramid to fit the prophecy is reminiscent of the very charge Russell directed at Second Adventists in *Studies in the Scriptures*:

Their attempts to apply prophecy to their false expectations often lead to twisting, stretching or whittling, according to the necessities of the case, in the endeavor to get all the prophecies to terminate at some one date. These friends should awake to their error in this direction; for one after another their expectations have failed, while we and they know that some of the prophecies they have used cannot be stretched into the future, but are in the past, and are now abandoned by them.[13]

Russell's followers have long since abandoned entirely the Pyramid prophecies which dominated Watchtower thinking for some fifty years.

Where did Charles Taze Russell get his teachings on the Pyramid in the first place? Egyptology had become popular in Western countries during the 1800s after French and then British military successes brought the land of the Nile under their respective spheres of influence and opened the way for their own archaeological explorations. Russell cites an unnamed 1859 work by John Taylor of England, then Prof. Piazzi Smyth, Astronomer-Royal for Scotland, and finally "a young Scotsman, Robert Menzies, who, when studying the scientific teachings of the Great Pyramid, discovered that prophetic and chronological teachings co-exist in it."[14] Very significantly, however, he fails to credit Apostle Orson Pratt of the Church of Jesus Christ of Latter-Day Saints. A comparison of what this Mormon leader published in 1880 with what the Watchtower Society published a year later and again a decade after that, will reveal these striking similarities:

- Both base prophecies on the Great Pyramid of Egypt.

- Both refer to the Pyramid as a "witness."

- Both interpret inches to mean years.

- Both include the "Step" of the "Grand Gallery" in their measurements.

- Both tie in Pyramid prophecies with the end of the "Gentile" times.

This is what the Mormon Church's Apostle was teaching in 1880*:

I have sometimes reflected upon a new witness that the Lord seems to have brought to light, by the opening of the Great Pyramid of Egypt. There are many things revealed by the opening of that Pyramid, nearly 3,000 years after it was built, that are great and marvellous, so far as I can understand them. There seems to be a prophetic spirit running through the construction of all that vast superstructure, pointing forward to the very end. Among the great events clearly portrayed by that Pyramid, was the organization of this Church on the sixth of April, 1830. This is expressed in the construction of the "GREAT STEP," in the Grand Gallery of that Pyramid. Time was measured in that ascending gallery by sacred cubit inches. The measurement from the birth of Christ to the upper edge of the "Step," which terminates the ascending passage, was exactly 1,829 cubit inches, and the fraction of another inch; that is, a little over the twenty-sixth hundredth part of an inch. Allowing one year to a cubit inch, it gives the sixth of April, 1830, as the exact time, corresponding to the upper edge of the "Great Step." At this point the Gallery ceases to ascend, and the passage becomes horizontal. This points out the very period of time when the Church was organized, and the

---

*Other than the preceding five points, the reader should not expect to grasp the significance of all that is contained in the following quotes. Too much is involved.

very day and month and year. Sixty-one cubit inches are measured off, from that point in a horizontal direction, until you come to the great impending wall, the end of the Gallery. What that means, I do not pretend to know. It may mean the closing up of the times of the Gentiles. Sixty-one years from the organization of the Church brings us, according to pyramidal testimony, to the end of something. Whether these pyramidal symbols are divine or not, there is one thing that I do know is true, namely, that the generation in which the fullness of the Gospel—the Book of Mormon—was brought forth, is the generation that will close up the times of the Gentiles.[15]

This is what C. T. Russell's *Watch Tower* magazine taught a year later, in 1881:

Thirty-three inches from the beginning of the grand gallery is a well, representing the death and resurrection of Jesus. From this well there is another downward passageway which connects with the entrance passage near the pit, and seems to teach the restoration of all men from the "horrible pit" of death, through and on account of Jesus' death.

The "grand gallery" measures 1,874 inches long at the top, 1,878 inches long at a groove cut in its sides about midway between bottom and top and 1,881 inches, at the bottom. (The upper end wall impends or slants forward.)

Now notice how aptly these three distinct dates (1874, 1878, 1881) are marked by the pyramid. . . .

Two other ways, in which the Pyramid corroborates scripture are these: At the top of the "grand gallery"—just where it measures 1,874 inches, there is an opening or passageway which seems to say, something might go out or come in here. For some time we thought this might represent the "change," or catching away of the church as spiritual beings; but it would have been due in 1874 and no translation took place; then it must mean something else. It seems plain and clear to us now that that opening can mean nothing else than what the Prophets have taught us, viz: that there the Bridegroom came [*sic*] a spiritual being. . . .

Secondly, we are claiming that our Lord's presence here, is to be to many in the nominal church "a stone of stumbling" and this too finds its illustration in the Pyramid, for at the upper end of the "Grand gallery" a huge block of stone juts out into the pathway. . . .[16]

And this is what the Watch Tower Bible and Tract Society published ten years later (again, note the similarities, but ignore the shifting dates):

Call to mind that the Scriptures showed us that the full end of Gentile power in the world, and the time of trouble which brings its overthrow, will be in the end of A.D. 1914, and that some time before that date the last members of the Church of Christ will have been "changed," glorified. . . . Then look at the manner in which the stone "Witness" testifies to those same dates and illustrates the very same lessons. . . .

. . . One measure (a) is from the wall at the north end, measured to the "Step" and then—omitting its riser or front—along its upper surface, the walking surface of the "Grand Gallery's" floor. . . .

. . . Now we inquire, If the inches of the floor-lines of these passages represent a year, each, as claimed and admitted by Pyramid students, what date would these measures of the "Grand Gallery" indicate as the end of the high calling to the divine nature, which the "Grand Gallery" symbolizes? . . . [T]his date, 1910, indicated by the Pyramid, seems to harmonize well with the dates furnished by the Bible. It is but four years before the full close of the time of trouble which ends the Gentile times; and when we remember the Lord's words—that the overcomers shall be accounted worthy to escape the severest of the trouble coming upon the world, we may well accept as correct the testimony of the Great Pyramid, that the last members of the "body" or "bride" of Christ will have been tested and accepted and will have passed beyond the vail [*sic*] before the close of A.D. 1910.[17]

If plagiarism consists of appropriating and passing off as one's own the writings or ideas of another, it is appropriate to ask, Did Watchtower President Charles Taze Russell plagiarize the prophetic ideas of Mormon leader Orson Pratt? Or, did both of them copy from a common source, such as Scotsman Robert Menzies cited above? Most likely, both latched onto a popular fad that today we would call New Age. Further research in this area may prove revealing. For Jehovah's Witnesses, however, the greater concern is not the possibility of literary dishonesty but, rather, the origin of their teachings and beliefs. The Watchtower organization today regards Mormonism with great distaste, just as it did in Russell's day; so for Russell to have "borrowed" a Mormon or New Age teaching on the pyramids, and presented it as if it were from God, would be particularly disturbing news to JWs.

Years after Russell's death, and well into the 1920s, the Watchtower Society continued to teach that Jehovah God had designed the Pyramid:

In the passages of the Great Pyramid of Gizeh [*sic*] the agreement of
one or two measurements with the present-truth chronology might be
accidental, but the correspondency of dozens of measurements
proves that the same God designed both pyramid and plan. . . .[18]

The great Pyramid of Egypt, standing as a silent and inanimate
witness of the Lord, is a messenger; and its testimony speaks with
great eloquence concerning the divine plan.[19]

Then, suddenly and without warning, the November 15, 1928,
issue of the *Watch Tower* reversed the sect's beliefs regarding the Pyramid. (The reason for the reversal relates to second president J. F.
Rutherford's consolidating his hold on power and forcing die-hard Russellites out of the organization—an issue that our next chapter will
make more understandable. For now, let it suffice to note the dramatic
reversal.) The pyramid now became "Satan's Bible," and anyone following pyramid teachings was "not following after Christ":

If the pyramid is not mentioned in the Bible, then following its teachings is being led by vain philosophy and false science and not following after Christ.[20]

It is more reasonable to conclude that the great pyramid of Gizeh
[*sic*], as well as the other pyramids thereabout, also the sphinx, were
built by the rulers of Egypt and under the direction of Satan the
Devil. . . . Then Satan put his knowledge in dead stone, which may
be called Satan's Bible, and not God's stone witness. . . .

Those who have devoted themselves to the pyramid have failed
to see some of the most important things that God has revealed for
the benefit of his church. The mind of such was turned away from Jehovah and his Word.[21]

With the release of a new magazine God's Stone Witness was transformed into Satan's Bible. This illustrates one of the most amazing
facts about Jehovah's Witnesses: that a cherished belief may be overturned at any time on command from Brooklyn headquarters; and that
such a belief may be not simply abandoned, but may even be *reversed*.
What is good may become bad overnight. What is right may become
wrong. What is true may become false. Individual Witnesses are *required* to accept and wholeheartedly agree with such new teachings, or
face trial behind closed doors before a *judicial committee*, usually a group
of three elders empowered to enforce Watchtower law and to hand out
punishments—but more about that later. In actual practice most JWs
respond as they are supposed to and change their thinking on whatever

issue is addressed in such a doctrinal change.* Others give lip service to the new teaching. Only a few refuse to conform—less than 1 percent would be my estimate from my own personal observation.

How one views the Great Pyramid of Egypt—whether as God's Stone Witness or as Satan's Bible—is an academic issue, of course. Some people would find themselves troubled by the intellectual dishonesty of reversing beliefs on command, but most people would likely have no problem at all in adapting their view of the Pyramid to suit the demands of an accepted authority figure. After all, it would not make much difference in a practical sense to most of us whether the Pyramid belonged to God, to the Devil, or to a holding company. We wouldn't be affected personally for good or ill if it sank into the sand and disappeared. The real problem with changing beliefs on command from Brooklyn occurs when the command affects *you* or *your family*. During the years I spent in the organization, I saw new sets of instructions come out in *The Watchtower* that required friends of mine to quit their jobs, move out of their homes, or break off contact with close relatives. I will go into some detail in chapter 5, which deals with Nathan Homer Knorr and Frederick W. Franz—because those men headed the Society while I was a member—and in chapter 8.

Right now, let's put ourselves in the position of a loyal *Watch Tower* reader who has just received his November 15, 1928, issue of the magazine in the mail, has opened it up, and has discovered that God's Stone Witness has suddenly been declared to be Satan's Bible. How does he react? First the shock of this news sends him emotionally reeling for a few seconds. Then, as soon as he regains his composure, he runs through a mental checklist to see if the change is going to impact directly on his life. Yes, but it is a small thing: he does some public speaking, and one of the talks is prepared to deal with the pyramid; he will have to scrap that talk and prepare to speak on another subject. Next, he strides into the kitchen to share with his wife the new information Jehovah has provided through His organization.

With JWs whose understanding is on the shallow end, that is where the matter stops. *New light* on the subject of the pyramids is its own reason for rejoicing; it is evidence that Jehovah is leading the organization, because He is the one who makes the light keep getting brighter and brighter for his righteous people. Deeper thinkers, on the other hand,

---

*The unquestioning belief required of Witnesses is illustrated by the JW publication *Qualified To Be Ministers* (1955 ed.), p. 156: "If we have love for Jehovah and for the organization of his people we shall not be suspicious, but shall, as the Bible says, 'believe all things,' all the things that *The Watchtower* brings out."

mouth those same thoughts in the hearing of others at the meetings of the congregation, but might share their thoughts on what *really* happened with a close friend or a marriage partner. Discerning *Watch Tower* readers know what it is all about: Certain elements in the organization don't like Judge Rutherford and the changes he is introducing. They preferred Pastor Russell and the way things used to be done when he was president of the Society. In fact, they prefer to keep studying Pastor Russell's books, rather than move on to the new material Rutherford is providing. This move is Judge Rutherford's way—though loyal members see it as Jehovah's way—to silence those disgruntled elements. Now they will have to make a choice: either give up clinging to Pastor Russell's books with their pyramid lessons, or else quit the organization.

Following Russell's death many believers actually did leave the Watchtower over issues such as this. Independent congregations of Bible Students continued to study Russell's books and were holding regular meetings in many cities, in competition with those taking direction from Brooklyn. Indeed, they still looked to Russell as their pastor. (In fact, some of these groups are still in existence today, and are still distributing their own reprints of Pastor Russell's *Studies in the Scriptures*.) Declaring the Great Pyramid—which was central to Russell's teachings—to be Satan's Bible, was a power play on Rutherford's part to put distance between himself and the competition.

Jehovah's Witnesses today are left largely in ignorance of the entire fifty-year episode involving the pyramids. A May 15, 1956, *Watchtower* article devotes four pages to the Great Pyramid and mentions that "others" claimed it was built under divine inspiration "as a witness in stone to corroborate the Bible," naming some of these "others" as "John Taylor of London, Professor Smyth* and Dr. Edgar of Scotland"†—all advocates of the theory that pyramid measurements held biblical significance. Notably absent from the list are Charles Taze Russell and Joseph F. Rutherford. A small footnote to this discussion adds that "Bible Students also held to this thought prior to 1928,"[22] but no mention is made of the fact that Watchtower publications promoted Professor Smyth's theories and Watchtower offices distributed Dr. Edgar's books.[23]

The 1993 *Proclaimers* book—though purporting to "present a candid history"—similarly leaves JWs in the dark as to the important role these pyramid studies played in the development of their organization.

---

*Prof. C. Piazzi Smyth was ex-Astronomer Royal for Scotland, Russell's contemporary and an expert on the Great Pyramid.

†John Edgar popularized Smyth's theories through his own books on pyramid passages and chambers, replete with photographs.

Although seven hundred and fifty pages long, this book devotes only one paragraph to the subject:

> For some thirty-five years, Pastor Russell thought that the Great Pyramid of Gizeh [*sic*] was God's stone witness, corroborating biblical time periods. (Isa. 19:19) But Jehovah's Witnesses have abandoned the idea that an Egyptian pyramid has anything to do with true worship. (See "Watchtower" issues of November 15 and December 1, 1928).[24]

Brief references such as this and the one in 1956 are not meant to inform JWs of the facts; they serve rather to immunize them against outsiders' efforts to expose the organization's errors. Witnesses can respond, "Oh, yes! I know all about the pyramids. We used to believe that, but we don't any more. The light has gotten brighter." As a result, outside students of the movement generally know more about the role pyramidology played in Watchtower history than members themselves. Still, the seven-foot-tall pyramid at the center of the Watchtower Society's burial ground north of Pittsburgh stands as a permanent reminder of this episode in the history of Jehovah's Witnesses, just as the Great Pyramid of Egypt testifies to the religion of that ancient land.

THE PLEIADES AS GOD'S HOME

Another unusual aspect of old Watchtower teaching was the belief that God's heavenly home lay among the stars in the Pleiades cluster within the constellation Taurus, specifically on Alcyone, the brightest star of that cluster. This belief, too, bore a strange resemblance to the Mormon teaching that God came from the star Kolob to commence his creative work on the earth. Russell's teaching portrays God similarly as a limited being located within the confines of time and space. As part of his discussion of the pyramids in *Studies in the Scriptures*, he quoted an otherwise unidentified "Rev. Joseph Seiss, D.D.," to the effect that

> "The Great Pyramid speaks to us, not by hieroglyphics, nor by sketches, but only by its location, its construction and its measurements. . . . Alcyone, the central one of the renowned Pleiadic stars. . . . Alcyone, then, as far as science has been able to perceive, would seem to be "the midnight throne"* in which the whole system of gravitation

---

*Russell's quote of Rev. Seiss contains, in turn, Seiss's quote from "the distinguished German astronomer, Prof. J. H. Maedler."

has its central seat, and from which the Almighty governs his universe. And here is the wonderful corresponding fact, that at the date of the Great Pyramid's building, at midnight of the autumnal equinox, and hence the true beginning of the year as still preserved in the traditions of many nations, the Pleiades were distributed over the meridian of this Pyramid, with Alcyone (*n* Tauri) precisely on the line.[25]

In various articles in *Zion's Watch Tower* Russell indicated that the Pleiades cluster stands at the center of the universe, "that that center may be the heaven of heavens, the highest heaven, the throne of God."[26] That was in 1895, but twenty years later Russell still held the same belief, namely, that "the Pleiades may represent the residence of Jehovah, the place from which he governs the universe."[27]

This belief did not die with Pastor Russell, either. After his death Judge Rutherford perpetuated the teaching in his own writings:

> The constellation of the seven stars forming the Pleiades. . . . It has been suggested, and with much weight, that one of the stars of that group is the dwelling-place of Jehovah. . . . The constellation of the Pleiades is a small one compared with others. . . . But the greatness in size of other stars or planets is small when compared with the Pleiades in importance, because the Pleiades is the place of the eternal throne of God.[28]

Since the Pleiades were God's heavenly home, Watchtower followers believed Christ went there following his death on the cross and Easter morning resurrection, and they themselves hoped to go to heaven some day—by resurrection or rapture—to live with Jesus and Jehovah on the star Alcyone of the Pleiades cluster. Since this teaching remained in force until it was reversed in the early 1950s, I will have a bit more to say about it in chapter 10.

SOUL SLEEP

> The Watchtower *of August 1, 1982, reports the death of "fourteen-year-old Renata from Brazil," who died after repeatedly refusing blood transfusions, commenting that the doctor admitted, "her faith was unshakable" (p. 22).*

❧   ❧   ❧

One more teaching that should be mentioned here, because it helped separate *Watch Tower* readers from their mainstream Christian neighbors, is the concept of soul sleep. Russell interpreted Scripture to teach that there is no hell of torment, and that neither soul nor spirit survives the death of the body in a conscious afterlife; rather, death ends conscious existence. The dead are gone, totally gone—annihilated. He taught that the Christian's hope lies not in immortality, but in a future resurrection. Jehovah's Witnesses still hold to essentially the same belief—that the dead cease to exist until God recreates them—with some variations that will be mentioned as part of their later history.

In spite of all that has been said above, congregations of *Watch Tower* readers at the time of Russell's death were still very much like congregations of other believers within the realm of Christendom. They prayed to the God of the Bible, as they interpreted him to be; they opened and closed their meetings with hymns, including both traditional pieces and others of their own composition; and they promoted the basics of Christian conduct and Christian morality. I have described four major doctrinal differences in this chapter—opposition to trinitarianism, the Great Pyramid as God's Stone Witness, the Pleiades as God's home, and soul sleep—to highlight areas that set them apart from mainstream Christendom at the time of the transition from Pastor Russell to Judge Rutherford, the subject of the next chapter.

NOTES

1. *Jehovah's Witnesses—Proclaimers of God's Kingdom* (Brooklyn, N.Y.: Watchtower Society, 1993), p. 241.

2. *The Watchtower,* January 15, 1983, pp. 22 and 27.

3. *Jehovah's Witnesses—Proclaimers of God's Kingdom,* p. 319.

4. *Zion's Watch Tower,* March 1883, p. 458 Society Reprints.

5. *Zion's Watch Tower,* October 1883, p. 536 Society Reprints.

6. *Jehovah's Witnesses—Proclaimers of God's Kingdom,* p. 45.

7. *Zion's Watch Tower,* July/August 1881, p. 249 Society Reprints.

8. *Zion's Watch Tower,* July 1882, p. 369 Society Reprints.

9. *The Watch Tower,* June 1, 1910, pp. 179–80.

10. *Studies in the Scriptures* (Brooklyn, N.Y.: Watchtower Society, 1903 ed.), vol. 3, pp. 303, 314–15, 322.

11. Ibid., p. 342.

12. Ibid.

13. Ibid., vol. 2, p. 244.

14. Ibid., vol. 3, p. 320.

15. From a talk by Mormon leader Orson Pratt, reproduced in the *Fiftieth Annual Conference Report of the Church of Jesus Christ of Latter Day Saints,* 1880, pp. 86–87.

16. *Zion's Watch Tower,* May 1881, pp. 5–6.

17. *Studies in the Scriptures,* vol. 3, pp. 362–64.

18. *The Watch Tower,* June 15, 1915, p. 5710 Society Reprints.

19. *The Watch Tower,* May 15, 1925, p. 148.

20. *The Watch Tower,* November 15, 1928, p. 187.

21. Ibid., p. 344.

22. *The Watchtower,* May 15, 1956, p. 298.

23. *The Watch Tower,* August 1, 1910, p. 4658 Society Reprints. Also, volume 2 of *The Great Pyramid Passages* by John Edgar and Morton Edgar, privately published in Glasgow, Scotland, in 1913, mentions on the unnumbered page facing page 1 that "copies may be procured by applying to . . . The Watch Tower Bible and Tract Society, 13 Hicks Street, Brooklyn, N.Y., United States of America."

24. *Jehovah's Witnesses—Proclaimers of God's Kingdom,* p. 201.

25. *Studies in the Scriptures,* vol. 3, pp. 326–28.

26. *Zion's Watch Tower,* May 15, 1895, p. 1814 Society Reprints.

27. *The Watch Tower,* June 15, 1915, p. 5710 Society Reprints.

28. *Reconciliation* (Brooklyn, N.Y.: Watchtower Society, 1928), p. 14.

4

Joseph Franklin Rutherford Transforms Russellites into "Jehovah's Witnesses"

In Tallahassee, Florida, twenty-one-year-old pregnant Jehovah's Witness Bridget Virginia Warner "died after she refused a potentially life-saving blood transfusion for religious reasons," hospital officials told reporters, according to an Associated Press dispatch printed in The Morning Call *of April 28, 1986. "She even signed a refusal, that's how alert she was," said Ron Brafford, a spokesman for the Tallahassee Memorial Regional Medical Center.*

In sharp contrast to the urban prosperity of Charles Taze Russell's youth, Joseph Franklin Rutherford grew up in more humble circumstances in rural Morgan County, Missouri, where he was born on November 8, 1869, to hard-working, no-nonsense Baptist parents. Rutherford's father, unnamed by his biographers, expected his tall, big-boned son to follow in his footsteps as a dirt farmer, even though the boy himself had higher aspirations. Joseph was a reader and took full advantage of the educational opportunities provided through the public school system; his father allowed him to study and attend class as long as these activities did not interfere with his chores on the farm. However, when the ambitious youngster eventually expressed the desire to leave home to further his studies, his father laid down conditions that would have kept most boys plowing fields for life: the family would provide neither tuition nor living expenses, so sixteen-year-old Joe would have to pay his own way, and, on top of that, he would have to hire a workman to take his place on the family farm and would have to pay this farmhand's wages from his own pocket.

To everyone's amazement the young scholar found a way to meet these conditions. To get started he secured a loan from a friend, with no collateral to offer other than his promise that he would pay the money back. Once off the farm and enrolled in college, Rutherford found work selling encyclopedias door to door. Then he learned short-hand and secured part-time employment as a court stenographer. This enabled him both to fund his remaining years in school and to gain first-hand knowledge of the legal profession, which in nineteenth-century Missouri was often entered through apprenticeship.

Rutherford worked and studied for two years under Judge E. L. Edwards. At the age of twenty he became the official reporter for the courts of the Fourteenth Judicial Circuit in Missouri. Two years later he was admitted to the bar. Cooper Circuit Court granted Rutherford a license to practice law in Missouri on May 5, 1892, and he joined the Boonville law firm of Draffen and Wright. After gaining experience as a trial lawyer he served four years as public prosecutor, still in Boonville.

While earlier engaged in the challenging work of door-to-door encyclopedia sales, Rutherford had promised himself that, after he became a lawyer, if anyone came to his office selling books, he would help out the struggling salesman by buying them. He had his opportunity early in 1894 when two female admirers of Charles Taze Russell were engaging in "colporteur" work, canvassing the area with the pastor's books. Elizabeth Hettenbaugh took the lead in speaking to his law partner, whom she and her associate colporteur, "Sister" Beeler, encountered upon entering the outer office. He declined the offer of three *Millennial Dawn* volumes and dismissed the two ladies, but Rutherford overheard the conversation from his private office and called after the women to come back and speak with him. He then made the purchase and took the books home.

By this time Rutherford had married, and he and his wife, Mary, lived together in Boonville. The books sat for a few weeks on a shelf in their home until a brief illness left the young lawyer convalescing in bed with time for idle reading. As a boy at home he had argued with his Baptist family over the doctrine of hellfire, and now he found a pastor who agreed with him. Mary read the books, too, and welcomed Russell's unorthodox approach to Christianity. This prompted the attorney to write a letter of appreciation to the publisher.

There were no Russellite meetings being held in Boonville, so the Rutherfords' association with the sect remained rather loose and intermittent for a number of years. On occasion they would travel to another Missouri town for an important meeting. In 1904 they attended their first "Memorial"—as Jehovah's Witnesses call their annual Communion service*—and the fluent trial lawyer was the natural choice from among the few men in the group to address the gathering on the symbolism of the cup of wine and the broken bread they solemnly shared.

Direct contact with the sect's leadership began when one of Russell's frequent cross-country speaking tours brought him through Kansas City in 1905. The president's close associate, A. H. Macmillan, accepted the attorney's hospitality for a couple of days and used the opportunity to encourage greater involvement. Rutherford responded and, in 1906, attended a gathering in Saint Paul, Minnesota, where Macmillan personally baptized him and a hundred and forty-three others. The following year Rutherford became the Watch Tower Society's resident legal counsel, serving at its Pittsburgh headquarters office.

He was known from the start among the Russellites as "Judge" Rutherford although he had never held a permanent position with that title. On occasion, when the regular judge was ill, Rutherford would fill in on the bench as Special Judge in the Eighth Judicial Circuit Court of Missouri. Some Watchtower sources[1] say he held this temporary position in the Fourteenth Judicial District, but more reliable sources[2] name the Eighth Judicial Circuit. The latter appears to be correct because Witness writer Marley Cole includes the information in a detailed quote from Rutherford's successor as Watchtower counsel, Hayden Cooper Covington. Covington later gained fame as attorney and occasional spokesman for World Heavyweight Champion boxer Cassius Clay, later known as Muhammad Ali—more about that in chapter 6.

When C. T. Russell saw his following growing not only at home but also abroad and began to realize the international potential for his sect, he decided to move its operations to the more cosmopolitan city of New York. To replace the four-story Bible House in Allegheny (Pittsburgh), Russell selected the venerable four-story brownstone parsonage of abolitionist Henry Ward Beecher at 124 Columbia Heights in Brooklyn as a home for the Watchtower headquarters staff. Beecher's old study was selected as Russell's future office. He also chose the old Plymouth Bethel, a disconnected annex of Beecher's Plymouth Congregational Church, to be remodeled into an auditorium and office building. (The name "Bethel" stuck and is still used of the Society's offices and resident workers.) Attorney Rutherford got himself admitted to the New York bar so that he could practice law in that state, and then

---

*It is called a "Memorial" because Christ said to take Communion "in remembrance of me" (Luke 22:19).

accompanied Russell's other representatives to make the real estate purchases and necessary arrangements for transferring the sect's center of operations. From that small beginning the Brooklyn headquarters complex has since expanded into a mini-Vatican of thirty-odd buildings worth $186 million, as will be detailed in chapter 7.

To own real estate in New York State Russell had Rutherford incorporate the People's Pulpit Association there on February 23, 1909. This corporation's name was legally changed to Watchtower Bible and Tract Society, Inc., on February 6, 1939, and then again on January 16, 1956, to Watchtower Bible and Tract Society of New York, Inc.—its present designation. The Pennsylvania corporation, however, remained the parent body, with the New York corporation treated as a branch office running operations in the United States, even though both use the Brooklyn address.

According to instructions Russell left behind, his successor to the presidency would share power with an editorial committee and with the Watch Tower corporation's board of directors, whom Russell had appointed "for life." It was clear from the written documents he had drawn up that Russell intended his own one-man patriarchal rulership to be succeeded by a new collective leadership. In spite of this, Judge Rutherford soon set about concentrating all organizational authority in his own hands. Naturally, his election to the presidency carried with it some authority, but it came nowhere near conveying to him the respect and admiration C. T. Russell had enjoyed among the membership as the "faithful and wise servant" and God's final spokesman to humankind. Many Bible Students were willing for Rutherford to succeed to the corporate presidency but not for him to fill Russell's shoes. In particular, it soon became clear that the Society's seven-member board of directors was unwilling to give Rutherford the free hand he wanted in administering the organization's affairs.

This development finds a parallel in the early 1970s, when the directors, along with their associates on the expanded Governing Body of Jehovah's Witnesses, succeeded in limiting the authority of President Nathan Knorr; nowadays the president of the Watchtower Society is seen as clearly subordinate to the Governing Body, and any attempt by the president to act independently would be considered a sin of rebellion on his part. Rutherford, however, resisted the efforts of the board to limit his powers, and the outcome in his case was just the opposite of what happened over fifty years later.

As his days in office passed, tension grew between Rutherford and the opposing majority on the board of directors, as it was called then.

He saw himself as inheriting all the authority Russell had held, and began trying to exercise it; the board, in turn, saw him as a usurper and worked to restrain him. The struggle and growing hostility became public knowledge among the resident headquarters workers, who began choosing sides.

A. H. Macmillan, then a young member of the board who was part of the minority supporting Rutherford, later wrote about the conflict in his 1957 book, *Faith on the March*. Although published by Prentice-Hall, a major commercial house, this book was written with the express permission and approval of the third president, Nathan Knorr, who gave it his blessing in a one-page introduction; hence Macmillan presents the "official" version of events painted by the winning side. He relates that he was vice-president of the New York corporation at the time, and Rutherford left him in charge of the Brooklyn office while on a speaking engagement on the West Coast. Before departing, the judge had warned him that his rivals might cause trouble in his absence and instructed Macmillan specifically to "call a policeman" if necessary.[3]

So, when the four opposing directors showed up at the Hicks Street office and went upstairs to hold a business meeting in the chapel, Macmillan had his office manager, Robert J. Martin, do just as Rutherford had said. Martin went out to the street, found an old Irish cop who was a personal acquaintance of his, and told him he had a problem with unwanted trespassers. (The four directors were not regulars at the Hicks Street office like Macmillan and Martin, so they would not be familiar faces to an officer walking the beat there.) The lawman followed Martin up to the chapel, twirled his night stick in the air, according to Macmillan's account, and demanded to know what the four men were doing there. When the directors argued that it was their corporation and that they had a right to be there, Macmillan assured the policeman that they were trespassing. So, with a bit of a brogue, the officer broke up their meeting and ordered them out.

It is difficult, if not impossible, to find an objective account of the events that played out in this conflict. As far as I can determine, this is what happened[4]: The whole matter came to a head on the morning of July 17, 1917, when Rutherford addressed the headquarters staff who had assembled for breakfast. He announced to them the release of a new book, *The Finished Mystery*, which he presented as the seventh volume of Pastor Russell's *Studies in the Scriptures*—his posthumous work. Rutherford had had the work prepared and printed without the approval or knowledge of the opposing majority on the board of directors. They and their supporters saw this as another high-handed usurpation of authority.

Rutherford, however, dropped another, more devastating bomb-shell at this breakfast meeting. He announced that four members of the Society's board of directors had been removed and replaced by his supporters. Although they had been appointed by Russell to serve for life, Rutherford had obtained an outside attorney's opinion to the effect that their appointments were invalidated by an oversight: routine reelection by shareholders had been neglected. Of course, the judge and his two allies on the board, Macmillan and secretary-treasurer W. E. Van Amburgh, had not been reelected as directors either—the whole re-election process had been ignored for years as an unnecessary technicality—but Rutherford held that their election as *officers* validated their positions on the board. As president, he claimed authority to appoint men of his choosing to fill the other four seats until the next election. He had already processed the paperwork for the removals and replacements five days earlier, and simply made the devastating announcement as a *fait accompli*.

An uproar ensued in the headquarters dining hall, with charges and countercharges being shouted back and forth across the breakfast tables for five hours. Turmoil continued for over a week until the judge finally succeeded in having his leading opponents put out of the Bethel home. Thus he used legal trickery to unseat the Society's recalcitrant directors without calling a membership vote. Today's official account in the *Proclaimers* book—the only history of the movement most JWs will read nowadays—portrays the ousted directors as the troublemakers: "Four members of the board of directors of the Society went so far as to endeavor to wrest administrative control from Rutherford's hands."[5] Only those who look down at a footnote to this quotation in very small type on the previous page may notice that there were a total of seven on the board of directors; hence the four opposed to Rutherford made up the majority of what is now called the Governing Body, which today does exercise control over the current president—but few JWs would make the connection from the *Proclaimers* account.

The purge of the four directors from headquarters sent shock waves through the entire world Watchtower community. It contributed to the development of Russellite Bible Student groups independent of the Society and of Rutherford's control. Interestingly, the *Proclaimers* book observes that "the number of Bible Students reported as having some share in preaching the good news to others during 1918 decreased by 20 percent worldwide when compared with the report for 1914."[6] The book blames this on "harsh treatment meted out to them during the war years,"[7] but fails to acknowledge the possibility that some may have quit because the Society's predictions for 1914 proved false or because the organization's new president was driving out members offended by his power-grabbing ambitions and methods.

The Finished Mystery, which was released as the seventh volume of *Studies in the Scriptures* the same morning as the Brooklyn Bethel breakfast, created hostility not only among the Bible Student faction that supported the deposed majority of the board of directors, but also in the secular world at large. In less than a year it led to the arrest and imprisonment of Judge Rutherford; Macmillan; Van Amburgh; office manager Martin; the book's authors, Clayton J. Woodworth and George H. Fisher; and other high officials of the sect—most of them committed to the Atlanta federal penitentiary with twenty-year sentences.

What was their crime? Certain passages of *The Finished Mystery*, buried deep within some six hundred pages of biblical interpretation, were held to be in violation of the Espionage Act, a stringent piece of legislation drawn up in the patriotic fever surrounding the First World War. The Justice Department obtained arrest warrants on May 7, 1918, from the United States District Court for the Eastern District of New York. Arrests began the following day at Watch Tower headquarters. When the case was brought to trial in early June, portions of *The Finished Mystery*, along with certain other publications of the Society, were offered before the court as evidence of a conspiracy to hinder the war effort. The book condemned "a certain delusion which is best described by the word Patriotism, but which is in reality murder, the spirit of the very Devil," adding, "Nowhere in the New Testament is Patriotism (a narrow-minded hatred of other peoples) encouraged."[8] It predicted that

> God will pour out His wrath upon the worldly professing Christians. He will blow upon them fiery blasts of war, revolution, and anarchy. They shall be delivered into the hands of a revolted soldiery ... taught by Teutons and Allies to know the utmost efficiency in war. The Sword of the Spirit, the Word of God, too, will be in the hands of consecrated ones, seemingly but not actually cruel, skilled through Divine power to use it with telling effect.[9]

Such statements as these were placed in evidence by the federal prosecutor.

And such were the times that a guilty verdict was pushed through in spite of evidence that *The Finished Mystery* had been written before the Espionage Act became law and before the United States entered the war, in spite of constitutional guarantees regarding free speech and the principles of religious freedom and freedom of conscience. The jury took less than five hours to return a verdict of guilty on June 20, 1918. Sentence was pronounced the following day, and the convicted men were denied bail and hustled off to jail in spite of their appeal to a higher court. They spent a week in Brooklyn's Raymond Street jail, followed by a week in Long Island City prison, and then took the train to Atlanta penitentiary on the fourth of July.

After nine months, when the matter had been brought all the way to United States Supreme Court Justice Louis D. Brandeis, the Circuit Court of Appeals reconsidered and ordered the prisoners released on bail. Two months later the Circuit Court overturned the convictions and remanded the case for retrial. At that point, with the war over and the accompanying hysteria gone, the government decided not to prosecute a second time and dismissed the indictments.

In the midst of all this turmoil, the Watchtower Society offices in Brooklyn were closed and operations moved back to Pennsylvania temporarily. Still, the organization survived, and so did *The Finished Mystery*, which the sect continued to circulate for many years. Some of the older copies, however—including the 1917 and 1918 editions sitting in my office—survived with the offending pages cut out by intimidated members of the sect.

Even today *The Finished Mystery* is a fascinating book to read. It contains some of the most amazing teachings the Watchtower organization has ever presented as "the truth." For example, consider what it says about the "Great Company" or "great crowd, which no man was able to number," mentioned in the Bible at Revelation 7:9:

> The number of the Great Company will apparently exceed one hundred millions. Num. 4:46–48 and Ex. 28:1 indicate but one priest to each 2,860 Levites, which would make the number of the Great Company approximate 411,840,000.[10]

In contrast, the Watchtower Society numbers its "great crowd" today as just under five million active Witnesses, or slightly more than 1 percent of the number prophetically indicated in *The Finished Mystery*.

Even more amazingly,[11] the book converts into miles the distance that blood flowed out of the winepress in Revelation 14:20, interpreting this as 137.9 miles, the exact distance from Scranton, Pennsylvania, where the book was prepared, to Brooklyn Bethel—meticulously calculated on the basis of the number of city blocks inside Scranton, the trip via rail from the Lackawanna Railroad station in Scranton to Hoboken Terminal, and the remainder of the journey over ferry boats and New York streets—as if the Bible could predict the details of this route some two thousand years in advance. In different editions published between 1917 and 1926, the rail and ferry mileages were calculated somewhat differently, but always added up to the same total distance. While the 1926 edition of *The Finished Mystery* gave the "Official Railway Guide timetable distance from Scranton to Hoboken Terminal" as 133.0 miles, earlier editions pointed out that

> The mileage from Scranton to Hoboken Terminal is shown in timetables as 143.8 and this is the mileage charged to passengers, but in 1911, at an expense of $12,000,000, the Lackawanna Railroad completed its famous cut-off, saving 11 miles of the distance. From the day the cut-off was completed the trainmen have been allowed 11 miles less than the timetable shows, or a net distance of 132.8 mi.

Thus the book implies that God used his foreknowledge to incorporate all these tidbits of railroad trivia into the distance given in the Bible at Revelation 14:20.

In today's world, with a number of surviving independent Russellite Bible Student groups that closely resemble Jehovah's Witnesses and share many of their beliefs but reject the modern Watchtower organization, *The Finished Mystery* furnishes a convenient litmus test to distinguish the two factions instantly: Simply ask, "How many volumes make up the *Studies in the Scriptures*." Jehovah's Witnesses will invariably answer *seven*, while members of their kindred groups will answer *six*, since the latter recognize only the volumes written by Russell himself.

❧   ❧   ❧

A March 5, 1961, New York Times article stated that three-year-old John A. Perricone of Elizabeth, New Jersey, had died the previous day, just hours after doctors obtained a court order to administer a blood transfusion. The child had been taken from Elizabeth General Hospital to the Pollack Hospital in Jersey City, the Jehovah's Witness parents all the while refusing to permit a transfusion. By the time doctors succeeded in having the boy made a ward of the state, it was too late.

❧   ❧   ❧

Long before going to prison, Judge Rutherford had won complete control of the Brooklyn headquarters complex and the sect's corporate entities. After his release on March 25, 1919, he turned his attention to the rest of the organization. The whole process took nearly twenty years, but, step by step, he gradually replaced locally elected elders with his own appointees and transformed a loose collection of semi-autonomous, democratically run congregations into a tight-knit organizational machine run from his office. The first step came in 1919, when Rutherford announced publication of a new magazine, *The Golden Age*, to supplement Russell's original *Watch Tower*. (It was later renamed *Consolation*, and in 1946 was given the name *Awake!* which it bears today.) The new magazine would be a publicity tool to advertise God's kingdom, and congregations that wanted to share in distributing it would register with the Society as service organizations. Rutherford appointed a service director in each of these congregations to direct the work and to tally the results, which would then be reported to Brooklyn. This appointed director served alongside the congregation's democratically elected elders and deacons.

Between 1919 and 1938 articles in the various publications emanating from Brooklyn introduced teachings and practices that gradually weakened the hands of the elected elders and brought everyone in the local congregations under the authority of men centrally appointed. Finally, the June 15, 1938, *Watchtower* featured a resolution for local congregations to pass declaring, ". . . 'THE SOCIETY' is the visible representative of the Lord on earth, and we therefore request 'The Society' to organize this company for service and to appoint the various servants thereof. . . ."[12] In other words, the resolution abolished the locally elected positions and authorized the Society to appoint men to lead each congregation. This, in effect, gave the Brooklyn leadership status equal to that of the pope, "the vicar of Christ," in the eyes of Jehovah's Witnesses. It ended the remaining vestiges of democratic church government and placed control of the local congregations completely in the Society's hands. These groups that had *willingly* followed Russell were now bound by contract to follow Rutherford. Russell's spiritual authority was replaced by Rutherford's organizational dominance.

"Was Rutherford simply trying to gain greater control?" the *Proclaimers* book asks. It shoots down this charge by asserting that Rutherford actually "was not the leader of Jehovah's Witnesses, and he did not want to be."[13] God was in charge, and Rutherford was merely serving as His humble human representative. This is the same claim, of course, made by presumptive theocracies, both Christian and non-Christian, down through history.

During the transitional period some elected elders and their friends would not put up with Judge Rutherford's steady push toward autocratic rule. Among the splinter groups of independent Russellite "Bible Students" were the Chicago Bible Students, the Dawn Bible Students, and the Laymen's Home Missionary Movement, which continue to this day. But most Bible Students remained under Rutherford's control. In 1931, he renamed his followers "Jehovah's Witnesses" to distinguish them from these closely related competing groups.

Meanwhile, he shifted the sect's emphasis from the individual "character development" Russell had stressed to vigorous public witnessing work, distributing the Society's literature from house to house. By 1927 this door-to-door literature distribution had become an essential activity required of all members, with the appointed service director in charge of the work. The literature consisted primarily of Rutherford's unremitting series of attacks against government, Prohibition, "big business," and the Roman Catholic Church. He also forged a huge radio network and took to the airwaves, exploiting populist and anti-Catholic sentiment to draw thousands of additional converts. Rutherford's vitriolic attacks, blaring from portable phonographs carried to people's doors and from the loudspeakers placed on top of cars parked across from mainstream churches, also drew down upon the Witnesses mob violence and government persecution in many parts of the world.

Like Russell, Rutherford tried his hand at prophecy and predicted that the biblical patriarchs Abraham, Isaac, and Jacob would be resurrected in 1925 to rule as princes over the earth. In his 1920 booklet *Millions Now Living Will Never Die*, he declares,

> ... [W]e may expect 1925 to witness the return of these faithful men of Israel from the condition of death, being resurrected. . . . Therefore we may confidently expect that 1925 will mark the return of Abraham, Isaac, Jacob, and the faithful prophets of old.[14]

Rutherford adds that "1925 shall mark the resurrection of the faithful worthies of old. . . ."[15] They failed to show up, of course, and Rutherford thereafter quit predicting dates. In fact, referring to that prophetic failure he later admitted privately, "I made an ass of myself."[16]

Although he avoided naming another specific date, the Society's second president kept alive the idea that ancient Bible characters were soon to be resurrected. His 1939 book *Salvation* describes a mansion named Beth-Sarim that he had built in San Diego and declares that "the purpose of acquiring that property and building the house was that there might be some tangible proof that there are those on earth today . . . who believe that the faithful men of old will soon be resurrected by the Lord, be back on earth, and take charge of the visible affairs of earth."[17] The Society's 1942 book *The New World*, published anonymously months after Rutherford's death, says ". . . those faithful men of old may be expected back from the dead any day now. . . . In this expectation the house at San Diego, California, . . . was built, in 1930, and named 'Beth-Sarim,' meaning 'House of the Princes.' It is now held in trust for the occupancy of those princes on their return."[18] The 1930 deed to the property actually names King David, Gideon, Barak, Samson, and others as the intended residents of Beth-Sarim, with the Society holding it in trust for them. As matters turned out, it was Rutherford himself who occupied the mansion. He wintered there with a staff of servants, until his death in 1942. Needless to say, the princes who were expected "any day now" never arrived. To avoid further embarrassment, the Society quietly sold the property in 1948.

As mentioned in chapter 2, Rutherford promoted, through *The Finished Mystery*, the idea that the departed spirit of the late Pastor Russell was actually running the organization from beyond the grave. Why? Apparently to secure the obedience of at least some the pastor's followers—those who would not follow Rutherford or the Society unless they saw these as visible puppets directed by an invisible Russell. Actually, this was only a minor variation or extension of the teaching that Christ had returned invisibly in 1874 and thenceforth had used Russell as his visible spokesman; now Russell, too, was invisible and was using Rutherford. This teaching remained in effect until such time as the judge evidently felt he could command respect in his own right without leaning on Russell's invisible support. He then repudiated the teaching in his 1934 book *Jehovah*:

> No one of the temple company will be so foolish as to conclude that some brother (or brethren) at one time amongst them, and who has died and gone to heaven, is now instructing the saints on earth and directing them as to their work.[19]

The wording of this repudiation indicates not only that the Society's second president now felt he no longer needed his predecessor's invisible backing, but also that he felt free to denounce as "foolish" any followers who continued to believe a teaching he himself had been promoting until that very moment. Fear of losing readers or at least of losing credibility with readers would restrain most authors from insulting their audience's intelligence by reversing positions without making some apology, explanation, or at least an acknowledgment of the fact. Here Rutherford, however, doubly insults the reader by offering, instead of an apology, a denunciation of any who believed his own prior teaching.

❧ ❧ ❧

"I have never seen anyone die in these circumstances, and I hope never to see it again," the Boston Herald *of September 19, 1979, quoted Dr. Raymond Gagnon as saying concerning his patient Eleanor L. Maurer of Falmouth, Massachusetts. The thirty-one-year-old Jehovah's Witness woman began hemorrhaging during childbirth but persisted in refusing blood transfusions. She bled to death.*

❧ ❧ ❧

Why didn't Rutherford lose his audience? For essentially the same reasons that an abusive husband can insult and even slap his wife without fear of losing her: her low self-esteem makes her feel that she deserved it; she sees her husband as having the right to do this to her; she perceives that she has nowhere else to go; and the husband, for his part, has no wish to keep a woman who would stand up to him, but would gladly replace her with another who would accept his abuse. I saw this same mentality at work on a number of occasions during my thirteen years in the organization, as I will relate in later chapters. When "new truths" were introduced and prior teachings denounced as evil falsehoods, my friends and I would rejoice in this as evidence that "God is directing the organization," rather than as reason to doubt its authority. Any who had difficulty in accepting the new truths would conceal their doubts, ashamed to reveal what they would see as their own "weakness" or "lack of spiritual maturity." The few who did raise objections to doctrinal reversals were summarily dismissed from the organization, with the rest of us muttering clichés such as "good riddance to bad rubbish" as they went out the door.

Very few Jehovah's Witnesses today are aware that the organization claimed for seventeen years (1917–1934) to be directed from beyond the grave by Pastor Russell's ghost. If confronted with the facts, many would tremble inwardly and experience a personal crisis of faith, but to save face they would feel obligated to maintain an unperturbed outward appearance. They might even chuckle and attempt to brush aside this embarrassing episode of Watchtower history with the excuse that "the light has gotten brighter" since the days of Russell and Rutherford.

But has it? Or are the organization's followers still, as Rutherford put it, "so foolish" as to conclude that leaders who have died and gone to heaven are now instructing them from beyond the grave? Amazingly, the Watchtower book *Revelation— Its Grand Climax At Hand!* published in 1988 and still in use as authoritative, does in fact contain another very similar reference to communications from dead leaders. Indeed, it implies such a source for some of the sect's recent new truths, claiming that deceased "anointed ones already in heaven . . . may be involved in the communicating of divine truths today."[20] These "anointed ones" would include Russell, Rutherford, and subsequent leaders, such as Nathan Knorr, who have died in recent years. The anonymously authored book gives no indication of which specific new truths are believed to have come from this source, nor the means employed by the deceased in "communicating" truths today—a puzzle since JWs reject both séances and channeling spirits of the dead; they view both practices as demonic deceptions. If any of the Brooklyn headquarters staff claim to have received new truths as direct communications from deceased staff members, no specific mention of this has ever been made in the publications presenting those new teachings.

The organization today does not make much of this teaching, and the typical JW would deny that such an idea is taught. The commonly accepted view, repeated often in current publications, is that the organization receives its invisible guidance from God's active force or *holy spirit*—intentionally not capitalized to negate the traditional concept of the Holy Spirit or Holy Ghost as the third member of the Trinity, a doctrine JWs reject. Witnesses today are generally unaware that Rutherford claimed direction from *spirits* rather than the Holy Spirit (or active force). His teaching, unique in Watchtower history but dominant during his presidency, was that the Holy Spirit ceased to function in 1918* and had to be replaced by invisible spirit persons. Seldom mentioned today, this teaching found expression in various publications, but is per-

---

*Rutherford's reasoning was that "in times past the holy spirit was the comforter and helper of God's people . . . but now, since the coming of Christ Jesus . . . the faithful ones receive knowledge and understanding from the Word of God revealed to them through the Head of the temple organization." J. F. Rutherford, *Jehovah* (Brooklyn, N.Y.: Watchtower Society, 1934)

haps most clearly stated in Rutherford's 1932 book *Preservation*. In it Rutherford writes, "By his spirit, the holy spirit, Jehovah God guides or leads his people up to a certain point of time, and thus he did until the time when 'the comforter' was taken away . . . in 1918."[21] In the same vein *The Watchtower* of October 1, 1932, says: "The Lord Jesus came to his temple in 1918, and that would mark the time of the cessation of the work of the holy spirit as an advocate, helper and comforter of the members of the church on earth. There the holy spirit was taken away. . . ."[22] Angelic spirits would function in its place, Rutherford indicated in *Preservation*: "After the holy spirit as an advocate or paraclete ceased to function in behalf of the consecrated, then the angels are employed. . . ."[23]

Rutherford expressed the same thought elsewhere in various *Watchtower* articles: "Invisible messengers pass such instruction on to the remnant."[24] But, "Just how this is done is not necessary for us to understand."[25] The Society's president evidently feared that some would accuse him of "spiritism" for receiving his new truths from "invisible deputies" he believed were sent to him by God. Thus in *Light, Book One*, Rutherford wrote, "The Lord used *The Watch Tower* to announce these truths. Doubtless he used his invisible deputies to have much to do with it. This is not what some may regard as spiritism, by any means."[26] After Rutherford's death his successors quietly reintroduced the belief that it is primarily God's "holy spirit" that leads the organization, along with help from angelic spirit creatures.

The rare mention of help from spirits of the dead, however—whether Pastor Russell's ghost or "anointed ones" in heaven—highlights an interesting similarity between JW beliefs and the teachings of groups JWs denounce as false. The Watchtower Society has long condemned communication with the dead as a form of spiritism or demonism; because "the dead are not alive anywhere" such communications must actually come from wicked spirits or demons, JWs are taught.[27] How, then, could the Watchtower publications cited above make these claims that the late Pastor Russell or other departed spirits of the dead communicate with living Watchtower leaders?

They could do this because, while other dead persons are said to be truly dead and unable to communicate, the Society has long claimed that its own dead anointed ones have been resurrected as spirits to live in the spirit world. The current teaching is that this spirit resurrection took place in 1918, the year after publication of *The Finished Mystery* with its claim that Russell was leading the organization from beyond the grave. But for many years the Watchtower Society taught that this spirit resurrection of the faithful took place earlier, in 1878, which would make Russell's departed spirit conscious and able to lead the sect in 1917 when *The Finished Mystery* was published.*

Yet, the Society attacks other religious groups for similar teachings: "False religion enslaves people in other ways, too. For example, many people believe that the dead are alive in the spirit world."[28] What is the difference? How do Jehovah's Witnesses claim to be different from "false religions" that teach essentially the same thing on this point? The difference is this: JWs, we repeat, believe that dead Catholics, dead Shintoists, and dead Voodoo practicers are *really* dead—unconscious, annihilated, nonexistent—while dead Jehovah's Witnesses (of the anointed class)† are actually alive in the spirit world and therefore in a position to "communicate divine truths" to Watchtower leaders. This self-righteous sort of reasoning could, of course, be used by any religious group that assumes its own faithful members are the only ones who go to heaven, and that therefore it is permitted to communicate with them. Compare, for example, the Roman Catholic practice of petitioning saints—a practice JWs condemn—with *The Watch Tower*'s claim concerning its own saints (dead JWs in this case): "the Lord . . . would privilege the saints beyond the veil to have a part in the work on this side. . . ."[29] The beliefs are nearly parallel, but JWs are highly offended by any suggestion of similarity.

❦ ❦ ❦

The 1971 Yearbook of Jehovah's Witnesses *reported the case of an unnamed "zealous sister who died in March" in the Ellice Islands (now Tuvalu) in the Pacific. The* Yearbook *placed the blame on doctors, stating that "She had been suffering from internal bleeding for the previous two years and needed an operation," but "the doctors refused to perform this unless she consented to take a blood transfusion" (p. 131). It adds that "she died a faithful Witness."*

❦ ❦ ❦

---

*Although the bodily rapture predicted for 1878 by N. H. Barbour failed to occur, the belief was that dead Christians were raised invisibly to spirit life in that year, and Watchtower followers who died afterward lived on as spirits. Today JWs believe 1918 to be the date for these invisible events.

†The rest await Christ's thousand-year reign, when they will be resurrected bodily to a paradise on earth.

When Branch Davidian cult leader David Koresh promised to reveal to humankind the meaning of the Seven Seals in the book of Revelation, only a few followers took him seriously. I think most outside observers would agree with me that he was suffering from megalomania—a mental disorder in which the subject thinks himself great or exalted. Similarly, although *The Watchtower* of December 1, 1993, cites J. F. Rutherford as an example of "a humble man,"[30] the Society's second president saw dozens of Bible verses as foretelling what he personally would do or what would happen to him. For example, Rutherford taught that he was God's chosen instrument for disclosing to humankind the seven seals of Revelation, chapters 5–8*; that the seven angelic trumpet blasts in Revelation, chapters 8–11, foretold resolutions he presented to conventions held between 1922 and 1928; and that the pouring out of the seven bowls of God's wrath in Revelation chapter 16, foretold proclamations he presented at conventions.[31] Also, as the following quotes from his book *Light*, vol. 1, reveal, he believed that angels directed him, and that the ,1260 days predicted in Rev. 11:3 and Rev. 12:6 foretold what would happen to him and his close associates†:

> [As Rev. 11:3 foretold] . . . 1,260 days . . . beginning . . . November 7, 1914, would end on the 7th day of May, 1918 . . . all the officers of the Watch Tower Bible and Tract Society . . . were arrested.[32]
>
> . . . .the Lord through his angel directed the proceedings at that convention [which Rutherford directed!].[33]
>
> [As Rev. 12:6 foretold] . . . 1,260 days in the wilderness began March 27, 1919, and the end of that period came September 8, 1922. . . . On March 26, 1919, the imprisoned officers of the Society were released.[34]
>
> . . . [W]ithout any thought of the fulfilment of the prophetic dates, September 8 [when Rutherford spoke] was designated on the program as "The Day." . . . That date was exactly the end of the 1,260-day period in the wilderness experience [foretold at Rev. 12:6,14].[35]

---

*These and subsequently cited chapters of Revelation all depict heavenly scenes in which angels open seals, blow trumpets, and pour out the contents of bowls, with each such action followed by a disaster on earth such as plague, earthquake, or fire.

†"And I will give power unto my two witnesses and they shall prophesy a thousand two hundred and threescore days, clothed in sackcloth." (Rev. 11:3 King James version)

"And the woman fled into the wilderness, where she hath a place of God, that they should feed her there a thousand two hundred and threescore days." (Rev. 12:6 KJV)

Strange as it may seem, the Watchtower Society today still teaches essentially the same thing: that all these Bible verses, and others, foretold what Rutherford and his associates would do. For example, the November 1, 1993, *Watchtower* interpreted the "time, times, and an half (said to equal 1,260 days, the 1,290 days, and the 1,335 days of Daniel 12:7, 11–12*) as pinpointing, centuries in advance, the date Rutherford was sentenced to prison, the date he spoke at a convention in Ohio, and the date a book of his was released.[36]

In another area of doctrine, it is significant that it was under the presidency of J. F. Rutherford that the Watchtower organization quit celebrating Christmas. This was a notable reversal, since *Zion's Watch Tower* had earlier encouraged readers to offer sets of *Studies in the Scriptures* to people who wanted to purchase "beautiful, appropriate," and reasonably priced Christmas gifts for friends.[37] Pastor Russell had acknowledged that Jesus was not born on December 25, but urged followers not to "quibble" about the date but rather to join "in celebrating the grand event on the day which the majority celebrate—Christmas day."[38] As a result Watchtower headquarters workers decorated the Brooklyn Bethel dining hall for a festive dinner each year. Stern Judge Rutherford, however, did decide to quibble. Pointing to the pagan roots of certain Christmas customs, he instructed the office staff to quit observing the day, so that there was no Christmas dinner served in 1927 or thereafter. To persuade the membership in general to abandon the holiday, Rutherford had his magazine, *The Golden Age*, publish a hard-hitting exposé in its December 12, 1928, issue.

What was the real reason for the change? The *Proclaimers* book says that "further investigation of the subject" revealed "the God-dishonoring roots of Christmas" and showed that " 'St. Nicholas' (Santa Claus) was admittedly another name for the Devil himself."[39] A look at the larger context, however, reveals rejection of the holiday as directed not at St. Nicholas but at Christ. The move was part of a long, slow process of deemphasizing Christ. This steady doctrinal shift is observable in the Society's literature, not only during the Rutherford era,

---

*"And I heard the man clothed in linen, which was upon the waters of the river, when he held up his right hand and his left hand unto heaven, and sware by him that liveth for ever that it shall be for a time, times, and an half; and when he shall have accomplished to scatter the power of the holy people, all these things shall be finished." (Dan. 12:7 KJV) "And from the time that the daily sacrifice shall be taken away, and the abomination that maketh desolate set up, there shall be a thousand two hundred and ninety days. Blessed is he that waiteth, and cometh to the thousand three hundred and five and thirty days." (Dan. 12:11–12 KJV)

but even to the present. Although noticeable, such a slow slide away from Christ-centeredness over the years is difficult to quantify. Perhaps the closest anyone has come to measuring it is in an overview of the sect's hymnals in its own *Revelation—Its Grand Climax At Hand!* which notes that

> In the songbook produced by Jehovah's people in 1908, there were twice as many songs praising Jesus as there were songs praising Jehovah God. In their 1928 songbook, the number of songs extolling Jesus was about the same as the number extolling Jehovah. But in the latest songbook of 1984, Jehovah is honored by four times as many songs as is Jesus.[40]

A similar change was reflected in the focus of the sect's magazine articles, books, and study materials. Abandoning Christmas was just one step in this move away from being a Christ-centered religion. Russell had said, "We always refuse to be called by any other name" than "that of our Head—Christians,"[41] but Rutherford's renaming the sect as "Jehovah's Witnesses" meant a further shift in emphasis away from Christ.

The name change served an additional purpose for the Society's second president. Prior to this, when pressed for their denominational affiliation beyond the designation "Christians," Watchtower readers would identify themselves as International Bible Students, or simply Bible Students. The problem was that some of the break-away groups that rejected Rutherford's leadership and that still clung to Pastor Russell used such names as Dawn Bible Students, Chicago Bible Students, and so on. As far as the public was concerned, all of the Bible Students—including Rutherford's people—were "Russellites." To break that mold and to build a wall between his followers and the independent Bible Student groups, the judge renamed his followers by means of a resolution adopted at a Watchtower convention on July 26, 1931. The wording of the resolution itself helps to explain Rutherford's thinking:

> WHEREAS shortly following the death of Charles T. Russell a division arose between those associated with him in such work, resulting in a number of such withdrawing from the Watch Tower Bible & Tract Society, and who have since refused to cooperate with said Society and its work and who decline to concur in the truth as published by the Watch Tower Bible & Tract Society, in The Watch Tower and the other recent publications of the above-named corporations, and

have opposed and do now oppose the work of said Society in declaring the present message of God's kingdom and the day of the vengeance of our God against all parts of Satan's organization; and said opposing ones have formed themselves into divers and numerous companies and have taken and now bear such names as, to wit, "Bible Students," "Associated Bible Students," "Russellites teaching the truth as expounded by Pastor Russell," "Stand-Fasters," and like names, all of which tends to cause confusion and misunderstanding . . . therefore we joyfully embrace and take the name which the mouth of the Lord God has named, and we desire to be known as and called by the name, to wit, *Jehovah's witnesses*. (Emphasis in original)[42]

The new name ended that confusion; it was now perfectly clear that Jehovah's Witnesses followed the Watchtower Society, while those who retained the name Bible Students did not.

Watchtower publications often spelled the name without capitalizing the second word—thus, Jehovah's witnesses. This was not sloppy typography. It was done intentionally to convey the thought that this was not a mere denominational name, but rather a meaningful description of what they actually were: the witnesses or earthly representatives of Jehovah God. Witnesses still view themselves that way, even though today the Society's publications usually capitalize the word Witnesses. This is the reason why they will say, "I'm a Witness of Jehovah," rather than, "I'm a Jehovah's Witness." They think of Lutherans as followers of Martin Luther, Mennonites as followers of Menno Simons, but themselves as followers of God himself. Outsiders, of course, see this line of reasoning as no more convincing than the argument that a group calling itself the Church of God is therefore God's only true church, or that the Church of Christ is, by virtue of having that name, the one true Christian church.

Surprisingly, when he introduced the name Jehovah's Witnesses, Judge Rutherford did not intend for it to apply to all of his followers, but rather only to those of the spirit-anointed class chosen to rule as kings with Christ in heaven. Others of his followers, he believed, were merely companions of the anointed ones but not part of that class. These companions were destined to live forever on earth instead of going to heaven. In 1932 Rutherford began calling these people *Jonadabs*, a reference to a man who joined the ancient Israelite king Jehu as a companion. In 1935 he began teaching that these Jonadabs were the "great multitude" or "great crowd" spoken of in the Bible at Revelation 7:9–17. He did not consider them to be Jehovah's Witnesses, but rather mere companions of the Witnesses.[43]

In time the organization began to view Rutherford's 1935 lecture as the cutoff point for the anointed class; the door to heaven was then closed and would remain so. Only a hundred and forty-four thousand would go to heaven, and that number was filled as of 1935, so that new converts from that time forward would be more or less automatically shunted into the class with an earthly future. They would live forever on a paradise earth in healthy physical bodies, without aging. Today fewer than nine thousand JWs claim to be members of the anointed class—mostly elderly Witnesses who joined the sect prior to 1935—and the remaining millions believe themselves to be of the earthly great crowd, hence not Jehovah's Witnesses as the term was originally used. It was not until after Rutherford's death that the July 1, 1942, issue of the *Watchtower* broadened the definition of the term Jehovah's Witnesses to include persons with an earthly hope. If the original teaching had been retained there would be very few "Jehovah's Witnesses" today, since more than 99 percent of the nearly five million active JWs today believe themselves to be of the earthly class.

Actually, the idea of the door closing on the opportunity for a heavenly inheritance did not originate with J. F. Rutherford. As detailed in chapter 2, his predecessor, C. T. Russell, originally taught that Christ had returned invisibly to earth in early October 1874; along with this Russell also taught that Christ spent the next seven years selecting those who would join Him in heaven as the composite Bride of Christ. At the end of those seven years, October 2, 1881, the opportunity ended and Christ closed the door:

> The *favor* of the present (and which we believe will end in October 1881) is not to the nominal church but to *individuals* in her, that they may come *out* and receive the *present* Lord. . . . We have no desire to dogmatize nor to keep anyone out, but we *believe* (and therefore speak) that the *favor* which ends this fall, is that of entering the Bride *company.* We believe the *door of favor* is now open and any who consecrate *all* and give up *all,* can come in to the wedding and become members of the Bride, but that with this year the company will be reckoned *complete* and the *door* to that *high calling* (not the door of mercy) closed forever. (Emphasis in original)[44]

Persons who came into association with the Watchtower organization after the door was shut in 1881 would not be part of the "little flock" destined for heaven as the Bride of Christ, but rather would make up the "great company" excluded from receiving the kingdom:

Just *what* we should look for from October 1881 onward we can scarcely say, but expect that these seven years of the harvest, which altogether is forty years, have been a time of *favor* to the church, the succeeding years will show a *lack of favor*, and that consequently the nominal church will *rapidly fall to pieces*, and as a consequence, *many* who have heard of *these things* but dared not brave the frown of a popular and flourishing church organization, will then be set free and begin to knock and inquire. But while we shall be glad to greet them and to help them in every way in our power, we believe that they will not be recognized of the Lord as part of the *Bride*. It is not for us to judge, however; we understand this to be the teaching of His word, but will wait for him to tell them that they are a part of the "*great company*" and not of the "*little flock*" to whom "it is the Father's good pleasure to give . . . the kingdom." (Emphasis in original)[45]

Russell was certain of the October 1881 cutoff date, because he saw it confirmed not only in the Bible but also in the Great Pyramid of Egypt.* When October 1881 came and went with no visible change in the congregation,† Russell nevertheless believed that what he had predicted did in fact take place:

That which occurred in 1881, like that which occurred in 1874, can be discerned only by the eye of faith in the light of God's Word. It was the date of the close of the high calling, and hence the date for the beginning of restitution announcement,—the Jubilee trumpet. About that date the author, and, so far as he knows, no one else, had noticed the distinction between the call to divine nature, open during the Gospel age, and the opportunity for restitution of *human* perfection and all that was lost in Adam, due at the close of the Gospel high-calling." (Emphasis in original)[46]

For some time Russell continued to refer to "the distinction between the high-calling of the Gospel Church and the Restitution favors for the world in general . . . the date of the close of that high-calling as October 1881."[47] For some reason, however, the Watchtower Society's founder proved unable to shut the door of heavenly opportunity. Perhaps it was because other prophecies connected with the 1881 chronology proved false, or perhaps because the organization lacked the centralized control that would develop later, but persons newly associating with the sect continued to declare themselves part of the Bride of

---

*For the "prophetic" measuring of the Great Pyramid, see pp. 55–65.

†See Appendix B regarding the changing dates.

Christ headed for heaven. As time passed, however, the 1881 date was abandoned. Most Jehovah's Witnesses alive today are not aware that the organization once attached special significance to that year.

Rutherford was more successful at this than his predecessor. He was able to close the door to heaven, in the eyes of Jehovah's Witnesses, and to keep it closed. In recent decades the teaching has been that "the heavenly hope was held out, highlighted and stressed until about the year 1935. Then as 'light flashed up' to reveal clearly the identity of the 'great crowd' of Revelation 7:9, the emphasis began to be placed on the earthly hope."[48] With more authority to command its followers than in the days of C. T. Russell, the organization under Rutherford and his successors began to "emphasize" to new students that they had missed the deadline to enroll for the heavenly hope, and that they would have to settle for less—a place among the great multitude of other sheep inhabiting paradise earth:

> [T]he spiritual remnant are not envious so as to hold back anything profitable from those "other sheep" but have lovingly published worldwide that grand earthly hope, particularly since the year 1935. . . .
>
> Down to the spring of 1935 the dedicated, baptized witnesses of Jehovah had entertained in true faith the "one hope" that was set before them in Ephesians 4:4–6, as follows: "One body there is, and one spirit, even as you were called in the one hope to which you were called; one Lord, one faith, one baptism; one God and Father of all persons." But in that memorable year of 1935, at the convention held in Washington, D.C., the "great multitude," as visualized at Revelation 7:9–17 (*Authorized Version*), was identified. . . .[49]

What actually happened in 1935? According to the March 1, 1985, *Watchtower* the convention talk Judge Rutherford gave on this subject proved to be a "revelation": "[a] . . . historical discourse on 'The Great Multitude,' given May 31, 1935, by the president of the Watch Tower Society, J. F. Rutherford, at the Washington, D.C., convention of Jehovah's Witnesses. What a revelation of divine truth that was!"[50] Based on this supposed "revelation," the Society redefined its theology on heaven, and declared the door shut (again) in 1935. The *Proclaimers* book repeats an earlier JW *Yearbook* in referring to Rutherford's new teaching as a "revelation."[51] Indeed, the concept of assigning believers baptized after 1935 to earth instead of heaven would have to be a new revelation, since the date is found nowhere in the Bible. Yet, with the weight of the organization's authority behind them, it is easy for

JWs to teach new members an earthly hope rather than a heavenly one, based on the 1935 date. In most cases both teachers and the students alike are unfamiliar with Russell's 1881 date and the earlier cutoff dates set by his Millerite and Adventist predecessors. Moreover, they fail to apply to the Watchtower organization the accusation Jesus hurled against the Pharisees of his day: "You shut the door of the kingdom of Heaven in men's faces; you do not enter yourselves, and when others are entering, you stop them" (Matt. 23:13 *New English Bible*).

Rutherford's 1935 teaching is responsible for another oddity of Jehovah's Witnesses: their annual "Memorial" or communion services, in which the cup of wine and the plate of broken bread are passed from one to another in the audience with no one partaking in most congregations.* Only those of the heavenly class are supposed to take communion. The Society has to issue new converts such instructions for the last sixty years. So, today, there are only a few old-timers among Jehovah's Witnesses who partake of the communion loaf and cup:

> There is only a remnant of such spiritual sons now living, and these are the ones who properly partake of the emblems. This, then, accounts for the vast majority of Jehovah's Witnesses being observers and not partakers.[52]

Another change introduced during the Rutherford administration was the denunciation of vaccination during the 1930s and 1940s. Although obviously carried out with the judge's approval, the driving force behind initiating the campaign appears to be Clayton Woodworth, who co-authored *The Finished Mystery* and who served as editor of *The Golden Age*. Woodworth denied the germ theory of disease and objected to the contamination of the human body by injecting animal "pus." At the same time, however, he opened the pages of *The Golden Age* to numerous questionable remedies as suggested alternatives to standard medical procedure—evidently as part of his ongoing battle against the evil vaccinators of the medical profession. More will be said about this in chapter 10.

The Society's second president died at Beth-Sarim on January 8, 1942. The *Proclaimers* book mentions that

> Brother Rutherford was survived by his wife, Mary, and their son, Malcolm. Because Sister Rutherford had poor health and found win-

---

*Their 1996 *Yearbook*, p. 33, reports that 8,645 individuals partook at services held in 78,620 congregations.

ters in New York (where the Watch Tower Society's headquarters were located) difficult to endure, she and Malcolm had been residing in southern California, where the climate was better for her health.[53]*

Nothing is said to indicate that Mary and Malcolm might have lived at Beth-Sarim in San Diego, where J. F. Rutherford died and where he had wintered in the years leading up to his death. Nor do other references to Beth-Sarim allow for that possibility. Other references to Rutherford in the Society's publications imply that he lived alone or in the company of other men on the headquarters staff. According to he *1975 Yearbook of Jehovah's Witnesses*, "Sister Hazel Burford was one of the nurses who cared for Brother Rutherford during his final illness at Beth-Sarim, where he was taken in November 1941."[54] Three men from Brooklyn headquarters also spent time with Rutherford during his final days, but no mention is made of his wife or son. The *Proclaimers* book's rare admission that Rutherford had a wife and child who lived apart from him for years should be a matter of concern for Jehovah's Witnesses, since they generally view their leaders as holding to a higher standard than the membership as a whole, or at least to the same standard. Yet, it is questionable whether a man with such living arrangements today would be eligible to serve even as a local elder or ministerial servant in a JW congregation. "Health" is given as the reason for the separate living arrangements, but if a Watchtower missionary "sister" assigned to Central America with her husband is forced by illness to move back to the States, the Society does not permit the husband to remain on assignment; both are moved back together. Allowance is sometimes made for a man with a non-Witness mate who separates from him, since the blame automatically falls on the unbeliever, but the organization normally responds with skepticism when a man claims to qualify for a position of responsibility while living apart from a wife and child who are also JWs in good standing.

It was not only Rutherford's wife and son who suffered from the judge's apparent disdain for women and children. He taught men not to stand up from their seats or remove their hats in the presence of a woman; these customs were "a scheme of Satan to turn men away from God and from his announced rule of the proper position of man

---

*How strange that the *Proclaimers* book cites fragile health as the reason Mary Rutherford resided on the West Coast while Joseph lived in Brooklyn, at least until the end of his life! The climate in southern California truly must have benefited her health. She outlived her husband by twenty years, dying on December 17, 1962, at the age of ninety-three.

and woman," he insisted.[55] Moreover, "On the face of it the arrangement of 'Mother's Day' seems harmless and calculated to do good.
But the people are in ignorance of Satan's subtle hand in the matter,
and that he is back of the movement," Rutherford went on in a similar vein.[56]

I remember Jack Rupert, an elderly JW, quoting "the Judge" on
marriage. Jack, who took me under his wing early on during my membership and gave me some of the Society's old books and recordings of
Rutherford's talks, used to delight in tormenting his wife by quoting
his description of a woman as a mere "hank of hair and a bag of bones."
The judge took this description from *The Vampire* by Rudyard Kipling,
and used it to discourage young men from getting married in a talk he
gave at a JW convention in 1941 in St. Louis, Missouri. Jack would
quote the judge, laugh, and then sing, "I wish I were single again,"
while his submissive wife pretended not to be hurt. Rutherford actually broke up youth groups and special arrangements for children that
congregations had developed in some localities. "Right down to the
present, it remains the custom among Jehovah's Witnesses for the entire family to attend congregation meetings together," the *Proclaimers*
book states, explaining J. F. Rutherford's move to ban youth groups and
Sunday school classes for children during the 1930s because they did
"not contribute to unity."[57] It does not admit here that the children of
JWs have been largely neglected throughout most of the organization's
history, with emphasis instead on converting strangers from house to
house.

NOTES

1. *1975 Yearbook of Jehovah's Witnesses* (Brooklyn, N.Y.: Watchtower Society, 1975),
p. 81, and *Jehovah's Witnesses in the Divine Purpose* (Brooklyn, N.Y.: Watchtower Society,
1959), p. 65.

2. *Jehovah's Witnesses—Proclaimers of God's Kingdom* (Brooklyn, N.Y.: Watchtower
Society, 1993), p. 67, and Marley Cole, *Jehovah's Witnesses—The New World Society* (New
York: Vantage Press, 1955), p. 215.

3. A. H. Macmillan, *Faith on the March* (New York: Prentice-Hall, 1957), p. 78.

4. My brief summary of events is based largely on information gleaned from the
following sources: Macmillan, *Faith on the March*; M. James Penton, *Apocalypse Delayed:
The Story of Jehovah's Witnesses* (Toronto: University of Toronto Press, 1985); Raymond
V. Franz, *Crisis of Conscience* (Atlanta: Commentary Press, 1983); anon., *Jehovah's Witnesses—Proclaimers of God's Kingdom*; and anon., *Jehovah's Witnesses in the Divine Purpose*.

5. *Jehovah's Witnesses—Proclaimers of God's Kingdom*, p. 66.

6. Ibid., pp. 424–25.

7. Ibid.

8. *Studies in the Scriptures* (Brooklyn, N.Y.: Watchtower Society, 1917), vol 7, p. 247.

9. Ibid., p. 469.

10. Ibid., p. 107.

11. Ibid., p. 230.

12. *Jehovah's Witnesses—Proclaimers of God's Kingdom*, p. 219.

13. Ibid., p. 212.

14. J. F. Rutherford, *Millions Now Living Will Never Die* (Brooklyn, N.Y.: Watchtower Society, 1920), pp. 89–90.

15. Ibid., p. 97.

16. *The Watchtower,* October 1, 1984, p. 24.

17. J. K. Rutherford, *Salvation* (Brooklyn, N.Y.: Watchtower Society, 1939), p. 311.

18. *The New World* (Brooklyn, N.Y.: Watchtower Society, 1942), p. 104.

19. J. F. Rutherford, *Jehovah* (Brooklyn, N.Y.: Watchtower Society, 1934), p. 191.

20. *Revelation—Its Grand Climax At Hand!* (Brooklyn, N.Y.: Watchtower Society, 1988), p. 125.

21. J. F. Rutherford, *Preservation* (Brooklyn, N.Y.: Watchtower Society, 1932), pp. 193–94.

22. *The Watchtower,* October 1, 1932, p. 294.

23. Rutherford, *Preservation,* p. 51.

24. *The Watchtower,* September 13, 1938, p. 285.

25. *The Watchtower,* December 1, 1933, p. 364.

26. J. F. Rutherford, *Light, Book One* (Brooklyn, N.Y.: Watchtower Society, 1930), p. 64.

27. *The Watchtower,* April 1, 1992, p. 13.

28. Ibid., p. 5.

29. *The Watch Tower,* November 1, 1917, p. 6161 Society Reprints.

30. *The Watchtower,* December 1, 1993, p. 18.

31. Rutherford, *Light,* vol. 1, pp. 72, 73, 105–227; vol. 2, pp. 19–60.

32. Ibid., p. 199.

33. Ibid., p. 223.

34. Ibid., p. 249.

35. Ibid., p. 251.

36. *The Watchtower,* November 1, 1993, pp. 11–12.

37. *Zion's Watch Tower,* November 15, 1907, p. 4094 Society Reprints.

38. *Zion's Watch Tower,* December 1, 1904, p. 3468 Society Reprints.

39. *Jehovah's Witnesses—Proclaimers of God's Kingdom*, p. 199.

40. *Revelation—Its Grand Climax At Hand!* p. 36.

41. *The Watch Tower,* March 1883, p. 458 Society Reprints.

42. J. F. Rutherford, *The Kingdom, the Hope of the World* (Brooklyn, N.Y.: Watchtower Society, 1931), pp. 30–31.

43. *Jehovah's Witnesses—Proclaimers of God's Kingdom*, p. 83.

44. *Zion's Watch Tower,* May 1881, p. 224 Society Reprints.

45. Ibid., p. 225 Society Reprints.

46. *Studies in the Scriptures,* vol. 3 (1913 ed.), p. 367.

47. Ibid., p. 367n.

48. *The Watchtower,* February 1, 1982, p. 28.

49. *The Watchtower,* December 15, 1982, p. 19.
50. *The Watchtower,* March 1, 1985, p. 14.
51. *Jehovah's Witnesses—Proclaimers of God's Kingdom,* p. 84.
52. *The Watchtower,* February 15, 1985, p. 17.
53. *Jehovah's Witnesses—Proclaimers of God's Kingdom,* p. 89.
54. *1975 Yearbook of Jehovah's Witnesses,* p. 194.
55. J. K. Rutherford, *Vindication* (Brooklyn, N.Y.: Watchtower Society, 1931), pp. 156–57.
56. Ibid., p. 55.
57. *Jehovah's Witnesses—Proclaimers of God's Kingdom,* pp. 246–47.

5

Nathan Homer Knorr and Frederick W. Franz Claim My Allegiance for Thirteen Years

Young mother Anita Brown "died June 17 of hemorrhaging from a jaw tumor," according to a June 25, 1980, article in California's Contra Costa Times. *The tumor had continued to grow during a two-year period when she "was unable to find a surgeon who would operate on her without using blood transfusions, which are barred by her religion," according to the article.*

By unanimous vote of the Watchtower corporate board of directors, Vice President Nathan Homer Knorr inherited the presidency upon Rutherford's death in 1942 but left doctrinal matters largely in the hands of Frederick W. Franz, who joined the sect under Russell and who had been serving at the Brooklyn headquarters since 1920. When Franz himself later succeeded to the presidency in 1977, he left Knorr's programs largely intact. Since the two functioned as a team with Knorr handling the sect's administration and Franz its theology, their successive presidencies are considered together in this one chapter. My own active participation in the Jehovah's Witnesses from 1968 through 1982 also overlaps both periods, enabling me to comment more extensively from personal experience in addition to research.

Nathan Knorr was born April 23, 1905, in Bethlehem, Pennsylvania. His parents were of Dutch ancestry and raised him in the Reformed Church. At age sixteen, however, while still attending high school in Allentown, Nathan became associated with Jehovah's Witnesses. After attending their convention in Cedar Point, Ohio, in 1922, he resigned from his parents' church. The following year, on July 4, eighteen-year-old Nathan was baptized at a Witness service presided over by headquarters representative Frederick Franz. Two months later Knorr himself joined the Society's staff in Brooklyn as a full-time volunteer. He worked in the shipping department, then later in the printing factory itself, and was made plant manager in 1932. In 1934 he was elected a director of the New York corporation, and became its vice president the next year. He was made vice president of the Pennsylvania corporation in 1940. When Knorr became president of the Watchtower Society (its New York, Pennsylvania, and British corporations) in January 1942, he was only thirty-six years old and had lived all of his adult life as a resident of the headquarters complex.

Frederick William Franz was born September 12, 1893, in Covington, Kentucky. He was living in Cincinnati, Ohio, and studying at the University of Cincinnati in 1913, with the aim of becoming a Presbyterian minister, when his brother Albert sent him a booklet he had obtained from the Bible Students, which he then followed up with a set of the first three volumes of Russell's *Studies in the Scriptures*. Frederick resigned from the Presbyterian Church and was baptized at a Russellite service that November. In May 1914 he left the university to become a colporteur distributing the pastor's writings full time. Six years later Franz joined the Bethel headquarters family in Brooklyn, where he continued serving until his death at the age of ninety-nine.

Rutherford bequeathed to the new president, Nathan Knorr, an organization markedly different from the one he had inherited from Pastor Russell in 1917. "The judge" had taken over a loosely knit organization that had been held together largely by Russell's personal magnetism. Members who cherished the late pastor's memory and their own Christian freedom resented what they saw as Rutherford's high-handed power plays, and they resisted his efforts to assume greater control. As outlined in the previous chapter, Rutherford at first used the device of claiming that Russell's departed spirit was still in charge. Then he employed his own prowess as an attorney to seize control of the Watchtower corporations and his political prowess to transform a loose collection of independent, democratically run congregations into a "theocratic organization" tightly governed from the top down. By the time of his death Rutherford had also gained what he had lacked at the beginning of his presidency: the personal loyalty of Watchtower readers around the world. Still, the awe in which Jehovah's Witnesses held Judge Rutherford was not in any way an obstacle to the transfer of power to Nathan Knorr. The tight organizational structure allowed this mild, unassuming man to slip into the president's slot with full power at his command. If Rutherford had entered the presidency like a cowboy climbing onto the back of a spirited horse that bucked and reared to throw off its new rider, Knorr came into office like the recipient of a well-cared-for and finely tuned automobile that starts on the first crank and responds to its new owner's every move. Indeed, for Knorr, redirecting the organization was as easy as turning the steering wheel of a high-performance sports car.

Neither a prolific writer like Russell nor a fiery orator like Rutherford, Nathan Knorr was most comfortable sitting behind the CEO's desk, organizing and directing others. He retreated into the background and focused followers' devotion on the "mother" organization rather than on himself. Under his direction the Watchtower Society began producing literature that was written anonymously (by Franz and a crew of headquarters workers) purportedly so as not to "glorify" men or give them "a name of prominence" which would amount to "creative worship."[1]

Even correspondence from headquarters no longer carried the signature of the writer; letters to congregations or individual JWs were signed with a rubber stamp imprinting the Society's name in cursive letters. Yet the publications and the correspondence did not become impersonal, since the organization itself was virtually personified, and readers were directed to "show our respect for Jehovah's organization, for she is our mother and the beloved wife of our heavenly Father, Jehovah God."[2]

A superb administrator, Knorr shifted the sect's focus from dynamic leadership to dynamic membership. He initiated training programs to transform members into effective recruiters. Instead of carrying a portable phonograph from house to house, playing recordings of Judge Rutherford's lectures at people's doorsteps, the average Jehovah's Witness began receiving instruction on how to speak persuasively. The weekly ministry school program that Knorr added to the schedule of congregation meetings taught men, women, and children to give sermons at the doorstep on a variety of subjects. Whereas Russell and Rutherford had each resembled a captain personally leading a small band of men into battle, Knorr took on the role of a general marshaling a huge army and ordering it into the field.

ЖЖ   ЖЖ   ЖЖ

British magazine TV Quick *for the week of July 31 through August 6, 1993, reports the death of twenty-seven-year-old Susan Teeney who was op-*

erated on for inflammation of the colon. Problems during the week that followed required that she receive blood transfusions, but she refused and died as a result, according to the testimony of doctors at the inquest.

☙   ☙   ☙

Nathan Knorr had already been serving for four years as Watchtower president when I was born in Boston in 1946 to non-church-going parents. My mother, Rachel, was nominally Jewish, although during my youth she underwent baptism in a Baptist church and later joined the Unitarians. My father, Herbert, was raised by a mother who associated first with the Baptists, then the River Brethren, and finally Jehovah's Witnesses—but he himself followed neither his mother nor his wife in formally joining any of these groups. I took this to be a lack of religious inclination on his part until, when I got to know him better in later years, I found him to be a spiritual man whose relationship with the Deity was deeply personal.

The first contact I remember having with Witnesses was in 1959, when I was a thirteen-year-old in junior high school. Two dowdy-looking women came to our front door offering *Watchtower* and *Awake!* magazines. I shouted up the stairs asking Mama what to do, and then passed on her refusal to the saleswomen. We didn't need any. We were all set. We were Unitarians.

Unitarianism suited Mama well, as it stressed a Judeo-Christian heritage and presented Jesus as a man who was a great teacher but, alas, was only a man. She attended services regularly and sent my sister, Barbara, and me to junior church and Sunday school. My eighth grade Sunday School class consisted of a survey of other religious groups: we spent a week studying what a denomination believed and the next week visited its house of worship and actually sat in on its services. In this way I received a whirlwind introduction to Catholics, Quakers, Greek Orthodox, Christian Scientists, and a handful of other faiths represented in the Boston area in 1960. My conclusion at the time was that religion is the opiate of the people. It wasn't that our Sunday School teacher sought to instill in us that infamous opinion of Karl Marx, nor did anyone else in the class necessarily reach the same conclusion I did; but in my case this course combined with other factors in my life to turn me into an outspoken atheist by my fifteenth birthday.

I had begun taking a bus each week to visit Robert and Nancy Richards, a Dorchester couple in their fifties who lived in a third-floor flat near the transit system's Ashmont Station. *The Boston Globe* had run a human interest story on Robert as an amateur astronomer who made his three-inch refractor telescope available to neighborhood teens on Monday nights. With a little encouragement from Mama I made the necessary phone calls and found my way to the mini-observatory on the Richardses' hilltop back porch.

Through his telescope Robert introduced me to the moons of Jupiter, the rings of Saturn, and the craters of the moon. Simultaneously, through her conversation, Nancy introduced me to the politics of socialism and the philosophy of atheism. At first I argued for the existence of God and resisted these challenges to my cherished beliefs. But the Richardses would send me home each week loaded up with reading material on the subjects we had talked about: *Sky and Telescope* magazines; socialist newsletters; and books by such scientific minds as Charles Darwin, Julian Huxley, Ashley Montague, George Gamow, Harlow Shapley—even an English translation of *The Origin of Life on the Earth* by the Russian A. I. Oparin, an active member of the Academy of Sciences of the USSR. It was not so much that these science writers engaged in antireligious diatribes—for the most part they did not—but that they left the biblical Creator God out of the picture. If the weekly association with the Richardses wasn't enough to persuade me to their point of view, the time spent reading—and thus associating with Darwin, Huxley, Montague, Gamow, Shapley, Oparin, and others—began to reshape my thoughts. Religion did indeed seem to be the formalized canonization of ignorance. While humankind may have had an excuse for following religion in the past, modern science was fast making such superstitious beliefs outmoded.

Besides, if I owed my existence not to a judgmental Supreme Being's act of creation, but rather to an ignorant ape's blind act of evolution, what a liberation that would bring! What freedom I would have, with no angry God pointing his finger at me! What a comforting thought for a guilt-ridden teenager agonizing over newfound sexual passions! Wishful thinking is seldom admitted, let alone listed, as a prime motivational factor affecting major decisions in life. But I must admit that, in large measure, I wished God out of existence. After listening to intellectual and social arguments that came down forcefully on both sides of the question, I let my heart's desire cast the deciding ballot. Poof! God was gone! Instead of picturing Him watching me with disapproval during times of sexual arousal, I could call to mind my ignorant apelike ancestor or, better yet, the three monkeys with their hands over their eyes, ears, and mouth to indicate "See no evil, hear no evil, speak no evil." What a relief!

When I graduated from high school in 1964, my yearbook's class prophecy predicted that I would become a minister—an inside joke, as classmates knew me for my outspoken atheism. But I was an atheist who kept the Ten Commandments in most other respects (except, of course, for my secret sins known only to the now nonexistent God). I neither drank, nor smoked, never used foul language, and kept out of trouble. In fact, I maintained a straight "A" average all through high school, won a National Merit Scholarship in competitive testing, and was accepted with full scholarships at all four colleges I applied to: Harvard, MIT, Tufts, and Brown.

While Harvard's prestige drew me, its reputation as a hotbed of liberal and even radical politics exerted an even stronger pull. The Richardses had introduced me not only to atheism but also to political dissent. My high school years were a time when young Freedom Riders were joining African-Americans in their struggle against Ku Klux Klansmen, and when Berkeley students had switched from protesting the college's policy of *in loco parentis* to sitting on railroad tracks to block military supply trains. As Harvard offered opportunities for student activism and political expression, I began to view the Richardses as mere armchair radicals.

At the end of my freshman year, besides finding more compatible roommates, I also switched my major from mathematics to government (called political science at most other American colleges). I hoped to learn something useful in making this world a better place. But the droning lectures on eighteenth-century political theory and the endless pages of dry documentation proved no more relevant to the real world than counting the number of stars in some distant galaxy millions of light years away. How could I keep my nose in a book, reading about ancient political theories, when real-life battles were raging all around me? I felt the need to do something about war, poverty, and injustice *immediately*—not years later after graduation.

By the middle of my sophomore year I was devoting more time and mental energy to social activism and to socializing than to my studies. Through all of this I managed to remain on the Dean's List—Harvard's "A" and "B" honor roll—but staying in school to get my degree fell lower and lower on my list of priorities. When the fall term ended I requested a leave of absence. With what few belongings I could carry I took up residence on a communal farm in rural Connecticut, where I could devote my energies to things that seemed more relevant than academics. Farm life proved liberating, not merely freeing my mental energies, but also bringing me closer to nature than I had ever felt in my boyhood Boston or amidst the bus fumes of Harvard Square.

The year 1968 found me working on a small dairy farm in the mountains of eastern Pennsylvania, performing tasks as varied as milking cows, shoveling manure, and operating pasteurizing machines. My closest co-worker was Henry Schenck, a fellow about my own age who happened to be a Jehovah's Witness. The first thing I noticed about Henry was his effeminate features. He looked like a short, chubby girl with blond hair, rounded blue eyes, and a pimply chin. The second thing I learned about him was his religion, and the third was the name of his girlfriend, Harriet. It almost seemed as if he brought up the religion and the girlfriend right away to throw off any suspicion that he might be gay or transsexual. (In fact, he was plagued by men making passes at him, as I discovered later on.) But I soon found to my dismay that the real reason why Henry brought up his religion and his girlfriend right away was that those were the *only* subjects he ever brought up. He proved incapable of talking about anything else. Moreover, he proved unable to remain silent. All day long, whether sterilizing equipment, pitching silage, or washing udders before milking, Henry chattered constantly.

Like a TV in the mountains that could be tuned to only two channels, Henry could switch from Harriet to the Jehovah's Witnesses, and back again, but no other programs were available. I very quickly tired of hearing about Harriet—what she said, what she wore, what they did together (always something boring like canning vegetables)—so I kept switching Henry back to the religious channel. This was easy to accomplish. All I had to do was to ask a question and Henry would respond like a computer programmed with 120 megabytes of Bible trivia.

Actually, I was no more interested in Henry's religion than in his girlfriend. Both sounded hopelessly insipid. But at least there was some variety on his religion channel. A specific question would bring another answer, and a different question would bring another answer. If I had to listen to Henry's chatter all day long, at least I could get some variety by prompting him to talk on different religious subjects.

Where did Cain get his wife?

He married one of his sisters, one of the daughters of Adam and Eve mentioned in the Bible at Gen. 5:4.

How did a snake talk to Eve to tempt her to eat the forbidden fruit?

The real snake in the grass was Satan the Devil, according to Rev. 12:9, an invisible spirit creature who merely spoke through the visible snake the way a ventriloquist speaks through a dummy.

How did Noah's ark hold all the animals?

It was four hundred fifty feet long by seventy-five feet wide by forty-five feet high with three decks inside, according to Genesis, chapter 6, which works out to a total of more than a hundred thousand square feet of deck space and more than 4.5 million cubic feet of living space and storage space for food and other necessities. Besides, the Bible doesn't say Noah took in full-grown elephants and hippos; the weaned young of each animal species would suffice and would require much less living space and food.

Bible trivia certainly wasn't the subject of choice for an atheist like myself, but it sure beat hearing about Harriet all day.

As winter warmed into spring, my questions became more serious and more pressing. To my surprise, Henry was really supplying *answers* to my questions, rather than simply telling me to "have faith" as previous would-be religious mentors had always done. It seemed that Henry's wealth of biblical knowledge was inexhaustible. And his answers really impressed me. Each one was reasonable, logical, and backed up by a specific reference to Scripture. I began to see, too, that the answers all fit together into a big picture: a tightly reasoned comprehensive world view that promised to explain the mysteries of life.

Atheism no longer did that for me. Could a series of chemical accidents, followed by random mutations and natural selection, actually produce Mozart, Einstein, and Gandhi? A yes answer required a leap of faith—just as much as any of the unreasonable doctrines of any church. Moreover, even the most outstanding examples of human intellect, beauty, love, and compassion seemed merely to reflect our striving after more perfect ideals—ideals beyond ourselves that could be conceived but not achieved. How could we conceive of and strive for things better than what actually existed on this planet? Could those ideal qualities exist in God? Atheism no longer contained any better answers than religion, I found. But if there is a God, who is he? Could it be that he is the Jehovah of the Jehovah's Witnesses?

Suddenly I just *had* to find out if it was true. I began attending congregation meetings at Henry's Kingdom Hall, agreed to let him teach me the Bible twice each week after working hours, and started reading on my own—Watchtower publications plus the sect's *New World Translation of the Bible*.

"Here's a Bible for you," Henry said, handing me a green hardcover book. "It's the *New World Translation*. You'll understand it more easily. Besides, it uses Jehovah's name."

I did find it easier to understand—easier than the seventeenth-century English of the King James version I had read as an adolescent. It used modern language, although a bit stiff.

In our first lesson Henry explained the importance of knowing and using the divine name Jehovah: "Prayers addressed simply to "God" could be directed to Buddha or Allah, or even to the god of this wicked world, namely Satan the Devil." I recognized "Jehovah" since my grandmother had used that name when I was a little boy and had explained to me that it was God's name.

"You must address God by his name, Jehovah," Henry added, "in order to guarantee that he will hear your prayers."

That made sense to me. Although it felt strange at first, I began praying again—first to "God-if-you-are-really-there," and then more confidently, to "Jehovah God."

Seeing that name throughout the Bible seemed strange, too. Henry's explanation was that I was simply accustomed to the versions produced by Christendom with the title "LORD" substituted for God's name. "This was proof of the devil's influence in the churches—Satan's efforts to hide God's name," he told me.

I soon came to trust the *New World Translation*, and to rely on it exclusively as the only correct translation of the Bible. As I read, studied, and listened, things began to fall into place in my mind. Yes, the churches of Christendom had been wrong to deify Christ and to declare him part of a triune deity; my Unitarian Sunday School classes had taught me that. Only the Unitarians had failed to explain, as the Witnesses now did, that Jesus was the incarnation of Michael the Archangel, hence less than God but more than mere man. Yes, the world's governments, churches, and commercial institutions were all hopelessly corrupt; the Richardses and my radical friends at Harvard had taught me that, but they had left it for the Witnesses to supply the answer to all of humankind's problems: God's kingdom government by Christ that will destroy and replace all of humanity's corrupt institutions with a perfect and righteous rule forever.

And when would this marvelous change take place? When would the earth be restored to paradise by this divine new government superior to anything radical reformers or revolutionaries ever conceived? Bible chronology pointed to a date exactly six thousand years after the original sin of Adam and Eve in 4026 B.C.E., the Witnesses demonstrated by using Old Testament genealogies. The time for the end of the world and the beginning of God's rule over the earth was reduced to a simple formula pointing to the year 1975 C.E. (Proof: 4026 B.C. + 1975 C.E. = 6001, but 1 had to be subtracted since the calendar has no zero year between 1 B.C.E.. and 1 C.E., so the year 1975 marked the end of the prophesied six thousand years.)

❦   ❦   ❦

Herself a nurse as well as a Jehovah's Witness, Mrs. James F. Christian resisted "intensive" efforts on the part of her gynecologist to persuade her to accept a transfusion. An article in the Arizona Republic *of March 9, 1968, states that her condition continued to deteriorate and she soon lapsed into a coma and died. Attorneys for Good Samaritan Hospital in Phoenix had "wrestled with the possibility of forcing the treatment through court order," a step that, according to the article, "would have been simple" if the patient had been a child.*

❦   ❦   ❦

Unbeknownst to me Fred Franz and his associates at Bethel headquarters had been working behind the scenes to restore faith in the sect's chronological calculations, a subject largely ignored following Rutherford's prophetic failure in 1925. The revised chronology first established Christ's invisible return as having taken place in 1914 rather than 1874; then, during the 1960s, the Society's publications began pointing to the year 1975 as the likely time for Armageddon and the end of the world.

As already stated in chapter 2, when Charles Taze Russell broke with Nelson Barbour's Adventists and began publishing his own magazine in 1879, he titled it *Zion's Watch Tower* with the subtitle *and Herald of Christ's Presence*. Its purpose was to announce that Christ returned invisibly in 1874 and was invisibly present since then. The first hint that the Watchtower Society might abandon this teaching came in 1930 when *The Golden Age,* with no explanation, spoke of that presence beginning in 1914:

> In Matthew 24, Jesus gives His disciples some proofs that He would be present. . . . These tangible evidences will be the beginning of the work of destroying the present evil conditions and systems. This work of destruction began in 1914. . . .
> If it is true that Jesus has been present since the year 1914, then it must be admitted that nobody has seen Him with his natural eyes.[3]

The magazine plainly declares that "Jesus has been present since the year 1914," but fails to acknowledge that this represents a change in teaching, much less explain why the teaching was changed. No further reference is made to the subject until 1943, over a year after Judge Rutherford's death, when the anonymously written book *"The Truth Shall Make You Free"* declares that "Christ Jesus *came* to the Kingdom in

A.D. 1914, but unseen to men" (emphasis in original).[4] This book also features a chapter titled "The Count of Time" which calculates, "From Adam's creation to the end of A.D. 1943 is 5,971 years," and then concludes, "We are therefore near the end of six thousand years of human history."[5] Still, no mention is made of the fact that the new chronological system amounts to a rejection of what Watchtower publications had been teaching since their inception.

That a change occurred is finally admitted and explained in 1973 in the book *God's Kingdom of a Thousand Years Has Approached*:

> In the year 1943 the Watch Tower Bible and Tract Society published the book *The Truth Shall Make You Free*. In its chapter 11, entitled "The Count of Time," it did away with the insertion of 100 years into the period of the Judges. . . . Naturally, this did away with the year 1874 C.E. as the date of return of the Lord Jesus Christ and the beginning of his invisible presence or parousia.[6]

This book explains in great detail why relying upon modern Bible translations based on more ancient manuscripts yields a date for Adam's creation that is a hundred years later than the date C. T. Russell had figured. However, instead of moving Christ's invisible return to 1974— a hundred years in the future from 1874—the Society interprets the invisible event as occurring in 1914, to be followed a generation later, in 1975, by the end of this wicked world. (This arbitrary interpretation was apparently driven by the need to show Christ as already present, with the world's end drawing near.)

Jehovah's Witnesses really began to get excited about this prospect in 1966. Their own *Proclaimers* book explains it this way:

> The Witnesses had long shared the belief that the Thousand-Year Reign of Christ would follow after 6,000 years of human history. But when would 6,000 years of human existence end? The book *Life Everlasting—In Freedom of the Sons of God,* released at a series of district conventions held in 1966, pointed to 1975.[7]

The following two paragraphs attempt to minimize the implications by stressing that, when asked whether "the new book meant that by 1975 Armageddon would be finished," Fred Franz answered, "in essence: 'It could. But we are not saying.' " However, JW leaders were indeed "saying" in other places. The *Proclaimers* book acknowledges that "other statements were published on this subject, and some were likely more definite than advisable." They certainly were. In fact, the book itself, published a mere nine years before the supposed "end," says, "According to this trustworthy Bible chronology six thousand years from man's creation will end in 1975, and the seventh period of a thousand years of human history will begin in the fall of 1975 C.E."[8] It then adds, "It would not be by mere chance or accident but would be according to the loving purpose of Jehovah God for the reign of Jesus Christ, the 'Lord of the Sabbath,' to run parallel with the seventh millennium of man's existence."[9] This implies, of course, that the wicked world would end, and the millennial reign of Christ would commence, in the autumn of 1975.

In case any missed the importance of this "new truth" at the summer convention, *The Watchtower* of October 15, 1966, called it to their attention once again:

> It did not take the brothers very long to find the chart beginning on page 31 [of *Life Everlasting—In Freedom of the Sons of God*], showing that 6,000 years of man's existence end in 1975. Discussion of 1975 overshadowed about everything else. "The new book compels us to realize that Armageddon is, in fact, very close indeed," said a conventioner.[10]

The same month's *Awake!* magazine emphasized this point:

> This seventh day, God's rest day, has progressed nearly 6,000 years, and there is still the 1,000-year reign of Christ to go before its end. (Rev. 20:3, 7) This seventh 1,000-year period of human existence could well be likened to a great sabbath day. . . . In what year, then, would the first 6,000 years of man's existence and also the first 6,000 years of God's rest day come to an end? The year 1975. This is worthy of notice, particularly in view of the fact that the "last days" began in 1914, and that the physical facts of our day in fulfillment of prophecy mark this as the last generation of this wicked world. So we can expect the immediate future to be filled with thrilling events for those who rest their faith on God and his promises. It means that within relatively few years we will witness the fulfillment of the remaining prophecies that have to do with the "time of the end."[11]

After declaring that "the autumn of the year 1975 marks the end of 6,000 years of human experience," the May 1, 1967, *Watchtower* asked, "Will it be the time when God executes the wicked and starts off the thousand-year reign of his Son Jesus Christ?" The answer: "It very well could, but we will have to wait to see."[12]

The year 1968, when I began studying with Henry, saw perhaps the most intense emphasis on the 1975 date:

> Since it was also Jehovah's purpose for man to multiply and fill the earth, it is logical that he would create Eve soon after Adam, perhaps just a few weeks or months later in the same year, 4026 B.C.E. After her creation, God's rest day, the seventh period, immediately followed.
>
> Therefore, God's seventh day and the time man has been on earth apparently run parallel. . . . Thus, eight years remain to account for a full 6,000 years of the seventh day. Eight years from the autumn of 1967 would bring us to the autumn of 1975, fully 6,000 years into God's seventh day, his rest day. . . .
>
> Within a few years at most the final parts of Bible prophecy relative to these "last days" will undergo fulfillment, resulting in the liberation of surviving mankind into Christ's glorious 1,000-year reign. . . .
>
> Does this mean that the year 1975 will bring the Battle of Armageddon? No one can say with certainty what any particular year will bring.[13]

The August 15, 1968, *Watchtower* featured an article boldly titled "Why Are You Looking Forward to 1975?" which indicated that there might be a slight delay between the end of humanity's first six thousand years in autumn 1975 and the end of the world—corresponding to the interval of time between Adam's creation and Eve's—but which assured that the delay would be only a brief one:

> Are we to assume from this study that the battle of Armageddon will be all over by the autumn of 1975, and the long-looked-for thousand-year reign of Christ will begin by then? Possibly, but we wait to see how closely the seventh thousand-year period of man's existence coincides with the sabbathlike thousand-year reign of Christ. If these two periods run parallel with each other as to the calendar year, it will not be by mere chance or accident but will be according to Jehovah's loving and timely purposes. Our chronology, however, which is reasonably accurate (but admittedly not infallible), at the best only points to the autumn of 1975 as the end of 6,000 years of man's existence on earth. It does not necessarily mean that 1975 marks the end of the first 6,000 years of Jehovah's seventh creative "day." Why not? Because after his creation Adam lived some time during the "sixth day," which unknown amount of time would need to be subtracted from Adam's 930 years, to determine when the sixth seven-thousand-year period or "day" ended, and how long Adam lived into the "seventh day." And yet the end of that sixth creative "day" could end

within the same Gregorian calendar year of Adam's creation. It may involve only a difference of weeks or months, not years."[14]

Witnesses felt confident that the end would come in the final weeks of 1975 or no later than the early months of 1976.

❦   ❦   ❦

The Courier-Journal, *a Kentucky newspaper, reports in its issue of Sunday, July 19, 1981, that Kim Straton died of Hodgkins's disease at the age of thirty-three because his refusal to accept blood deterred doctors from performing surgery that could have arrested the cancer.*

❦   ❦   ❦

As I studied with Henry Schenck, I became convinced that the Bible predicted that the world was about to end, with the angry God Jehovah destroying everyone living on the planet except His Witnesses. The survivors would rebuild paradise. When I learned this in 1968 it seemed too good to be true. But Henry and his friends could prove everything from Scripture, step by step, piece by piece; and when all the little pieces of the puzzle were assembled, the big picture they painted was that God was going to step into human affairs again, after watching humankind struggle unsuccessfully for six thousand years. All the calculations clearly pointed to 1975 as the appointed time for the apocalyptic battle of Armageddon. In order to survive, I had to become a Jehovah's Witness. And to save the lives of my family and friends, I had to convert them, too.

When I approached long-time friends with these strange arguments—which I seemed to have come up with overnight—some simply backed off and avoided me. Others cautioned me that I was getting involved with a cult, but none could offer any convincing evidence for such a charge. My mother, on the other hand, showed interest and agreed to let me teach her what I was learning. So did my sister, Barbara, and I secured my mother's permission to teach my younger brothers Jonathan, Daniel, and Aaron. Dad was apathetic but acknowledged his own JW ground and, when I moved back home to share my new faith with the family, he ended up taking all of us to Kingdom Hall in his station wagon; occasionally he attended himself, but usually just dropped us off.

The first time I went there alone, on a Sunday morning in February 1969, Dad simply dropped me at the door of the Brockton, Massachusetts, Kingdom Hall. Designed to be inconspicuous in a residential neighborhood, it was a single-story brick building with sloping roof, shaped much like the front-to-back split-level homes surrounding it on a tree-covered hill at the north end of the city. A young blue spruce stood about eight feet high in the center of its front lawn. The tree had been planted by Jean-Paul Audette, a tall, gaunt, transplaced French man with white hair who greeted me outside the door. Standing atop the half-dozen steps leading to the entrance, with a black full-length coat hung over his shoulders like a cape, this foreign figure struck me as if he had just flown in from vampire country in Transylvania.

"You must be Dayveed Reed, who called on the telephone for diyrayctions," he intoned in a drawn-out sing-song that, I later learned, was peculiar to him rather than to Franco-Americans in general.

I quickly became the protégé of this oddly imposing figure whose simple greeting concealed the fact that that he was the Congregation Overseer, the man in charge. Also a "pioneer," appointed by the Watchtower Society in Brooklyn to preach full time from house to house, Jean-Paul disciplined me and trained me in the door-to-door work. He took a special liking to me, apparently on account of my scholarly nature and because I learned so quickly. The clincher was when he administered my oral exam before baptism—eighty catechism questions from the sect's *Lamp* book, normally discussed with the book open on the candidate's lap; I kept my book shut but scored 100 percent anyway. Jean-Paul prophesied that I would become a Circuit Overseer (the next rank above Congregation Overseer, with supervision over some sixteen congregations).

As I worked closely with Jean-Paul and his wife, Marie, on a daily basis, offering JW literature from house to house, I learned that his almost cringing appearance—a caricature of meekness—cloaked a rock-hard interior. His brief career as a chemical engineer had ended almost thirty years earlier when the Third Reich invaded France. Patriotism propelled Jean-Paul into the underground resistance movement, where he rose to the rank of lieutenant. His specialty was assassinations. He was what we now call a hit man.

Masquerading as a German officer—complete with fake moustache and phony ID—Jean-Paul would go right among the Nazis, armed with a photo of his intended target and a concealed dagger destined for the victim's heart. This, I learned, was the meaning of the red thread he wore tied loosely onto his gold watch band: it served as a constant reminder of his bloodguilt. Nothing in this world could intimidate

Jean-Paul, but fear that God would punish him for his many murders kept this guilt-ridden man bowed down before the Watchtower organization. He saw it as a place of protection shielding him from God's wrath, the only thing standing between him and eternal condemnation.

Marie was a veterinarian by profession but now spent her days going door to door full time as a pioneer. Jean-Paul and I usually worked together from house to house, but she accompanied us into the field in their car, either going to doors by herself or leading a female protégée of her own. Marie was quiet and totally submissive to Jean-Paul, a major concession for a woman built like a tank who was, in many ways, her husband's superior. During her own machine gun-toting days in the French underground, Marie had personally freed Jean-Paul from a Nazi death camp as part of an assault team. After the war, when they had made their way first to Italy and then to the United States, it was Marie who kept them supplied with food and shelter through her veterinary skills. Jean-Paul proved unable to find employment in chemistry and had trouble keeping the jobs he did find, but Marie built a successful practice.

In fact, it was the savings accrued from the combination of their Spartan lifestyle and Marie's abundant earnings that enabled them both now to devote all their time to volunteer preaching work. Shortly after my arrival back home in Brockton, the Audettes had driven to Brooklyn to discuss the future with friends at Watchtower headquarters. Bible chronology indicated that the battle of Armageddon would bring the world's end on or about October 4 or 5, 1975, and simple mathematics revealed that the money in their bank account would suffice to feed them until that date. So, she closed her office, he quit his job, and together they set off on the quest for eternal life by committing themselves completely to work for the Watchtower.

The training Jean-Paul gave me on our rounds door to door consisted of our taking turns—he spoke at one door, and I spoke at the next—followed by his analysis of our presentations as we strolled along between houses. It soon became clear to me that Jean-Paul's success in ministry came solely from the volume of time and effort he poured into it, rather than from any notable communications skills on his part. He and Marie still spoke French to each other, except in the presence of others, and it was obvious that they both still thought in their mother tongue as well. Householders strained to make out what Jean-Paul was saying and kept their doors open, due not to interest in his message, but simply because it took them several minutes to figure out who he was and why he was calling at their door. By the same token,

when he paused long enough for the listener to say a few words in response, Jean-Paul often failed to grasp either the meaning of what was
said or the householder's emotional overtones.

I recall one morning in particular when Jean-Paul was presenting
a sermon door to door in which he compared this doomed world with
the ancient civilization wiped out by the global deluge of Noah's day,
as reported in the book of Genesis. Speaking to a night-shift worker he
had just awakened at ten in the morning, Jean-Paul began by asking
the barely tolerant man, "Do you reemember thee flood?"

"Sure, the big flood in Taunton a few years ago," the bleary-eyed fellow obliged, citing the only inundation he was familiar with locally.
"Yeah, I remember the flood." Mind reading would have been required
for him to realize that Jean-Paul had in mind a bigger flood than that.

"Good!" Jean-Paul exclaimed, missing the point that the man had
missed *his* point. "Well, thee world today ees een thee same situation
as thee world before thee flood."

The householder leaning against the doorpost in his pajama bot-
toms rolled his sleepy eyes at this statement that, to Jean-Paul, was a
warning of impending disaster, but that left him wondering why two
men in suits would ring his doorbell at ten in the morning.

"Are you fellas selling flood insurance?" he asked, in all sincerity.

On other occasions when Jean-Paul or Marie did find success in
their door-to-door work—getting invited inside, starting a weekly study
in a home, or bringing a newcomer to Kingdom Hall—it was usually attributable to bold persistence and the law of averages. If you spend
your whole life knocking on doors and pour your whole energy into
pushing your message onto anyone willing to listen, sooner or later you
are bound to come across someone sufficiently vulnerable or easily
led. Door-to-door salesmen eventually find someone to buy the vacuum cleaner or the set of encyclopedias, and Jean-Paul and Marie
would, every so often, find someone they could bring to Kingdom Hall
the following week—typically a man out of work due to emotional
handicaps or a mother of three young children eager to do anything for
a break from the kids.

There were other strange ones like the Audettes at Kingdom Hall,
as well as lots of losers who had been badgered into coming to meetings, but I must admit that most of the people I met at Kingdom Hall
were plain, ordinary folk who had become convinced, either through
parental influence or later in life, that Jehovah's Witnesses taught the
truth. Women tended to get involved more than men, which is probably true of most religions; but there were still many traditional family

units represented in the auditorium on a typical Sunday morning. The audience did not appear, at first glance, to be any different from the flock gathered at any other church in town.

The people answering our knock at the door saw two conservatively groomed men standing on their front steps in sportcoat and tie, carrying leather portfolios. If they permitted, we spoke briefly about world conditions and Bible prophecies and then offered them a small book or two magazines for a few pennies—usually less than a dollar. To them we were simply magazine salesmen and book vendors offering our wares.

But Jean-Paul Audette and I saw ourselves quite differently. In our own eyes we were God's messengers performing a life-saving work. We were warning the world that the Almighty was about to intervene in human affairs once again, as He had done before in the fiery destruction of Sodom and Gomorrah and in the flood of Noah's day. Just as the passengers aboard Noah's Ark were the only survivors of that global deluge, so it would be necessary for people now to come aboard the organization of Jehovah's Witnesses in order to survive the imminent annihilation of today's world.

To us it was not in the least presumptuous to tell people that the imminent destruction would spare only the members of our sect, wiping out the remainder of the planet's population. After all, our name "Jehovah's Witnesses" was not a mere denominational designation but rather an accurate description of what we were: the witnesses, or testimony-bearers, belonging to the God of the Bible, whose name is Jehovah. We belonged to God and served as His spokesmen, while the other religions only pretended to do so and therefore belonged to the enemy of God, Satan the Devil. It was only reasonable that God would preserve His people alive, while destroying the impostors.

Our call at the door, therefore, was of utmost importance. If the people who lived there responded favorably to our message, they would be starting out on the road to everlasting life in a restored earthly paradise. If they rejected our message or dismissed us without listening they might have another chance or, because the end was so close at hand, they might be sealing their doom.

Still, in its outward form at least, our activity was very much like any ordinary door-to-door sales work. Our day started with a brief sales meeting, followed by methodical canvassing of our territory, and then later in the day we made return calls with an experienced closer to close deals at those houses where our initial canvassing had uncovered interest.

We termed the sales meeting our "meeting for field service." It convened at 9:15 A.M. at Kingdom Hall on weekdays. (On Saturday mornings and Sunday afternoons, when more people were able to participate, several meetings for field service were held throughout the city at the same private homes where Congregation Book Study meetings were held on Tuesday nights—close to the blocks and neighborhoods they would be canvassing.) Jean-Paul was usually quite punctual, starting the meeting on time and concluding at 9:30 sharp. He was eager to get out into the work so that he could start "counting his time" toward his monthly goal of one hundred hours in field service.

He opened the fifteen-minute meeting by turning to the day's text in the current *Yearbook of Jehovah's Witnesses*—a single verse from the Bible followed by a one- or two-paragraph discussion quoted from a recent *Watchtower* magazine. The *Yearbook* featured a text for each day of the year. Jean-Paul might solicit a comment or two from the handful of people assembled for service, or he might have something relevant to say himself, with discussion usually focusing on the *Watchtower* commentary rather than on the Bible verse.

Next, Jean-Paul would pull the current *Kingdom Ministry* newsletter* from his book bag and mention "the offer" for the month—usually a recent book—to be featured at the doors. Saturday was magazine day, devoted to offering the latest *Watchtower* and *Awake!* magazines as a matched set for ten cents, and one or two months out of the year might be devoted to offering annual subscriptions to the semimonthly publications. December was Bible month, when we would offer a green hardcover copy of the Society's *New World Translation* for a dollar, but most other months the weekday offer was a small book that we could later use to start a home Bible study with a prospective convert.

I would pay twenty cents per copy at the Kingdom Hall book room for *The Truth that Leads to Eternal Life*, the blue pocket-size volume Henry had used to convert me, and would sell copies at the doors for twenty-five cents—this at a time when similar hardbound books were selling in book stores for three or four dollars. Still, a morning when I would "place" half a dozen copies was exceptional, with one or two "placements" being the norm. (We avoided the words "sell" and "sales" because that sort of transaction would have obligated us to collect sales tax; instead, we "placed" literature and received "contributions" to cover the cost.) Individually, it might not have seemed that we were accomplishing very much, but the overall effect was spectacular. In 1969, the first year I shared in the work, more than 1.3 million Wit-

---

*This is a members-only monthly featuring instructions and suggestions for door-to-door work, such as which items to offer, how to introduce the material, and how to handle various situations that could come up.

nesses participated, devoting some 240 million person-hours and placing more than 200 million pieces of literature, mostly magazines. Published in 1968, the book *The Truth That Leads to Eternal Life* was listed under "Highest Printings" in the 1982 *Guinness Book of World Records*, when its distribution had reached 102 million copies in 116 languages. With JW factories now turning out nearly 19 million *Watchtower* and 16 million *Awake!* magazines twice a month, the more than 800 million copies sold in 1996 can reasonably be expected to bring the organization between one-quarter and one-half a billion dollars in income. Adding books, tapes, and other products yields a staggering total that is discussed in chapter 10.

After noting the day's offer, Jean-Paul continued the meeting for field service by either demonstrating how to present it door to door or inviting someone else to do so. The *Kingdom Ministry* suggested two or three possible ways to do it, some involving a five-minute sermonette complete with Scripture readings, and others that could be recited by rote in thirty to sixty seconds. The least ambitious or least capable Witnesses would not attempt to vary their presentations but would always repeat the same simple formula they had memorized, such as, "Good morning! We're Jehovah's Witnesses, calling to offer you the latest *Watchtower* and *Awake!* magazines for ten cents. Here they are, if you would like to have them." Most, though, addressed the subject matter of the particular magazine issues and made some attempt to stimulate interest.

Following the daily text and discussion of the offer and how to present it, Jean-Paul would look at those assembled and calculate quickly whether it would be more practical to go together in a single automobile or to split up into two or more car groups. Witnesses generally purchased their automobiles with field service in mind, so only the most selfish or "untheocratic" (not submissive to God's rulership) JWs owned small two-door cars. Jean-Paul's black Oldsmobile Eighty-Eight could transport six comfortably.

More was involved, though, than mere numbers. People had to be paired compatibly, preferably with a capable "brother" directing each group. A spiritually minded "sister" could be used to direct a car group, but only if no suitable man was available. Also, the destination territory had to be taken into consideration. Was it large enough to support the activity of so many people for the morning, or was it so congested that we would be getting in each other's way?

Jean-Paul always seemed to make the necessary arrangements so smoothly, but when I had to fill in on occasion I realized how much thought went into it: The Timilty twins were too young to work alone, so each needed an adult partner. Brother and sister Smith had to go together in the same car, of course. Sister Jackson came with Sister Rose and would have to meet up with her at the end of the morning for her ride home, and so on. Poor arrangements would cause ill feeling, and some arrangements would not work at all.*

At the conclusion of each day we would use a small preprinted form to record the number of hours we had spent in service, as well as the numbers of books, magazines, and booklets placed, and the number of "back-calls" or return visits we had made to people who had shown interest on previous occasions. This "time slip" would be used to accumulate a week's or a month's figures and would then be dropped into a slot in a wooden box at Kingdom Hall that was set aside for these reports. Because the primary emphasis was on hours rather than placements, our work proceeded at a rather leisurely pace. In contrast to the vacuum cleaner vendor or the encyclopedia salesman spurred on by the hope of earning commissions, we moved more slowly, like hourly workers. We were indeed being "paid" by the hour. Our hours counted up as brownie points with God.

Logic would dictate that my closest friends at Kingdom Hall should be the young men around my own age, and there were several of these: strikingly handsome pioneer and part-time storm window salesman Dan Wessel, whose fine features matched a melodious voice, and who seemed coldly detached while being wooed by sultry Diana from nearby Weymouth congregation; his brother-in-law Jerry who was wrapped up with raising a young family; rough-hewn Wilbur, newly estranged from his unbelieving wife, who worked full time in a laboratory at Massachusetts General Hospital and whose companionship would have proved intellectually stimulating. But somehow we never clicked.

Dan Wessel and his pioneer friends from nearby congregations went out in full-time service to meet their pioneer goal of a hundred hours per month, but they whiled away most of those hours analyzing territory maps, flipping pages of back-call books, or sipping coffee during frequent breaks at local donut shops. Pioneer service, which auto-

---

*I can remember a time when Jean-Paul was ill and Douglas Newton—a middle-aged man out of work on disability leave, but able to go door to door—ran the meeting for field service. Rather than assign each car group to a different street or block and send them off to their respective destinations, he had the other two cars follow him to the territory. We pulled into the residential street like a motorcade. Then Douglas got out and started shouting instructions, pointing up and down the street, sending pairs of Witnesses in all directions. By then it seemed that half the people in the neighborhood were watching from their windows, wondering what all the commotion was about.

matically earned one an exemption from the draft under a 4-D minister's classification from the local draft board, was the most acceptable
way for young men to cope with their military obligations. (Witness
boys who accepted their draft board's call to enter the army or even to
perform civilian alternative-service work in a local hospital, were tried
in absentia by a judicial committee of elders, where they faced the automatic verdict of being labeled "disassociated persons" who must be
shunned.) So there were many young male pioneers who, having secured the desired draft classification, went about the actual work of pioneering with a zeal that was half-hearted at best. Their work habits
were mirrored by the girls who signed on as pioneers with the aim of
catching one of the eligible guys.*

Unlike these young people who had been raised in the organization
through no choice of their own, dragged to meetings by their parents
for years, and forced to sit quietly through endless hours of adult-ori-
ented religious lectures, I was a new convert on fire for the message to
which I had just been converted. My zeal corresponded closely with
that of the old ladies who persisted in pioneering for decades despite
health problems, financial difficulties, outside ridicule, and a gauntlet
of other obstacles. So I found myself going door to door with them,
rather than with those in my own age group.

These tough old veterans of the door-to-door work, in their sixties,
seventies, and even eighties, were always on the go, covering their ter-
ritories with *Watchtower* and *Awake!* magazines, calling back where they
found interest, and starting Bible studies. They were drawn to me because, once I had acquired an automobile of my own, I was a depend-
able source of transportation; and I was drawn to them because they
were dedicated, no-nonsense professionals in the witnessing work with
decades of experience and wisdom to draw upon.

So it was in this manner that wrinkled old Agatha Paulson became
one of my companions. Her age impressed me most forcefully one day
when she had me drive her to see an interested "young man" with
whom she hoped I could start a Bible study. She rattled on about him
as I followed her directions heading south on Main Street, right onto
Forest Avenue, then left onto Ash Street, and right again onto one of
the many tree-lined residential side streets crossing that thoroughfare.
I expected to meet a bright-eyed college boy but instead encountered
a retired gentleman rocking gently with a cat on his lap on the front
porch of his dilapidated wood-frame home. This senior citizen was in-

---

*For more on JWs and military service, see pp. 223–24.

deed a "young man" to octogenarian Agatha, but thereafter I questioned her more carefully whenever she used that term.

I often found myself working alone with Agatha from house to house, especially during wet weather that kept other Witnesses indoors or on summer afternoons when the heat had sent others home early. She and I had to get in our pioneer hours, and, more importantly, we had "sheep" in need of shepherding. Born and raised on Prince Edward Island before the turn of the century, Agatha resembled one of the crags jutting out into the sea along the Canadian Maritime coast—not only in her facial features, but also in the rock-hard way she faced down opponents and critics encountered at the doors. Agatha never raised her voice or hurried her speech to win an argument. Rather, she took command of a conversation by whispering her words so softly and slowly that the other party was forced to stop and listen. "Yesssss," she would add at the end of her presentation in a trailing hiss that attested to her words like the drawn-out Amen concluding a hymn.

In winter Agatha wore woolen gloves pinned to the ends of her coat sleeves like a child's mittens. At first I marveled at how she ignored the cold, letting her gloves dangle from their pins while I wore mine and still found my fingers growing too stiff to turn *Watchtower* pages on windy doorsteps. Then I learned her secret: a miniature purse-like portable heater with smoldering wick inside—like a slow-burning cigarette lighter—that she kept tucked away in her pocket. Whenever her hands started to get cold, she would plunge one into her pocket and grip the little heater for a while before passing it to the other hand. From then on I feared fire whenever she was in my car, all the while envying her hidden source of warmth.

Ellie Clifford, nearly ninety years old, was as soft and gentle as Agatha was wizened and hard. Agatha's contemporary, but a late bloomer in that she had not been baptized as a Witness until after 1935, Ellie had lived her younger years as a Methodist and raised her children in that church. Her sons were already retired when I met her, but Ellie was still driving a ten-year-old white Chevy and living on her own on the Brockton-Avon line. Baptism after 1935 meant that Ellie was part of the "great crowd" of "other sheep" consigned to live forever on earth after second *Watchtower* president, Judge Rutherford, closed the door to the heavenly class. When Witness acquaintances assumed from her age that she was one of the hundred and forty-four thousand "anointed ones" going to heaven, Ellie would wave them off with a smile and explain, "No, I always wanted to plant a garden. And that's what I'll do in the paradise earth."

For months all of my JW friends and acquaintances had been buzzing with excitement about the "Peace on Earth" International Assemblies scheduled for the summer of 1969, and eventually the time arrived. Summer district conventions were annual events for Jehovah's Witnesses, with large stadiums rented for seven or eight days of Bible lectures with near-capacity crowds. But every few years the gatherings were given an international flavor with missionaries brought home from foreign lands and ordinary Witnesses encouraged to visit convention sites in other countries. (For the regular yearly district conventions each congregation was assigned to attend a particular stadium in its home state or nearby.) My twelve-year-old brother, Jonathan, and I could not afford to visit London or Paris; but, instead of simply attending the nearest convention at Yankee Stadium, we accepted an invitation to ride a bit farther to Buffalo, New York, with Carl Hess, a divorced man in his forties who handled magazine distribution at our Kingdom Hall. At the time I was between cars—my first few were old clunkers purchased for under a hundred dollars, capable of taking us out in service, but not reliable enough to drive out of state—and Carl was looking for riders. He needed someone to share expenses, and the gas money he required for the longer trip to Buffalo would be slightly less than bus fare to New York City, so the arrangement was mutually agreeable.

Chubby in spite of living once more as a bachelor, Carl Hess concealed his belly under well-tailored suits, but he found it impossible (or never really tried) to conceal his temper; like lightning followed by thunder, first his face would flush and then his sharp tongue would lash out. He was a very precise person who carefully pronounced every syllable of every word, harshly corrected others for the smallest mistakes, and insisted that his car be kept immaculate. The trip was not going to be fun. But I was eagerly looking forward to the convention.

Our magazines and congregation meetings had whipped up anticipation by discussing the excitement of travel to unfamiliar places and the fact that full-costume Bible dramas were to be presented. The titles or themes of the dramas and convention talks, however, were kept top secret until Witnesses actually arrived at their convention sites and received copies of the program. This secrecy added to everyone's sense of anticipation. But the assembly feature most looked forward to—especially by long-time Witnesses—was the bringing out of "new truths" in the course of the talks. Whenever the Watchtower Society received new revelations from God, these would be announced during one of the talks. That alone was sufficient reason to pay close attention to every talk, because there was no way of knowing just when such a new truth would be presented.

Brother Hess was a long-time Witness, at least by my standards, and—although he seemed rather annoyed by our presence, and I had the distinct feeling that he had agreed to our company solely to share the cost of his travel expenses—he used the long hours of turnpike driving to review with Jonathan and me some of the conventions he had attended in the past. Of course, there were many new truths learned during the course of his twenty-plus years in the organization. A new truth might involve a new interpretation of an obscure Bible verse, and could be purely academic. Or, it could impact on lives. A new truth brought out in 1944 revealed that God prohibited blood transfusions; henceforth, Witnesses would not be taking blood. Another new truth in 1967 banned cornea and kidney transplants, and other operations involving donor-provided organs. Sometimes such new information came out in a *Watchtower* article, but most new truths were announced first at the large assemblies.

ᴥ   ᴥ   ᴥ

"Mom Bled to Death," reads the front page headline of the Province, *a Vancouver, British Columbia, newspaper, of December 9, 1987, with the subtitle "Jehovah's Witness rejected transfusion." Thirty-one-year-old Jehovah's Witness Audrey Lawson died in Burnaby Hospital in Burnaby, British Columbia, Canada. "She went into cardiac arrest due to severe blood loss after refusing a transfusion following the birth of . . . twins by Caesarean section and a subsequent tubal ligation," according to a news clipping from the* Edmonton Journal *sent to us with the date cut off. The victim's mother, Helen Sorenson, a Roman Catholic, pressured the provincial government to open an inquest into the death. "She said she is particularly interested in knowing whether the Jehovah's Witnesses who were present in the hospital before Lawson died unduly influenced her decision to refuse treatment." A December 18, 1992, report in the* Vancouver Sun *indicates that the inquest was finally held that month. It lasted eight days but failed to find anyone guilty of criminal misconduct. Meanwhile, Mrs. Sorenson had "spent all her life's savings—almost $40,000 in legal fees and another $18,000 still owing—fighting the court battles."*

ᴥ   ᴥ   ᴥ

Jehovah's Witnesses received important new information in the November 15, 1967, issue of their *Watchtower* magazine. An article in the

"Questions from Readers" section presented a new ruling handed down from Brooklyn headquarters to the effect that "sustaining one's life by means of the body or part of the body of another human . . . would be cannibalism, a practice abhorrent to all civilized people" and condemned by God. The article explained that organ transplants were "simply a short cut" to cannibalistically chewing and eating human flesh.[15]

This pronouncement, in effect, banned organ transplant operations for Jehovah's Witnesses. No longer could a JW with renal failure accept a kidney transplant to keep him or her alive; nor could someone losing his vision receive a new cornea. Bone marrow, skin, or anything else taken from another person could no longer be received in a medical procedure. The transplant issue immediately took its place alongside the blood issue as a life-or-death matter for Witnesses hospitalized for illnesses or accidents.

Like the ban on blood, the new ban on organ transplants was presented as eternal and permanent. The same Bible verses from the book of Genesis were cited, indicating that it was included in instructions God gave Noah after the worldwide flood, and hence applicable to the whole human race descended from Noah. The prohibition was meant to apply not just to the Jewish nation for a period of time, but to all humankind forever.

In actuality, however, the Watchtower Society's ban on organ transplants lasted a bit under thirteen years. In 1980, it was quietly repealed. The March 15, 1980, *Watchtower* stated blandly, "there is no biblical command pointedly forbidding the taking in of other human tissue."[16]

What of those who went blind refusing a cornea transplant during the thirteen-year ban? What of those who died refusing a kidney or other vital organ? No apologies were given to the suffering individuals still alive, nor to the JW families who lost loved ones. The prohibition on such medical procedures was quietly dropped and then no longer mentioned, as if it had never been. Recent Watchtower Society publications applaud transplants as procedures that have "helped" people.[17] Still, JWs who submit to such operations must do so without benefit of blood transfusions.

A former JW elder interviewed in England related that he resigned after a woman in his congregation refused a cornea transplant and went blind in obedience to the organization's command. My wife and I attended the wake of Witness elder Martin Davis who refused a kidney transplant in obedience to the Watchtower Society and died of kidney failure in 1977. Newspapers reported neither his story nor that of the above-mentioned woman who went blind. So, it is reasonable to assume that other similar cases among Jehovah's Witnesses across the United States and around the world likewise went unnoticed and unreported by the media.

How many such cases were there? Unfortunately, there is no way to know for sure. Even the Watchtower Society kept no records of JWs who died refusing transplants. I know, because I served for a while during the late 1970s as secretary in my local congregation, the elder responsible for handling all correspondence with Brooklyn headquarters. Standard procedures called for reporting meeting attendance figures, hours spent in door-to-door work, numbers of books and magazines distributed to the public, and various other pieces of information, but not a word about Witnesses dying from the transplant ban then in force. Deaths related to refusing blood transfusions were not reported either, at that time, although today the sect has Hospital Liaison Committees that keep close tabs on such matters.

Kidney transplants represented the largest share of the over fifteen thousand kidney, heart, liver, lung, and pancreas transplant operations performed in 1990 (with an additional nineteen thousand people on the waiting list) according to *Grolier's Academic American Encyclopedia*. Such procedures were still relatively new in 1967, when they were declared off-limits to Jehovah's Witnesses, but kidney transplants were fairly routine by 1980. The numbers of JWs who died as a result of refusing such procedures were certainly fewer than those who died over the blood issue, but the numbers were still no doubt significant.

As stated in chapter 1, the ban on blood transfusions was first announced in the mid-1940s. It actually constituted a reversal of sorts, since objections were not raised against the practice during the first seven decades of publishing *The Watchtower.* Physicians down through the centuries experimented with blood transfusion, but success was hampered by lack of knowledge concerning blood-borne diseases and blood-type incompatibility. (Austrian pathologist Karl Landsteiner classified the major blood types in 1901.) Standard reference works and medical history books reveal that doctors were performing blood transfusions in the United States throughout the nineteenth century—usually with the donor lying beside the recipient and their circulatory systems connected with tubes, since refrigeration and proper blood storage methods had not yet been developed.[18]

With improved methods of refrigeration and sterilization, the first U.S. blood bank was established in 1937, at Cook County Hospital in

Chicago, and the December 25, 1940, issue of *Consolation* contained an upbeat report on a blood transfusion administered to a New York City housewife. But only a few years later, JW condemnations of the procedure began to appear in its publications.[19] By the early 1980s doctors in the United States were administering more than ten million transfusions of blood or components annually, with the JW element of the population routinely refusing.

References to blood in the Bible actually center around two areas: diet and sacrifice. In the Old Testament Noah and his offspring were commanded not to eat the blood of animals they killed for food (Gen. 9:4). The nation of Israel was repeatedly instructed not to eat "any fat or any blood," because these portions of their animal sacrifices were set aside for God (Lev. 3:17 *New World Translation*). And, in the New Testament when friction developed between Jewish and Gentile converts to Christianity, and the question arose as to whether or not Gentile Christians had to be circumcised and keep the Law of Moses, the apostles' decision did not require them to follow a complete kosher diet but did include instructions that they abstain from meat offered to idols, from animals that were killed by strangulation, and from blood (Acts 15:20, 29).

Under the new administration of President Nathan Knorr the Watchtower Society began to interpret these verses as a divine command prohibiting blood transfusions—a position at variance with Orthodox Jews and with mainstream Christians, as well as with previous Watchtower leaders.

❧　　❧　　❧

"A Jehovah's Witness bled to death after heart surgery because he refused a blood transfusion, an inquest heard yesterday," according to a report in the Sun, *a British tabloid, of January 19, 1989. The paper reports that insurance consultant Christopher Burke, age forty-seven, "left instructions forbidding doctors" to give him blood.*

❧　　❧　　❧

At long last, we arrived at our destination: the home of a gray-haired Baptist lady on the outskirts of Buffalo. The convention Rooming Department had found lodging there for Jonathan and me at two dollars each per night, with separate bedrooms and a shared bath. (Months before the convention local Witnesses supplemented their house-to-

their seats for the afternoon session, I felt like a disloyal apostate and a man lacking faith as Jonathan and I stole across the street once more to the worldly diner. I knew we needed lunch if we were to make it to five o'clock, but I felt guilty leaving the convention once again for food. My shame grew as I remembered the Bible verse about the wicked men "whose god is their belly." After all, where were my priorities?

We grew weary as the eight-day convention wore on, but at least we were getting to the sessions on time after the first day and, by leaping to our feet while each "Amen" still reverberated in the air, we were guaranteeing ourselves a place at the lunch and dinner tables.

On the third or fourth day, a message reached us through the Rooming Department summoning me to the News Service Desk. Someone had alerted the News Service Department that a Harvard man who had been newly baptized was attending his first large JW assembly. I was going to be interviewed. The privilege inflated my ego and blinded me to the incongruity of a sect presenting its newly converted Harvard man to the media, while prohibiting its own people from sending their kids to college.* Witnesses viewed the dichotomy as a victory: the Watchtower had captured a Harvard man as a trophy, thus proving that its "godly wisdom" was superior to this wicked world's "higher education." Little did I or anyone else know then that the organization would reverse itself twenty-three years later and that a new truth in 1992 would suddenly allow Witnesses to begin attending college on a limited basis, if necessary to obtain decent employment in a given locale and economic climate.

In any case, I was floating on clouds as I made my way to the News Service Desk. When I arrived, I found it unstaffed, but, after a while, someone returned and located in a wooden file box an index card requesting that I return at 11:30 the next morning to be driven to a local television studio for an interview that would be shown later on the evening news.

The next day I deposited Jonathan for safekeeping with a mature Witness I had met at the convention and arrived early at the News Service Desk. As Circuit Overseers and Department personnel from Brooklyn headquarters greeted one another and introduced themselves to unfamiliar faces, I grasped that convention spokesmen would also be interviewed, that a whole convoy of cars would be going to the TV sta-

---

*The approved goal set before high school kids was to graduate and sign up for full-time pioneer work—not for college or the military, both of which competed with the organization's interests. In any case, the world would likely end before a college student could reap benefits from the time and money invested.

tion, and that I would be in the company of organizational VIPs who were going along for the ride. Word that we would be "doing lunch" together first impressed me almost as much as if I had been invited to dinner with Moses and Elijah; the importance of the interview paled as I began looking forward to spiritual discussions—perhaps even new truths—from these mid-level leaders.

Several shook hands with me but, upon learning my rank as a lowly distributor of literature, covered their retreat with a brief blessing and turned to their peers for fellowship. My feelings were hurt, of course, but I still looked forward to hearing words of wisdom even if I would be merely *over*hearing them as these higher-ups conversed with one another in my presence.

Assuming we would all eat together in an isolated section of the cafeteria, as I had seen the Circuit Overseer do with certain elders at a smaller circuit assembly, I was surprised when those who knew what was happening ushered me into a car and we drove to a local restaurant. It seemed strange that these dignitaries should do the very thing that I had been ashamed of doing with Jonathan, namely, leave the convention site to obtain a meal from worldly sources.

The dinner-table conversations at first centered around who among them and their mutual acquaintances was being transferred, who was being promoted, who had been demoted—organizational tidbits that I accepted as necessary things to get out of the way before spiritual discussions could begin. The talk then shifted to automobiles. Brother Chambers just got a brand new Mercury four-door. Tom Southerland outdid that with his new top-of-the-line Chrysler. "Oh, really? Pass the mayo, please! Well, Jerry Montour got himself a new Cadillac with leather upholstery!" another Circuit Overseer shot back to top them all.

After that the topics bounced back and forth from the hefty inheritance Jack Simmons fell into from his uncle, to the pretty pioneer girl Chris Goddard just married; from the Becketts' unfortunate divorce, to the trouble Brother Ramos got into for driving his automobile without insurance in his Massachusetts circuit; from the fabulous stock brokering business Peter Frankel was operating on the side, to the free Bermuda vacation Harry Demp was treated to by a wealthy widow. Perhaps I was naive to have expected that these men would sit prayerfully with their hands pressed together analyzing Bible verses, but the raucous laughter and mundane gossip struck me as somehow irreverent.

The actual TV interview was anticlimactic. Four of us appeared before the cameras, and I answered two or three questions. I never got to see the broadcast when it was aired on the local evening news. What impacted on me more forcefully was the time spent in company with the JW convention functionaries in the car and at lunch. The effect on me was as if I had been present in the Land of Oz when Dorothy's little dog Toto pulled aside the curtain and exposed the powerful Wizard as a frail old man. It forever colored my view of the organization's midlevel management, perhaps paving the way for the challenges that I would much later throw in the faces of circuit and district overseers and my fellow elders. But, in the meantime, I failed to extrapolate to those ranking above them the coarse worldliness beneath a veneer of spirituality that I observed among these men. I still had faith in the sect's top leaders, conceiving of them as truly spiritual men aloof from corruption and the selfish concerns of this world.

After returning home from the Buffalo convention, I settled into a comfortable routine: part-time secular employment on a Brockton Hospital cleaning crew three nights a week, JW meetings two other nights plus Sunday mornings, and door-to-door witnessing seven days a week. The routine suited me, but I wasn't happy. Eventually I would realize that I needed a mate, but not without an emotional and spiritual struggle over the matter.

Unlike Mormons, who are encouraged by their religion to marry and bear children, Jehovah's Witnesses are dissuaded from both. During the late 1930s and early 1940s the admonition to remain single was worded strongly, and as a result many young Witnesses followed it. The encouragement was never intended to doom members to a long, lonely life; rather, the thought was simply to put off marriage until "after Armageddon": God's final war to rid the earth of wickedness was just around the corner. Those who had the faith to wait patiently would soon be able to marry under happier conditions and to raise children in a better world. "Spiritually strong" individuals followed this counsel and remained single so as to devote their time and energies, in the meantime, to the full-time preaching work. Some of the unmarried old pioneers I met, who had accepted this teaching decades earlier and were still waiting, seemed to have found fulfillment in this service— or at least that was the image they projected for public consumption. Others, it was plain to see, spent their final years alone and bitter.

Interestingly, the leaders who promoted such teachings were men who had had problems with women. Charles Taze Russell died childless and, as detailed above, lived his last twenty years estranged from his wife. Judge Rutherford publicly described woman as a mere "hank of hair and a bag of bones" and lived apart from his wife after fathering their child. Fred Franz remained a bachelor throughout his life.

Most Witnesses, though, try as they might to fight the temptation, married anyway, bore children, and then labored under a burden of guilt, always trying to compensate for these manifestations of "spiritual weakness." Some succeeded in postponing marriage for years, marrying late in life. Nathan Knorr remained celibate until his forty-seventh year. His marriage at that time opened the way for other headquarters workers to marry and softened the teaching somewhat, but left it in place as the preferred course.

I struggled to convince myself that I should follow that course. I still imagined that I possessed "the gift of singleness" when a mutual friend, Tim, introduced me to Penni Scaggs. Tim told me ahead of time that Penni's college background and her devotion to full-time ministry would make her a good match for me. Penni, a native of Michigan, had been raised "in the Truth" by parents who started studying with the JWs when she was in the fifth grade. Because they were "weak" Witnesses, they sent Penni to college to become a school-teacher. After teaching briefly in Michigan public schools, she moved to Boston where her sister's husband had been transferred by the Coast Guard. Here Penni taught part time in the Boston school system and served as a JW pioneer. We were married in the spring of 1971 at her Kingdom Hall in the Hyde Park section of the city.

Although I still saw marriage as somewhat of a compromise of faith, I did believe it to be Jehovah's will in my case—but I was determined not to have children right away. Penni agreed. It would make the best sense for us to devote our time and energies to field service now and to postpone having a family until after Armageddon, when the children would have a safer and gentler world to grow up in. In the meantime we would concentrate on starting home Bible studies with interested people. If they responded well and came into the Truth, they would become not only our spiritual brothers and sisters, but also our spiritual children in that we would have helped them find everlasting life. During our remaining years in the organization Penni and I both conducted studies with dozens of people, including some couples with whom we studied together and individuals we visited separately. Many of them responded, and between the two of us we gave birth to approximately twenty-five spiritual children.

ⵞ   ⵞ   ⵞ

Twenty-three-year-old Cedric Thames, an auto accident victim, "died eighteen hours after the 1991 crash because his relatives wouldn't allow transfusions

needed for surgery," according to attorney Gary Geisler, as quoted in the Au-
gust 14, 1992, Orlando Sentinel *of Orlando, Florida. An Associated Press*
dispatch printed in many newspapers on August 13 adds that "family mem-
bers were asked eight times about transfusions and refused them each time,"
explaining that the family "refused to permit him to receive transfusions be-
cause he was a Jehovah's Witness."

🌿   🌿   🌿

During the 1970s changes began taking place at Watchtower headquarters that Penni and I were largely unaware of. They involved presidential power. First it became accepted in theory that the Christian
Church (which Jehovah's Witnesses see their organization as encom-
passing) should not be under one-man rule, but rather governed by a
body similar to the twelve apostles. The seven-member board of directors of the Watch Tower Bible and Tract Society of Pennsylvania
had previously been viewed as fulfilling this role, but in 1971 an expanded Governing Body was created with a total of eleven members,
including the president and the six other directors. The aim was to
demonstrate that the leadership of Jehovah's Witnesses derived authority from an apostolic source, rather than from Pennsylvania corporate law, and that the organization itself—"God's organization," as Witnesses are taught to view it—is a spiritual entity larger than the various
corporations that own its real estate and manage its financial affairs.

Notable among the four men who joined the seven corporate directors as added Governing Body members was Raymond V. Franz,
nephew of President Frederick W. Franz. He was a third-generation
Witness, raised in the religion of his parents and three of his four grand-
parents. A serious-minded youngster, he began devoting twenty to thirty
hours per month to field service as a teenager. Upon graduating from
high school in 1940, he entered the witnessing activity full time. By
1946, he had already served a year and a half visiting congregations in
the Southwest as a Circuit Overseer and then received an assignment to
Puerto Rico as a Watchtower missionary. Shortly after President Knorr's
marriage and the policy change permitting missionaries to marry, Raymond Franz wed. In 1965 he was called to serve at Brooklyn headquarters in the writing department. His appointment to life membership on
the Governing Body in 1971 is noteworthy, because nine years later he
experienced a "crisis of conscience" over his role there.[20] Franz's troubled conscience resulted in a leave of absence in 1980, then his forced
resignation from the body and subsequent expulsion from the sect.

It was research that Raymond Franz had done as a member of the writing department that helped precipitate the 1971 administrative changes in the first place, according to the behind-the-scenes account in his book. Since the scenario he presents is in agreement with known facts, and none of the other parties involved has commented publicly, either to agree or to disagree with the version of events he presents, we have no alternative but to accept Raymond's account of what actually happened.

President Knorr had assigned him to prepare a Bible dictionary for the sect.* In researching the subject of "elders" for this project, Raymond pieced together abundant evidence that Christian churches in New Testament times were governed by bodies of elders rather than by a single individual as was then the practice among Jehovah's Witnesses. Karl Adams, head of the writing department, realized the implications of publishing such material and therefore took it to President Knorr. After reading it, Knorr showed it to Frederick Franz. At first, Franz saw no necessity to restructure the congregations after the pattern his nephew had drawn, but later he reconsidered, and the Society eventually announced as a "new truth" just such a switch to collective leadership—both locally and at headquarters.

The new eleven-member Governing Body was displayed as further evidence of the sect's being the one true church, now restored to the apostolic pattern of church government.† Similar collective leadership by a body of elders was also established in the local congregations to replace the one-man rule Judge Rutherford had imposed in 1938. Like the new local bodies of elders, the Governing Body at headquarters had a rotating chairmanship.

In actuality, however, Nathan Knorr continued to rule Jehovah's Witnesses much as Russell and Rutherford had done before him—with full power to act independently and inform the Governing Body after the fact. Collective leadership became a fact on the local level, with bodies of elders now exercising authority in the congregations, but the

---

*The biblical reference works generally available in bookstores were not useful to Witnesses, because they invariably contained references to the Trinity, hellfire, the deity of Christ, and other doctrines the sect rejected. Like the *New World Translation* of the Bible, which the sect published to eliminate verses that conflicted with Watchtower doctrines, a Bible dictionary that would be harmonious with Witness thinking now had to be produced.

†Collective leadership is the key here, not a specific number; with new appointments, deaths, and resignations, the number on the Body has varied, with as many as seventeen members during 1975–1977.

Governing Body at headquarters served as mere window dressing: a decision-making body on paper but not in practice. According to Ray Franz, that remained the case until 1975, when several Governing Body members began asserting their right to use those powers granted to them in theory, which, up to that time, they had never exercised. Over the objections of Fred Franz the body that he had approved in theory and that he had helped to create on paper actually began governing. As a result, when Nathan Knorr died in 1977, Franz inherited an emasculated presidency.

ᴥ   ᴥ   ᴥ

Second-degree criminal trespass charges were filed against three Jehovah's Witnesses arrested for physically blocking a JW patient's court-ordered blood transfusion, according to a report in the Williamsport, Pennsylvania, Sun-Gazette of December 31, 1988. The three were arrested after fifteen Jehovah's Witnesses circled the hospital bed of a patient in the intensive care unit of Long Island's Brookhaven Memorial Hospital in Patchogue, New York.

ᴥ   ᴥ   ᴥ

Penni and I shared with our spiritual brothers and sisters the hope that the world's end would come in late 1975 or early 1976. The confidence most Witnesses had in this prophecy is reflected in the May 1974 issue of *Kingdom Ministry*:

Reports are heard of brothers selling their homes and property and planning to finish out the rest of their days in this old system in the pioneer service. Certainly this is a fine way to spend the short time remaining before the wicked world's end.[21]

JWs who sold their homes and quit their jobs to go selling Watchtower literature in the "short time remaining" were commended and set before other Witnesses as an example to follow. Penni and I displayed the same spirit by postponing until after Armageddon any plans for a home of our own. One of the older pioneers in the congregation found us a three-room apartment on the third floor of a seven-family house in what was known as the "Lithuanian Village" section of Brockton. A gas log built into the kitchen stove provided the apartment's only heat, but it was clean and quiet. Half of the building's inhabitants were little old ladies in babushkas who swept the street as if it were their living room.

I painted and papered our apartment, and Penni decorated it tastefully. It wasn't paradise, but we were happy there; after all, it was going to be our home until Armageddon, when we would find ourselves in the real earthly paradise.

A family and home of our own weren't all my wife and I postponed until the new world dawned. We kept all of our material wants to a minimum so that we could spend as little time as possible in secular employment and devote all our remaining time to field service. We patched together an old car instead of buying a new one. When teeth developed cavities, we told the dentist to pull them instead of paying for expensive root canals and caps. After all, our bodies, including our teeth, would be restored to perfection after Armageddon, when there would be no more sickness, no more death.

As events transpired, however, the autumn of 1975 came and went without the world coming to an end. We were disappointed, but still confident that the destruction would occur at any moment. When nearly a year had gone by and the same old world was still here, *The Watchtower* finally addressed the subject in its issue of July 15, 1976. In an article designed to be studied by means of questions and answers, one of the questions asks, "If a person has regulated his life with the view that the end would come on a certain date, what should he now do?" The corresponding answer states:

> But it is not advisable for us to set our sights on a certain date, neglecting everyday things we would ordinarily care for as Christians, such as things that we and our families really need. . . . If anyone has been disappointed through not following this line of thought, he should now concentrate on adjusting his viewpoint, seeing that it was not the word of God that failed or deceived him and brought disappointment, but that his own understanding was based on wrong premises.[22]

Instead of admitting that the organization had "deceived" its followers, the church leadership blamed the followers themselves and told each one that it was "his own understanding" that brought disappointment. This approach was reminiscent of what the organization had done in 1928, when it reversed itself on the role of the Great Pyramid and condemned readers for following the prior teaching (see chapter 3), and in 1934, when it ridiculed as "foolish" those who believed its earlier teaching on the late Pastor Russell's continuing organizational activities in heaven (see chapter 4).

Stuck in a syndrome similar to that of an abused wife, many JWs accepted this official rebuke and blamed themselves rather than the organization for their disappointment. Others, however, like Penni and me, looked back at what the publications had predicted. (The references given above represent only a small sampling from dozens of references to 1975.) They saw the evidence before them in black and white, and they knew that the leadership was at fault. Penni and I excused them due to their "human imperfection" and trusted that God would still fulfill the prophecy before many more months passed.

When Nathan Knorr died of a brain tumor on June 8, 1977, at the age of seventy-two, Frederick Franz inherited an organization troubled by discontent. The hitherto fast-growing sect actually began losing members for the first time in decades, as people who had expected Armageddon in 1975 became disillusioned.* The prophecy itself had actually been responsible for accelerated growth through much of the prior decade. Between 1960 and 1966 the sect had been baptizing an average of sixty to sixty-five thousand new members each year. After the 1975 date for the end of the world was announced, baptisms jumped to approximately seventy-five thousand in 1967 and eighty-three thousand in 1968. The more emphatic statements concerning "the end" published that year pushed baptisms up to a hundred twenty thousand in 1969 and a hundred sixty-five thousand in 1970. With the autumn of 1975 fast approaching, baptisms in 1974 exceeded the quarter-million mark and actually reached just under three hundred thousand for that year and for 1975 itself. The number of Witnesses actively preaching increased by 13.5 percent in 1974 and by 9.7 percent in 1975. But after the prediction proved false and disappointment swept over the organization, the worldwide total for active Witnesses actually dropped 1 percent in 1977 and 1.4 percent in 1978. (Figures appear in the January 1 *Watchtower* each year, and in the annual yearbook.)

Even more demonstrative of the membership loss triggered by the 1975 failed prediction is a comparison between new members baptized and the resulting increase in active Witnesses. Except for a small attrition due to the deaths of elderly JWs, the addition of new members should be reflected by a corresponding increase in the number of active members ("publishers"). If the Witnesses baptized ten new mem-

---

*JWs don't keep "membership" figures per se; instead they publish the number of "publishers," i.e., Witnesses actively engaging in door-to-door work proclaiming the "good news" (Mark 5:2).

bers, for example, but this resulted in only six more publishers, the difference indicates that four members ceased their activity or left the organization. Or, again, if ten new members were added but the total of active Witnesses did not increase at all, this would mean that ten old members were lost at the same time. Applying such comparison to figures published in annual JW *Yearbooks* yields the following results:

Year	New Witnesses Baptized	Average "Publisher" Increase	Difference = JWs Leaving
1974	297,872	224,040	73,832
1975	295,073	180,736	114,337
1976	196,656	76,088	120,568
1977	124,459	−21,343	145,802
1978	95,052	−30,496	125,548
1979	113,672	10,372	103,300
1980	113,779	78,416	35,363
1981	119,836	72,083	47,753
1982	138,540	95,148	43,392
1983	161,896	159,088	2,808
1984	179,421	178,552	869
totals	1,836,256	1,022,684	813,572

As shown above, JW *Yearbook* figures indicate that while 1,836,256 new followers were added through baptism between 1974 and 1984, the number of active Witnesses increased by only 1,022,684. Simple subtraction reveals a loss of 813,572 individuals during that eleven-year period.* The exodus reached a peak in 1977, when the organization baptized 124,459 new converts but experienced a decrease of 21,343 "average publishers" compared with the previous year, for a total net loss of 145,802 members. The departure of half a million Witnesses between 1975 and 1979 can be traced directly to disillusionment over the failed prophecy. Their *Proclaimers* book admits the decrease in membership, although it tries to downplay the actual cause: "1977/78 re-

---

*Although some were expelled for openly challenging beliefs or for misconduct, and others "disassociated" themselves with a formal letter of resignation, most of these quietly stopped their door-to-door activity and quit attending meetings. They were allowed to slip away. New rules instituted in 1982 put a stop to that by authorizing elders to take action against such individuals. Faced with possible judicial confrontation and shunning, many who would have liked to slip away quietly instead kept plugging along in the organization.

flected a decrease in the number sharing in the preaching work. Was the decrease at least partly due to disappointed expectations concerning 1975? Perhaps."[23]

Thus did Frederick Franz, the Society's fourth president, face the unwelcome task of cleaning up after his failed prophecy. The little groups at Brooklyn headquarters that were meeting privately for Bible study started to question not only the 1914-based chronology that had produced the erroneous 1975 deadline, but also the related teaching that the "heavenly calling" ended in 1935, with new converts after that date consigned to an earthly paradise for their eternal reward. Similar questions troubled thinking Witnesses around the world. Some waited patiently for "new truths" to clarify matters, while others went off to find another religion. When membership loss grew into the hundreds of thousands, as detailed above, Franz and the conservative majority on the Governing Body began to panic. In the spring of 1980 they initiated a crackdown on suspected dissidents, breaking up the independent Bible study groups at headquarters, and forming "judicial committees" to have those seen as ringleaders put on trial for "disloyalty" and "apostasy." The *Proclaimers* book refers to them this way:

> By 1980, a number of persons who had shared in the activities of Jehovah's Witnesses for some years, including some who had served prominently in the organization, had been in various ways trying to cause division and oppose the work Jehovah's Witnesses were doing.[24]

It indicates that *The Watchtower* featured special articles to counter the "apostate influence," but does not speak of the accompanying purge.

By the time this mini-Inquisition culminated in the forced resignation and subsequent excommunication of the president's nephew and fellow Governing Body member, Raymond V. Franz—a development *Time* magazine found worthy of a full-page article[25]—a siege mentality had taken hold on the worldwide organization. Even Witnesses who left quietly and voluntarily for personal reasons were denounced as disloyal and made to be strictly shunned, with former friends forbidden to say as much as "a simple 'Hello' " to them.[26]

If leadership had passed to other hands following the 1975 prophecy's failure, new leaders could have denounced the old teaching and substituted a new one. However, it was the very one who had crafted the chronology behind the 1975 date who became president in 1977. Frederick W. Franz was eighty-three years of age when he took office—a time of life when men, if they are still alive, typically defend their life's work rather than strike off in a new direction. True, the Governing Body held the reigns of power at this time, but its members, too, were old-guard conservatives, unwilling to change. For the most part, they were the president's contemporaries or slightly younger cronies, who themselves had likewise spent a lifetime promoting the prophecy and its chronological dating system. Therefore, instead of accepting responsibility for the slowdown in JW activity, they blamed the apostates who had not yet been cleaned out of the organization:

> Loyal Witnesses moved forward vigorously into the 1980s! Likely the presence of a small number of apostates had contributed to the slowing down of Jehovah's work during the last half of the 1970s—when the average yearly increase in the active ranks of Jehovah's Witnesses fell to less than 1 percent.[27]

Jehovah's Witness Ernestine Gregory was seventeen when she was diagnosed as having leukemia. When she and her mother refused to consent to transfusions, the Cook County state's attorney's office sought a court order, according to a front-page article in the March 13, 1989, Chicago Tribune. *Juvenile Court Judge Harry Aron ordered that Ernestine be given the transfusions. After undergoing several of them, her condition improved and her leukemia went into remission. But she and her parents continued to fight the transfusions in court.*

Like a stranger on a mountaintop viewing a peaceful valley below, who, as he turns to leave, casually tosses a pebble into the void, and who continues on his way, unaware that the pebble dislodged two other pebbles, which unbalanced a small stone, which in turn set other stones in motion until a major avalanche rumbled down the mountainside, forever altering the valley scene he viewed—just such a stranger set in motion a series of events that eventually brought turmoil to Penni and me, and permanently changed our lives.

The initial pebble was a picket sign carried by one of five individuals walking in a small circle on the sidewalk outside the Providence, Rhode Island, Civic Center in July 1977. Penni and I were inside, comfortably surrounded by more than ten thousand fellow Jehovah's Witnesses gathered for an annual four-day convention. Like the other Witnesses, we felt insulted that people, even if a mere handful, were picketing us. We assumed they were "evil slaves," a contemptuous term JWs use for former members who turn against the organization. Neither Penni nor I felt any sympathy for the demonstrators, but one of their signs made Penni a bit uncomfortable. She told me about it that evening when we were alone in our car driving home.

"That sign bothered me," she said, leaving me to ask which one and why. "The one that said, 'Read the Bible, not The Watchtower!' There's a certain amount of truth in that. Not that we shouldn't read *The Watchtower*, of course. But that we really should be reading the Bible, too."

Penni and I both had to admit to each other that we never read the Bible. Of course, we looked up verses here and there, and we often read a chapter assigned in connection with the Thursday night Theocratic School meeting. But we never sat down with the Bible alone to read it on a regular basis. Why? Well, we were too busy reading Watchtower Society publications. (Later, after leaving the organization, we actually added up the pages of all the *Watchtower* and *Awake!* magazines, books, booklets, *Kingdom Ministry* bulletins, study articles, and other materials assigned for Witnesses to read each year and compared that total with the pages of Bible reading officially assigned through the Theocratic School. The numbers turned out to be thousands of pages of the Watchtower Society's materials as compared with fewer than two hundred pages of the Bible annually.) We knew that only the most conscientious Witnesses came close to covering all of this material, and that the average JW gave priority to publications used for question-and-answer sessions at the meetings, so that very few engaged in personal Bible reading. I myself had read the JW *New World Translation* through once before baptism, but stopped after that, and I knew from private conversation with my fellow elders on the local body—men viewed as the congregation's Bible teachers—that some of them had *never* read the Scriptures from cover to cover.

During that drive home from Rhode Island, Penni and I resolved, therefore, to start reading the Bible on a regular basis—not as a move away from the Watchtower organization, but to become better Jehovah's Witnesses. We knew, after all, that a large illuminated sign on one of the Society's buildings in Brooklyn admonished the general public to "read God's Word the Bible daily." So, there could not possibly be anything wrong with our taking that admonition seriously ourselves.

To facilitate such reading by making it more interesting, we decided to obtain another translation. The sect's *New World Translation of the Holy Scriptures* was the one we always used for looking up verses referred to at Kingdom Hall meetings and in personal study, but the wording of the Watchtower Society's favorite verses that we looked up over and over again in that version was so familiar to us that we could recite the words by heart. We felt we would be assisted to meditate more on the meaning if we read the familiar verses in a different translation. However, our indoctrination had convinced us it was wrong to omit God's name, as the most popular translations do by replacing the name with the title LORD in small capital letters. We were aware that the Hebrew Tetragrammaton or four-lettered name for God is actually transliterated YHWH (or, more familiarly, *Yahweh*), and that the form *Jehovah* resulted from a medieval scribe's error—a fact admitted occasionally in Watchtower literature.[28] But we still felt comfortable only with that familiar rendering, Jehovah, that Witnesses always used. So, we decided to obtain a copy of *The Way*, a Catholic edition of *The Living Bible*, which, for some unexplained reason, features the name Jehovah throughout the Old Testament. A friend at Kingdom Hall had pointed this out to us as a helpful tool for witnessing to Roman Catholics, so we felt doubly justified in taking the unusual step necessary to purchase such a volume.

That "unusual step" consisted of crossing the threshold of a "Christian bookstore," a place normally off-limits to JWs. Reading literature by other denominations is strongly discouraged, and books by apostate ex-Witnesses are strictly forbidden. (A Jehovah's Witness caught reading this book that you are now reading can be put on trial behind closed doors for such a crime and punished severely—totally shunned by family and friends. In this case, however, Penni and I felt we could safely enter a nearby Christian bookstore in Whitman, Massachusetts, to obtain a *Living Bible*, since it would equip us to be better Witnesses and to speak more effectively to Roman Catholics. We wouldn't look at any forbidden books.

And we didn't. In fact, we boldly identified ourselves as Jehovah's Witnesses to the bespectacled lady at the counter, as if that would somehow ward off the evil of the place. (It was filled with crucifixes, praying hands, and haloed portraits of Jesus, all of which gave us the creeps; such symbols are as spooky to JWs as skulls and shrunken heads are to other people, because they view them as demon-infested false idols.) Not wanting the salesclerk to think we were compromising our faith, we told her we were buying that Catholic Bible because it contained God's name Jehovah. She simply smiled, said "That's nice, praise the Lord!" and sent us on our way.

I had been the more eager to buy it, but Penni soon took over *The*

Way Bible and kept it by her bedside for nightly reading; she loved the way its idiomatic paraphrases made each scene come alive. Often she would blurt out to me, as I was undressing or eating a bedtime snack, "Listen to what Peter said!" or "Here's what Paul said!" I still stayed primarily in our familiar JW version, but reading the New Testament in either form had the same effect on both of us: we fell in love with Jesus!

For me, this was actually the rekindling of an old love. I had first grown fond of Jesus when I read the Bible as a teenager as an assignment for the Boy Scout "God and Country" award, if I remember correctly. I was bothered back then by his presenting himself as the Son of God, but otherwise he was a real hero. He stood up for the underdog, denounced high officials' hypocrisy to their faces, and took Gandhian nonviolent direct action. Even as a budding atheist I couldn't picture Jesus intentionally lying or misleading people, so I assumed the "Son of God" stuff he spouted was symptomatic of a mental disturbance, or else a product of his culture. But again, how could such a strong and clearsighted mind be mentally unbalanced? And wasn't Jesus obviously so far ahead of his times as to be free from cultural biases?

Yes, I had loved Jesus as a teenager, but he had always made me uncomfortable. Now as a Jehovah's Witness I saw him as the incarnation of Michael the Archangel, so the supernatural stuff made more sense. Yes, as the first angel God created, Jesus could rightly be called the Son of God, and doubly so after his life was miraculously transferred by Jehovah to the Virgin Mary's womb for human birth. All of that made sense to me now. I could love him even better than I had before.

Yet, little did Penni and I realize at that time that our growing affection for Jesus would eventually get us thrown out of our religious organization; that responding to his invitation, "Come, follow me!" would lead us into a head-on clash with Watchtower headquarters.

The clash would never have come had we not been such zealous Witnesses, busy in the work of recruiting others to join the sect. Between the two of us, Penni and I had started and conducted dozens of "free home Bible studies" with people we found in our door-to-door work, and we succeeded in leading approximately twenty-five of these all the way to baptism as full-fledged Jehovah's Witnesses. Our converts included single young people, married couples, and the elderly. It was our activity among younger people that eventually brought us into conflict with the organization.

Kate Van Drise, a Witness in her mid-sixties, had brought me with her to meet Tony Almonte, a young man who had shown interest when she knocked at his parents' door. Kate hoped that I would be able to start a weekly Bible study with Tony and lead him "into the Truth." Tony turned out to be a handsome seventeen-year-old with fine blond hair that he wore in a long ponytail. His intense blue eyes lit up as Kate gushed over him in grandmotherly fashion. I wondered how long he would last studying with a grim-faced guy like me. But he took well to my less effusive personality and accepted my commendations for correct answers as gladly as he had accepted Kate's exclamations about his good looks. In a matter of weeks Tony began to respond to what he was learning. He renounced Catholicism, his parent's nominal religion, and started sharing "the Truth" with his friends at school.

One of these friends, Al, wanted a home Bible study of his own. So Tony introduced us and I began visiting Al each week on a different evening. Both young men responded well to the lessons I conducted with them. They began cleaning up their lives. When I pointed out satanic lyrics in their heavy-metal rock music, they trashed offending albums. The glow-in-the-dark plastic skulls that had adorned Tony's bedroom disappeared. Although both Tony and Al practiced Transcendental Meditation as a scientific relaxation technique to relieve tension, when I showed them that the "meaningless" mantras they recited were actually Sanskrit invocations to demonic deities, they both recognized TM as Hinduism traveling incognito, and both quit the practice entirely.

All went well, until the first meeting that I got them to attend at Kingdom Hall. Arriving late, they were unable to sit with Penni and me, but found seats together near the back of the hall. When the meeting was over, many Witnesses shook their hands and introduced themselves to the obvious newcomers. One of the "sisters" even offered to give Tony one of her son's white dress shirts, which she was sure would fit him—and that's where the problem arose. Tony told me at our next study that he was sure he would never fit in at Kingdom Hall. Even if he were to shed his jeans suit, decorated black tee shirt, and worn-out sneakers on Thursday nights in exchange for a white shirt and tie, blue blazer, and dress shoes, there would still be the problem of his ponytail.

"Did anyone come up to you and suggest to you that you needed a haircut?" I asked, fearing that someone may have already been so bold. A "theocratic haircut"—hair trimmed above the ears and collar—was a prerequisite for men speaking from the platform or sharing in door-to-door work, but tact and good sense argued against confronting a nonconforming first-time visitor with these rules.

"No," Tony admitted. "Nobody said anything about my hair, but they didn't have to. It's obvious, man! All the guys at the meeting had 1950s haircuts—every last one, except me and Al!"

I knew that Tony was right, but at the same time I knew he should have been wrong. I realized full well that his ponytail would never be accepted at Kingdom Hall, but I also recalled that biblical superhero Samson wore his hair in seven braids and had only one haircut in his life—a foolish mistake that eventually cost the strong man his life. I knew that Samuel the prophet *never* cut his hair; that king David's son Absalom saw a barber once a year; that the Nazarites in ancient Israel let their hair grow as many months or years as they were under a vow of dedication to God; and that John the Baptist was a Nazarite for life. Could God have written approvingly of all these long-haired men in the Bible and yet reject these boys if they kept their ponytails? I stumbled around, not knowing how to answer Tony. However, I still encouraged him to attend Kingdom Hall meetings.

"It's pointless!" he answered. "I could never become a Jehovah's Witness with my ponytail, and I'm not going to cut it off."

Tony and Al soon stopped keeping their appointments for the studies I was conducting with them, and we eventually lost contact. I was devastated, because this meant that they would miss out not simply on joining our denomination, but also on everlasting life. When the Battle of Armageddon soon swept across the face of the earth, with God's angelic executioners ridding the planet of the wicked and preserving alive only those who had taken refuge in Jehovah's organization, these two boys would lose their lives. They would be annihilated, with no chance of a resurrection.

Other Witnesses who heard about Tony and Al dismissed them with the wave of a hand: "Too bad for them! If they love their hair more than they love God, then good riddance! If they die at Armageddon, it's their own fault. They deserve it."

I couldn't dismiss them that easily, however. To me, the hair length rules we followed were not biblical requirements, nor even organizational requirements imposed from Brooklyn headquarters. I believed them to be standards set by the local elders in our congregation and in the surrounding area. I began to see these elders as men who were capable of error. Yes, I heard them quote 1 Corinthians 11:14–15 (JW *New World Translation*), "Does not nature itself teach you that if a man has long hair, it is a dishonor to him; but if a woman has long hair, it is a glory to her?" but I knew that verse was written in a culture where a woman's hair was left uncut, and that its author, the Apostle Paul, was a Jewish Christian who honored Samson and Samuel. All his life, Paul had kept the Jewish law which commanded, "You must not cut your sidelocks short around, and you must not destroy the extremity of your beard" (Lev. 19:27). Yet, a man who followed that grooming style would not be allowed to pass out magazines at our Kingdom Hall, let alone serve as an apostle! It seemed wrong for our elders to interpret "long hair" in the context of the 1940s and 1950s they had grown up in, rather than in the historical context in which the verse had been written.

I even called to mind the words our Circuit Overseer, Ed Burke, had spoken to me months earlier over dinner; concerning the standards we elders should follow in recommending individuals for positions of responsibility in the congregation, he said, "Of course, you can't refuse to appoint a man because you don't like the way he parts his hair." It occurred to me that some boys with Beatles-style or Dutch-boy haircuts actually had shorter hair than some of the elders who used creams or lotions to keep theirs combed straight back. If gray-haired brother Richards, a prominent Assembly Overseer, were to part his down the middle and comb it to the sides, it would more than cover his ears, while if those boys with the unacceptable haircuts were to use plenty of oil and comb theirs straight back, they would suddenly pass the test. We were actually judging a man according to the way he *parted* his hair, after all.

This really bothered me, because I was in the habit of confronting Roman Catholics I met at the doors with the words of Matthew 15:9, "It is in vain that they keep worshiping me, because they teach commands of men as doctrines." I would identify eating fish on Fridays and priestly celibacy as man-made doctrines, and use the quoted verse to declare their Catholic worship to be "in vain." Now I suddenly saw myself as teaching tacitly, and by my personal example, the commands of men regarding hairstyles and beards. Jesus was my hero, and he condemned this. What would he do in my place?

While this question was still on my mind, I had occasion to work from door to door with two other local elders from neighboring congregations. One of them mentioned that he was conducting a study with a young man who was making good progress and who expressed the desire to start sharing in house-to-house preaching. The only obstacle was that the fellow wore a little goatee on his chin. Before I could say anything, the third elder answered decisively, "You'll just have to tell him he can't take part in the witnessing work until he shaves it off!" I felt sick and kept quiet. Here we were again, teaching the commands of men as doctrines. As Jews under the Law of Moses, Jesus and all twelve of his apostles obviously wore beards, yet we would not allow such a man to preach. (I was unaware at the time that illustrations in JW publications from 1942 through early 1968 pictured a beardless Christ, but Jesus' facial hair was restored just before I began associating with the sect that summer.)

I remained silent in the company of these elders, but on March 6, 1978, I decided to write to the Society's Brooklyn headquarters about the matter. I began:

> This letter is in regard to a matter that I fear may be a cause for stumbling, discouraging persons from examining the truth. The obstacle is the insistence on the part of some that brothers groom themselves according to the styles that were popular in the world during the '40s, '50s and '60s.

The answer came in the form of an April 11, 1978, letter on the New York corporation's letterhead, signed with a rubber-stamped "Watchtower B. & T. Society" in cursive script. The official letter declared plainly,

> The grooming of one's hair just as the wearing of a beard or a mustache is a personal decision. (Rom. 5:2) We know of no Scripture that speaks against wearing a beard when it is kept neat and trim making the individual presentable.

Well, that definitely answered my question. As I suspected, it was not the Society but rather the local elders who were insisting on the outdated styles. How could I avoid sharing with them in their error? I resolved in my mind that I would follow the example of Jesus, who healed a man on the Sabbath to refute a man-made doctrine of his contemporaries: I would grow my hair longer to refute the theocratic haircut doctrine of the local elders.

By this time I was a respected elder myself: a prominent teacher in our local congregation, well-liked by other elders, and a public speaker frequently invited to address neighboring congregations on Sunday mornings. Like the other elders, I took my turn by rotation serving as presiding overseer, or head of the congregation for a year at a time. If I wore my hair over my ears and collar, how could the other local elders continue to badger youngsters into getting theocratic haircuts? Obviously, they couldn't; the kids would be able to point at me and say, "Brother Reed wears his hair this way, so it must be okay."

Some months after this, Penni began conducting a weekly study with Gloria Hagar, a young Jewish divorcée. Gloria was a brilliant woman raising a ten-year-old boy and a thirteen-year-old girl while working full time as an oceanologist at Woods Hole. Her scientific mind was fascinated with the Watchtower Society's chronological calculations and their relationship to the predictions of her own Hebrew prophets. The New Testament was a whole new world to Gloria. She gladly accepted Penni's invitation to attend Kingdom Hall.

At their next study, however, Gloria was furious with my wife. "Why didn't you tell me I needed to wear a dress?" she demanded. Built like a model, the professional woman had a closet full of pantsuits that she looked stunning in, and she had worn one of these to the meeting. Gloria quickly realized, however, that she was out of place.

"You don't need to wear a dress," Penni replied, drawing on Scripture for what she said next: "God says he is 'the One examining hearts,' not wardrobes."

"Look! I'm not stupid," Gloria continued, angered even more by Penni's denial. "I was the only woman there in pants. With more than a hundred people present, the majority female, *someone* else would have had on pants if it weren't against your rules."

Penni knew there was no biblical basis for requiring dresses, so she kept repeating that it didn't matter to God. After all, like most of the other women in the congregation, Penni had pants outfits that she wore downtown or to the mall, although not to Kingdom Hall. She also knew that Gloria's wardrobe consisted entirely of pantsuits; the woman didn't own a dress and would have to go out and buy some if they were required for her to become a Witness.

"Well, even if God doesn't require a dress, why should I face the embarrassment of being the only woman there in pants? I would feel everyone would be looking down on me," Gloria went on. "If God doesn't disapprove of pantsuits, why don't you wear one of yours, too? Then I won't be the only one. If pants are really acceptable with God, then you wear them, too!"

Penni accepted the challenge. She wore a pantsuit to the next meeting. Some people there murmured and grumbled, but others were pleased with her move. If an elder's wife could wear pants, then they could as well, they reasoned. One Witness around fifty-five years old wore pants to work but had not been attending meetings because she did not want people to see the varicose veins on her legs that a dress would expose (like pants, an ankle-length skirt was also considered extreme and avoided by Witnesses); when a friend told her pants were now all right, she started coming back to Kingdom Hall. Another JW, a woman in her eighties, had been staying home on cold days, but now started attending meetings wearing long-johns and pants.

Not everyone was pleased with these developments, however. When word about my longer hair and Penni's pantsuits reached them— and such news travels fast in JW circles—elders in neighboring congregations were outraged. How could they keep their kids wearing short hair and stop their women from wearing pants if this was going on in the congregation next door? Immediately the elders in surrounding Kingdom Halls began canceling my scheduled Sunday morning speaking engagements. Our Circuit Overseer, Ed Burke, who was about to be transferred elsewhere, also took away a teaching assignment he had given me for the upcoming circuit convention, even though it was he who had told me months earlier over dinner that "you can't refuse to appoint a man because you don't like the way he parts his hair."

Pressure from neighboring elders soon led the elders in our congregation to begin reexamining my qualifications to continue on this body, but the new Circuit Overseer, Tom Halloran, intervened and told them that my grooming was not objectionable. Shortly afterward a speaker from Bethel headquarters came to the area for a special one-day assembly. In one of his talks he singled out the elders in the audience for some strong counsel: "You are driving the young people out of the Truth," he told them, "by enforcing rules on dress and grooming that are not biblical." Then the Society's magazines began featuring illustrations of Witness men and boys with longer, up-to-date hairstyles.[29] Obviously, the elders in our area were the ones who were out of step with the Society, or so it seemed.

Then came the February 1981 visit of our Circuit Overseer, Tom Halloran. At our Friday evening elders' meeting with him the matter of women wearing pantsuits came up, but the body's decision was not to make an issue of it. Brother Halloran brought up for discussion his recommendation that we remove as an elder Brother Hank Rimmer, the fifth member of our body, who was then wintering in Florida. The grounds for removal, he suggested, would be the fact that Brother Rimmer had missed most of the last Kingdom Ministry School (for elders) as well as some circuit assembly elders' meetings. I strongly disagreed, pointing out that Brother Rimmer's failure to attend as expected must have been due to his health problems. He was in his seventies, had a bad heart, and suffered from angina. Eventually, the body decided to let the matter drop, but Halloran was obviously displeased that my arguments had contributed to blocking his attempt to remove this older man for whom he had expressed a dislike for some time. The subject of my haircut was not brought up by anyone at the elders' meeting.

Then on Sunday morning, February 8, an elder told me that Halloran wanted to hold a special meeting with the body at 2:30 that afternoon to consider his charge that I was "leading a rebellious movement" on dress and grooming in the congregation. I was puzzled, since he was the one who had come to my defense over this issue on prior occasions. Surely enough, however, when the door closed behind me and I was alone with the other elders and the Circuit Overseer, they informed me that they were about to call in two witnesses to testify against me. The charge? My haircut and Penni's pantsuits were "stumbling" people, offending them to the point of causing harm. I was flabbergasted as I listened to two young men offer their solemn testimony to that effect. All of this had come without warning. Halloran gave me little opportunity to respond to the charges, and virtually no opportunity to prepare in advance. After denouncing my grooming and my wife's style of dress for four hours, they sent me out of the room so they could discuss my case, and then called me back in to announce their verdict. They were writing the Society to recommend my removal as an elder. Here follow some excerpts of their letter to headquarters:

> . . . Bro. Reed was asked to walk to the back of the room and as he did so he was observed by the body. All stated that they couldn't tell if it was a man or a woman from the back.
> . . . His 'inordinate desire to glorify himself and his opinions' and his 'fanatical and stubborn zeal for his own views' [12/1/78 WT pp. 23–24*] were disqualifying traits for an elder.
> . . . We saw no evidence of repentance at all.

The following Thursday evening the elders called me into the library after the Service Meeting, demanded that I turn in my territory map, and told me I was no longer eligible to do the door-to-door witnessing work.

I was in a state of shock. Not only were they stripping me of my position in the congregation, but also condemning me to destruction. In the eyes of Jehovah God, anyone not doing the witnessing work is not one of His Witnesses, and so is in line for eternal destruction at Armageddon. I couldn't believe that the Circuit Overseer and elders were doing this to me over less than an inch of hair, and in opposition

---

*This *Watchtower* article concerned characteristics that would disqualify a man from serving as an elder.

to the Society's position on dress and grooming. As soon as the shock wore off, I wrote to headquarters a detailed letter outlining what had happened. The rest of the story relates to the sect's enforcement procedures and what happens when a Witness tries to leave, so I will continue with what happened in my own case in chapter 8.

🌿 🌿 🌿

An article in the Florida Sun-Sentinel *of July 9, 1992, concerning a court-ordered transfusion for a young mother, comments that "Florida courts generally have upheld an adult's right to refuse medical treatment based on his religious beliefs," and gives the example of a March 1991 ruling that "construction worker Thomas Poole, thirty-seven, critically injured in a fall from the unfinished Broward Center for the Performing Arts, could not be forced to have a transfusion. He later died." According to a story in the* Miami Herald *of March 7, 1991, the doctor who performed an autopsy on Poole said his decision to refuse blood "contributed to his death."*

🌿 🌿 🌿

It would be inappropriate to close this chapter on Nathan Knorr and Frederick Franz without mentioning the outcome of another prophecy promoted during Knorr's presidency but doubtless the work of theologian Franz. The 1958 book *"Your Will Be Done on Earth"* gives the Watchtower Society's scenario of end-times events. Concentrating on the struggle between "the king of the south" and "the king of the north" in Daniel, chapter 11, it identifies the modern king of the south as the combined alliance of "Britain and America"[30] and the king of the north as "the Soviet Union, the Communist power that, since it seized power in Russia in 1917, has held world domination as its aim to this day."[31] The book prophesies that "Down to the 'time of the end' at Armageddon there will be competitive coexistence between the 'two kings' "[32]—that is, between the Communist USSR and the British-American combine—and that "Jehovah's angel foretold further aggressions by the Communist king of the north before his end in Armageddon."[33] However, as events actually transpired, the early 1990s saw the collapse of the Communist empire and the dissolution of the Soviet Union.

Moreover, *The Watchtower* of April 1, 1984, referred readers to *"Your Will Be Done on Earth"* as still current information, and stressed that the Soviet Union is an "atheistic" power. Yet, well before the breakup of the USSR, religion began blossoming anew in its various republics.

Before meeting his own end on December 22, 1992, President F. W. Franz lived to see the facts demolish his prophecy that an atheistic, Communistic Soviet Union would survive to meet its "end in Armageddon." Ironically, another prophetic book produced under his direction had said (concerning others), "Jehovah, the God of the true prophets, will put all false prophets to shame either by not fulfilling the false prediction of such self-assuming prophets or by having His own prophecies fulfilled in a way opposite to that predicted by the false prophets."[34]

NOTES

1. *The Watchtower,* October 1, 1959, p. 607.

2. *The Watchtower,* May 1, 1957, p. 285.

3. *The Golden Age,* April 30, 1930, p. 503.

4. *"The Truth Shall Make You Free"* (Brooklyn, N.Y.: Watchtower Society, 1945), p. 300.

5. Ibid., p. 152.

6. *God's Kingdom of a Thousand Years Has Approached* (Brooklyn, N.Y.: Watchtower Society, 1973), pp. 209–10.

7. *Jehovah's Witnesses—Proclaimers of God's Kingdom* (Brooklyn, N.Y.: Watchtower Society, 1993), p. 104.

8. Ibid., p. 29.

9. Ibid., p. 30.

10. *The Watchtower,* October 15, 1966, pp. 628–29.

11. *Awake!* October 8, 1966, pp. 19–20.

12. *The Watchtower,* May 1, 1967, p. 262.

13. *The Watchtower,* May 1, 1968, pp. 271–73.

14. *The Watchtower,* August 15, 1968, p. 499.

15. *The Watchtower,* November 15, 1967, pp. 703–704.

16. *The Watchtower,* March 15, 1980, p. 31.

17. *Awake!* August 22, 1969, p. 6.

18. *The Universal Standard Encyclopedia* (New York: Standard Reference Works Publishing Co., 1957), pp. 912–14 and 8551–53.

19. *Consolation,* December 1943, p. 23, and *The Watchtower,* December 1, 1944; the July 1, 1945, issue of *The Watchtower* stated a clearly defined prohibition against members accepting blood.

20. Franz recounted this experience in his book *Crisis of Conscience* (Atlanta: Commentary Press, 1983).

21. *Kingdom Ministry,* May 1974, p. 3

22. *The Watchtower,* July 15, 1976, p. 441.

23. *Jehovah's Witnesses—Proclaimers of God's Kingdom,* p. 110.

24. Ibid., p. 111.

25. "Witness under Prosecution," *Time,* February 22, 1982, p. 66.

26. *The Watchtower*, September 15, 1981, pp. 23, 25.

27. *The Watchtower*, December 15, 1986, p. 20.

28. "As to the Old Testament name of God, certainly the spelling and pronunciation 'Jehovah' were originally a blunder." Translator's Preface by Steven T. Byington, *The Bible in Living English* (Brooklyn, N.Y.: Watchtower Society, 1972), p. 7.

29. *The Watchtower*, July 15, 1978, p. 24; December 15, 1980, p. 1; March 1, 1981, p. 1; *Awake!* November 8, 1979, p. 16; November 22, 1980, p. 11.

30. *"Your Will Be Done on Earth"* (Brooklyn, N.Y.: Watchtower Society, 1958), p. 263.

31. Ibid., p. 278.

32. Ibid., p. 297.

33. Ibid., p. 300.

34. *Paradise Restored to Mankind—by Theocracy!* (Brooklyn, N.Y.: Watchtower Society, 1972), p. 353.

6

Milton G. Henschel: Last of the Old Guard

John Richard Alson, a forty-seven-year-old Jehovah's Witness from French Camp, California, died in August 1992, "because he lost too much blood after the main artery in his left leg was severed" in an accident at his place of employment in Manteca, according to an article in The Modesto Bee. *"The doctor told both Alson and his wife that if he would not take blood transfusions, he would die," says the report. A later article in the August 16 issue of the same paper quotes Alson's wife as saying, "Well, I may lose him here but I won't lose him to eternity," according to a report of their conversation by Dr. Kenneth Young, chief of orthopedics at San Joaquin General Hospital in Stockton. The story also quotes the doctor as adding, concerning his patient, that, "I'm quite confident he would be alive today," if he had accepted the transfusion.*

Milton G. Henschel was named fifth Watchtower president on December 30, 1992, to succeed Frederick Franz who died December 22 at the age of ninety-nine. Henschel was born a third-generation Jehovah's Witness in Pomona, New Jersey, in 1920 and was baptized in 1934. He served at Watchtower headquarters in various capacities, including the vice presidency, for some fifty years. As a younger man Henschel was personal secretary to Nathan Knorr and toured northern Europe with him in late 1945 and early 1946. Eventually, as a Governing Body member during the final years of Knorr's presidency, Henschel did administrative work. He has served on the Governing Body's Service Committee and as Coordinator of the Publishing Committee, overseeing the corporation's many factories.

152

Although Milton Henschel is now president of both the Watchtower Bible and Tract Society of New York, Inc., and the parent corporation, the Watch Tower Bible and Tract Society of Pennsylvania, the presidency has never recovered from the trimming of powers that occurred during Nathan Knorr's declining years, so Henschel is not the significant figure that Russell and Rutherford were. Real power rests with the eleven-member Governing Body as a whole. To supervise the organization's day-to-day operations, this group breaks up into five overlapping committees, with five or more members serving on each.

The Personnel Committee handles issues involving the more than fifteen thousand "Bethel family" members, the volunteer staff residing at the headquarters complex and at more than a hundred branch offices, farms, and factory facilities worldwide. The Publishing Committee supervises the factory operations. The Service Committee oversees the work of the district and circuit overseers, who in turn give direction to local elders; it also serves as the ultimate judicial authority issuing guidelines and even directed verdicts through church courts. The Teaching Committee oversees all of the sect's training programs and teaching seminars. The Writing Committee determines the content of the Society's publications, including books and magazines. The annually rotating chairmanship of the Governing Body itself results in a sixth committee, different from the others. The Chairman's Committee, with continuity as its aim, consists of the present chairman, his predecessor, and the man next in line.

In addition to Henschel the members of the Governing Body, as of this writing, are Ted Jaracz, age seventy; Dan Sydlik, seventy-six; Lloyd Barry, seventy-nine; Jack Barr, eighty-two; Albert Schroeder, eighty-four; Lyman Swingle, eighty-five; Carey Barber, ninety;. Karl Klein, ninety; John Booth, ninety-three; and 1994 appointee Gerrit Lösch, fifty-four.

At seventy-six Henschel is the third-youngest member of the Governing Body, whose median age was eighty-four before the recent addition of much younger Gerrit Lösch, who brings it down to eighty. With members in their eighties and nineties prone to sleep through meetings and to vote on matters upon being awakened,[1] the group is losing its ability to provide purposeful and decisive leadership. Henschel was no doubt chosen to be president in part due to his youthful vitality when compared to other members of the Governing Body. Obviously, these aging leaders will not be able to hold the reigns of power much longer. The men who shared in building the Watchtower into what it is today will soon leave it behind for others to run.

The April 15, 1992, *Watchtower* announced what may eventually prove to be the first step in such a leadership transition, although, at this stage, it serves more as a prop to brace up the existing structure:

> . . . [I]t has been decided to invite several helpers, mainly from among the great crowd, to share in the meetings of each of the Governing Body Committees, that is, the Personnel, Publishing, Service, Teaching, and Writing Committees. . . . Under the direction of the Governing Body committee members, these assistants will take part in discussions and will carry out various assignments given them by the committee.[2]

There is no indication that these "assistants" would attend the meetings of the Governing Body itself, where doctrinal changes are approved—only the more routine committee meetings. And, even at the committee meetings, they will serve "under the direction" of those who are actual members of the Governing Body.

Two tedious "study articles" in this same issue of *The Watchtower*[3] provide the supposed scriptural justification for this minor organizational adjustment, drawing alleged parallels with non-Jewish temple servants following the return of ancient Israel from Babylonian exile.

The desperately needed appointment of younger men to the Governing Body itself has, however, largely been blocked by the unique Witness doctrine that leaders must come from the "anointed remnant" of the hundred and forty-four thousand supposedly in line for heaven. Hayden C. Covington (later, attorney for Muhammad Ali) took office as vice president of the Society's New York and Pennsylvania corporations in 1942, but resigned less than four years later, in the autumn of 1945, "to comply with what appeared to be the Lord's will, namely, that all the members of the directorate and the officers be of the anointed remnant," since attorney Covington was "one of the 'other sheep,' with prospects of life on earth."[4] Today, of the more than twelve million people attending Kingdom Halls worldwide, fewer than 8,700 claim to be of this "remnant" from which the leaders must be chosen. (They signify this claim by partaking of the wine and bread at the sect's annual Memorial, or communion service, which the remaining millions attend only as observers, and the count of partakers is published in the January 1 *Watchtower* each year.) Most of these members who predate the 1935 cut-off date for the heavenly class are women, automatically barred from leadership roles.

Initial reports of the appointment of Gerrit Lösch sparked speculation that the Society might have abandoned its teaching that Governing Body members must be of "the anointed class"—which would require abandoning dozens of other teachings, since that doctrine is tied in with the 1914 "invisible return of Christ" and related chronological interpretations and prophecies. However, a September 8, 1994, letter from Brooklyn headquarters reaffirmed that "all" on the Governing Body "are spirit anointed Christians." Responding to a writer from New Jersey (who shared it with me), the anonymous official letter from the Society's Writing Department explained it this way:

> As discussed in *The Watchtower* of February 1, 1982, a person's being of the anointed is a personal matter between that one and Jehovah God. It is not a matter concerning which a Christian may judge his brother. (Rom. 14:10) It is true that since about 1935 the general call for spirit-anointed brothers of Jesus has ceased to go out. But, should one of the anointed prove unfaithful since that time and before having completed his earthly course, it is reasonable to conclude that his position would have to be filled by a replacement. In this regard, please note what is stated on page 383 of the June 15, 1970, issue of *The Watchtower.* In paragraph 1, it points out that favor would be given to the time-tested person over the novice in selecting such a replacement from among the "great crowd." This is especially reasonable in view of Jesus' statement to his disciples: "However, you are the ones that have stuck with me in my trials." (Luke 22:28) Brother Lösch has been a dedicated servant of Jehovah for over three decades and professes to be of the anointed.
>
> "This Governing Body," says the *Live Forever* book, page 195, "is made up of 'the faithful and discreet slave.' It serves as a spokesman for that faithful 'slave.' " All of them, then, are spirit anointed Christians. The *Live Forever* book goes on to say: "The men of that Governing Body, like the apostles and older men in Jerusalem, have many years of experience in God's service." Be assured that Brother Gerrit Lösch, recently appointed as a member of the Governing Body, meets these requirements.

So, Lösch is one of the rare breed of younger Witnesses who, as JWs put it, "profess to be of the anointed." Such a claim is usually greeted with silent skepticism by fellow Witnesses. They commonly say of a JW baptized before 1935 that "Sister So-and-so is of the anointed," but of a younger person that "Brother So-and-so *professes* to be of the anointed"—with extra emphasis on the word "professes," and sometimes even a wry smile, a raising of the eyebrows, or a sarcastic laugh.

My own observation from years with the organization is that persons baptized after 1935 who claim to be of the anointed class generally fall into one of three categories: First, some are emotionally unstable men and women who tend to exhibit unconventional behavior in other areas of life as well. For example, one such woman in my wife's former congregation habitually arrived at the annual Memorial (communion) service dressed in white from head to toe, which she felt suited her as a member of "the bride of Christ." Second, there are a few sincere folk who grasp the Bible's invitation to come into the same relationship with Jesus Christ as first-century Christians, and who extend this invitation to themselves. Third, there are a number of arrogant men with huge egos who think it only natural that they should occupy a position of superiority and who are eagerly "reaching out" for greater authority within the organization.

It is unlikely, of course, that an odd duck from the first category would climb very high in the hierarchy of an organization where conformity is an exalted virtue. If Gerrit Lösch falls into the second or third category, his appointment to the JW Governing Body should give rise to some interesting developments. If he is a sincere Bible believer attempting to follow Scripture more closely than organizational tradition, he may eventually follow the footsteps of Raymond Franz in experiencing a "crisis of conscience," followed by an abrupt departure from Brooklyn headquarters. Or, he may attempt to swing official doctrine back toward mainstream Christianity. If, on the other hand, he is a man from the third category with a mammoth ego, he may fight to bring the organization under his own one-man rule reminiscent of Judge Rutherford's days.

While it seems fairly certain that the role of Gerrit Lösch on the Governing Body will be a prominent one, that body's future is unclear. Continued adherence to the doctrine of leaders chosen from the remnant of men baptized before 1935 is, by definition, self-limiting. It will eventually prove impossible as these men die off or become totally incapacitated by age. Appointment of additional younger exceptions like Lösch is a possibility, but too many exceptions would void the rule. Either way—allowing exceptions or allowing more time to pass—the doctrine will soon be canceled out.

However, replacing this teaching with a new leadership doctrine will not be easy. The problem is that the present doctrine, which allows a small heaven-bound elite to command an earth-bound "great crowd" of followers, is tied closely with many other key teachings. Trying to replace just this one doctrine would be like trying to replace the bottom apple in a pile of apples on a grocery store shelf—the whole pile would come tumbling down. Why? The teaching is that Christ appointed this leadership class over all his earthly interests in 1919 as one step in a whole series of events tied in to his returning invisibly in 1914 and fulfilling prophecies through J. F. Rutherford and his associates, as noted earlier in chapter 4. Other events in the series include the commencement of the First World War in 1914, the imprisonment of the Society's officers during the war, their release and the resumption of the public preaching work after the war, specific announcements made at annual conventions from 1922 through 1928, the selection of the name Jehovah's Witnesses in 1931, and the announcement of an earthly hope for new converts after 1935, as related in detail in *Revelation: Its Grand Climax at Hand* and many other Watchtower publications. Changing the leadership doctrine would call into question whether Christ really returned, whether the millions of believers really have only an earthly hope instead of a heavenly one, whether they might not *all* be qualified to lead, and whether the organization really speaks for God.

As noted earlier, the teaching that Christ appointed the Watchtower's leadership class is not the only element of Frederick Franz's chronological structure that is running out of time. As of this writing, his prediction of "a peaceful and secure new world before the generation that saw the events of 1914 passes away," still appears in the masthead of each new *Awake!* magazine.* Originally, the final "generation" was calculated with respect to the 1975 date. "Youngsters fifteen years of age" in 1914 would be "nearly 70 years old" in 1968, and near to passing away by 1975.[5] Later, the Society began speaking of "babies" born in 1914 who were "now 70 years old or older" in 1984.[6] Yet those same babies would be in their eighties now. "The Hebrews . . . reckon seventy-five years as one generation," *Awake!* said in its issue of April 8, 1988.[7] So, by that Hebrew reckoning, and most others, "the generation that saw the events of 1914" has passed away, and the few surviving individuals representing that generation will soon be gone. At that point the entire JW chronological system, along with all of its related doctrines, will be like food whose freshness date has expired, and has started to rot and to stink.

It will have to be replaced, along with its leadership doctrine.

---

*As this book was being prepared, the sect officially dropped this teaching. The October 22, 1995, *Awake!* was the last issue to feature this prediction that the end would come before the 1914 generation passed away.

When new, younger men take over, as they inevitably must, the ban on blood transfusions could well be dropped also. In the meantime, however, Jehovah's Witnesses face death daily in the misguided belief that God forbids this medical practice.

NOTES

1. Raymond Franz, *Crisis of Conscience* (Atlanta: Commentary Press, 1983), p. 40.
2. *The Watchtower*, April 15, 1992, p. 31.
3. Ibid., pp. 7–17.
4. *Jehovah's Witnesses in the Divine Purpose* (Brooklyn, N.Y.: Watchtower Society, 1959), p. 197.
5. See the lengthy presentation in *Awake!* October 8, 1968.
6. *The Watchtower*, May 15, 1984, p. 5.
7. *Awake!* April, 8, 1988, p. 14.

7

The Kingdom and the Empire

A four-year-old boy identified only as "S" was undergoing chemotherapy treatment for leukemia at Freedom Fields Hospital in Plymouth, England, when his condition weakened and doctors turned to the courts for permission to give him blood over the objection of his Jehovah's Witness parents. The Independent *of July 30, 1992, reports that "Mr. Justice Thorpe" of "Bristol High Court" ruled that the boy "be treated with blood or blood products at the discretion of doctors."*

"Thy kingdom come. Thy will be done in earth, as it is in heaven." Those familiar words from the Lord's Prayer mean different things to the hundreds of millions of people who utter them daily. Some who repeat this prayer envision a literal millennial reign of Christ as king; others see the kingdom as a change coming over human hearts as individuals adopt Jesus' way of love; and still others repeat the words by rote but have a nebulous concept of the kingdom, or puzzle over what it means. Jehovah's Witnesses superstitiously avoid repeating the words of the Lord's prayer, lest they incur divine wrath for indulging in the "vain repetitions" Jesus warned against before uttering the supplication (Matt. 6:7); but they do pray—in their own words—for God's kingdom to come. And when they do, they have something concrete in mind; namely, that their organization will take over the world when Jehovah God destroys all other religious and governmental organizations and kills off every man, woman, and child not loyally adhering to the Watchtower Society. Then the kingdom organization that

159

is already ruling over part of the earth—its Witness population—will, by default, take over the planet as its only remaining government.

"God's Kingdom is a real, operating government having a ruler and subjects," according to the recent JW publication *Knowledge That Leads to Everlasting Life*.[1] Since the invisible head of this government is Jehovah God, it is a theocracy, or a theocratic organization. God has appointed as his chief executive officer in this government the first spirit creature or angel that he created, namely, Michael the archangel, who took on the name Jesus when he was born as a human and the title Christ when he was baptized thirty years later. Jesus Christ rules from heaven with the aid of a hundred forty-four thousand associate rulers taken from earth for the express purpose of *ruling with him in heaven*. From the first century through the year 1935 a mere hundred forty-four thousand people around the world proved faithful as Christians—primarily the apostles and their close associates in the early apostolic church during the first century, in addition to the early Watchtower believers in modern times, with only a relative handful of real Christians alive on earth at any one time during the intervening centuries. These individuals, and these only, will go to heaven to live and *rule* with Christ. All other faithful believers constitute the kingdom's earthly subjects.

Today this kingdom rules from heaven, as JWs see it, like a government-in-exile that already claims the loyalty of a portion of the population. While waiting for the opportune moment to topple the existing regime, it busily gathers more earthly citizens to its side. Its supporters give their loyalty and allegiance to this shadow government rather than to the old regime, and the government-in-exile has already set up a functioning bureaucracy to provide essential services for its partisans. The Watchtower Society's Brooklyn headquarters complex contains the shadow government's Executive Mansion or White House, its Supreme Court, and its Capitol or legislative chambers. Local Kingdom Halls are its town halls, and the volunteer quick-build crews that amaze outsiders by erecting a Kingdom Hall on a weekend constitute its public works department. Congregation elders constitute its town officers and policemen, and the judicial committees of elders are its local courts. Ministerial servants in the congregations staff its bureaucracy. The ministry school programs established by Nathan Knorr constitute its public schools. This entire apparatus already governs its loyal supporters (Jehovah's Witnesses) and looks eagerly to the day when its armed forces (angels) will attack and destroy the old regime that still governs the rest of the world's population. God's kingdom will wipe out Satan's puppet governments that currently rule from Washington, London, Moscow, Beijing, and other capitals.

So, God's kingdom is very real to Jehovah's Witnesses. They deal with its officials and bureaucrats on a daily basis, and they visit its buildings to receive an education and to perform their civic duties. Occasionally, they even visit its earthly capital in Brooklyn and tour its central government buildings. These edifices are truly impressive, as one might expect of a government that now claims some five million loyal citizens (full-fledged active JWs) and that actually exercises dominion over a total of some twelve million subjects (Kingdom Hall attendees). Far more extensive than the hundred thousand followers Judge Rutherford ruled over in 1941, today's Watchtower empire has a population exceeding that of many United Nations member countries.

I myself had been a baptized Witness only a short time when in 1970 I made the pilgrimage to tour the earthly capital of God's kingdom—the Watchtower Bible and Tract Society's world headquarters offices, known affectionately to Jehovah's Witnesses as "Brooklyn Bethel"—and I was truly impressed by what I saw. The Witness headquarters establishment in the Brooklyn Heights section of New York City consists of some thirty buildings with a combined real estate value of $186 million, according to *The New York Times*.[2] The nonprofit status of this property takes $7.3 million off the New York City tax rolls, according to the *Times* article, which states that all of the remaining property in Brooklyn Heights yields $35.6 million in taxes annually. The ratio between these two numbers implies that the sect owns roughly one sixth of the neighborhood's real estate, at least in terms of tax-base dollars.

Except for a brief interval during the First World War, the Watchtower Society has had ongoing operations in this area since shortly after the turn of the century, with real estate accumulating steadily over the years. There were far fewer than thirty buildings making up the complex when I visited it in 1970, and I entered only a handful of them. Some twenty years later, with the assistance of my friend Preston Walter, a former headquarters worker who still lives in the area, I put together the crude visual catalogue of buildings on pp. 162–63.

Among the newest additions to major Watchtower properties in Brooklyn are the "sliver building" (so called because the twenty-six-story structure is less than twenty-three feet wide) at 67 Livingston Street, which the Society purchased in April 1989 for $6.2 million, and a thirty-story residence at 90 Sands Street, recently constructed to house a thousand volunteer workers.

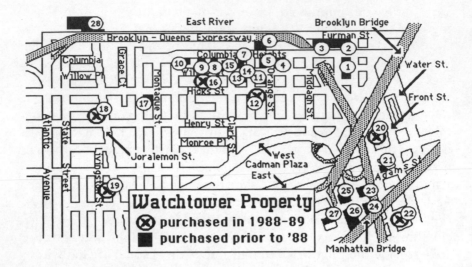

Watchtower Headquarters Complex, Brooklyn, N.Y.

Key to Watchtower Property in Brooklyn Heights
(Total real estate value: $186 million)

1. 25 Columbia Heights, the chief headquarters office, part of the former Squibb Pharmaceutical complex

2. 30 Columbia Hts., also part of the former Squibb property

3. 58 Columbia Hts., a storage and supply building

4. 97 Columbia Hts., a modern eleven-story residential building

5. 107 Columbia Hts., containing residences, offices, a library, the Bethel garden, and a Kingdom Hall

6. 122–124–126 Columbia Hts., formerly the chief headquarters office, now converted to residences, a library, and dining halls

7. 119 Columbia Hts., a residential building

8. 161 Columbia Hts., a residential building

9. 167-169-171 Columbia Hts., a twelve-story building, formerly the Standish Arms Hotel

10. 183 Columbia Hts., a residential building

11. 30 Orange St., a residential building

12. 50 Orange St. and 89 Hicks St., both residential buildings

13. 79–99 Willow St., a residence with a dining hall in the basement, formerly the Towers Hotel

14. 76 and 80 Willow St., both residential buildings

15. 8–10 Clark St., a residential building

16. 105 Willow St., a residential building

17. 98 Montague St., the twelve-story former Bossert Hotel, purchased by Cohi Towers Assoc. (a Watchtower front) in 1983 and resold to the Society in 1988

18. 108 Joralemon St., a residential building

19. 67 Livingston St., the twenty-six-story "sliver building" purchased in 1989 for $6.2 million as a residence

20. A parking lot facing Front St., Main St., and York St.

21. 74 Adams St., the Society's garage and auto repair shop

22. 85 Jay St., a factory building filling the entire city block

23. 55 Prospect St., a factory building with a Kingdom Hall

24. 81 Prospect St., a factory building next to the Manhattan Bridge

25. 117 Adams St., a factory building

26. 77 Sands St., a factory building filling a city block

27. 175 Pearl St./74 Sands St., a factory building

28. 360 Furman St., an immense structure housing offices, tape duplication and recording studios, the shipping department, and other facilities

29. 90 Sands St. (not shown), a new thirty-story residence building constructed in 1993

Indeed, approximately two-thirds of the thirty-odd buildings are residences accommodating thousands of headquarters workers who serve in exchange for room and board plus a small monthly allowance (ninety dollars as of this writing). Underground tunnels connect the Towers Hotel (79–99 Willow St.) and the office buildings at 124 Columbia Heights, 107 Columbia Heights and 119 Columbia Heights— allowing nearly three thousand of the "Bethel family" to pass from building to building without having to step out onto city streets. The April 22, 1989, *Awake!* magazine announced intentions to add 97 Columbia Heights to the tunnel network.

According to the *1995 Yearbook of Jehovah's Witnesses* there are now five thousand eighty-two full-time volunteers residing at Brooklyn headquarters and "at nearby facilities," which likely includes Watchtower Farm in Wallkill, New York, to be described below. Most of them work in the Society's factories producing books and magazines, or in related service and support roles, while a smaller number share in the organization's administration. Rank-and-file JW "publishers" regard these "Bethelites" in much the same way that ordinary Roman Catholics regard the inhabitants of Vatican City. "All of them are members of the Order of Special Full-Time Servants," the *Yearbook* declares, "a religious order that is devoted exclusively to the ministry."[3] Creation of this religious order is a new development aimed at gaining tax exemptions for workers who would normally be taxed on room and board received from the organization—taxes that their small monthly cash allowance would not even cover. The *Proclaimers* book states:

> Those who are accepted for special full-time service at the world headquarters of Jehovah's Witnesses all subscribe to a vow of poverty, as have all the members of the Governing Body and all the other members of the Bethel family there.[4]

Worldwide the sect has a total of 15,145 full-time volunteers living in the residence buildings of its various office, factory, and farm facilities.[5]

As of 1992 the factory and office facilities alone at Brooklyn Bethel covered eight city blocks and included 2,476,460 square feet of floor space.[6] This does not include the living space for the five thousand volunteers. Using the latest high-speed full-color web offset presses and book binding equipment, workers produce roughly twenty thousand complete books per day. The shipping facility in the former Squibb Pharmaceutical building sends out more than thirty million pounds of materials per year to countries around the world.

Besides the Brooklyn properties, the sect maintains a huge factory, residence, office and farm complex at Watchtower Farm in Wallkill, New York, which I visited as part of a Witness tour group in the late 1970s. Started in 1963 to supply inexpensive food to the headquarters facility, by 1973 the 1,700-acre farm was producing eighty thousand gallons of milk annually, fifty thousand pounds of cheese, three hundred thousand pounds of meat and poultry—beef, pork, and chicken—and seven hundred twenty thousand eggs.[7] As a result of this in-house food supply the management at Brooklyn headquarters calculated it cost them only thirty cents per meal that year to feed their factory and office workers. The Society's land holdings in Ulster County, where Watchtower Farm is located, total nearly $81 million, according to a report in the Middletown, New York, *Sunday Record*.[8]

The organization is also completing construction of a $125 million Watchtower Educational Center—comparable to an entire college—on a seven-hundred-acre parcel of land along Route 22 near Patterson, New York. Volunteer JW construction workers are furnishing virtually all of the labor for the project, the largest the Society has yet undertaken on its own. The initial phase, completed in 1996, includes six multi-story apartment houses with a total of 624 apartments, a 450-car garage, a 144-room hotel, an office building, a classroom building, several service buildings, and a dining hall capable of serving 1,600 people at one sitting.

Moreover, the Watchtower Society has branch office buildings in nearly a hundred foreign countries. Some of these branches have their own large factory complexes in addition to offices and residence buildings. For example, the branch in the Philippines requires an eleven-story structure to house its many workers. The branch facility in the poor African country of Nigeria was recently constructed on a 140-acre parcel of land and includes a 450-foot-by-225-foot factory building, plus residences for over four hundred people. The complex completed in 1981 at Cesario Lange, Brazil, included eight buildings with half a million square feet of floor space, yet a major expansion project was undertaken less than ten years later.[9] Mammoth construction projects are currently under way in Germany, Colombia, Poland, and Korea.

Besides all this, the organization controls numerous large assembly halls, most with capacity for an audience of some two thousand to four thousand people. The twenty-five thousand square-foot assembly hall on Vancouver Island in Canada was built in nine days by volunteer labor.[10]

Other real estate holdings include the countless Kingdom Halls serving more than seventy-five thousand local congregations of Jehovah's Witnesses worldwide, all controlled from Brooklyn. More than ten thousand of these congregations are in the United States alone. Although some congregations meet in rented facilities or share a Kingdom Hall with one or more others, many own the buildings where they meet.

According to the published figures listed above the large Watchtower properties in New York State alone total nearly $400 million in value. If the Society has tallied up the value of its remaining real estate in the United States and worldwide, the figure is kept top secret. In any case, it is obvious that the organization's total wealth is measured in the many hundreds of millions, if not billions, of dollars.

Fixed assets in the form of real estate comprise only part of that wealth. The factory buildings contain huge printing presses and other state-of-the-art production equipment valued in the millions of dollars. Moreover, this equipment manned by thousands of volunteer workers generates significant income for the organization. In fact, a confidential credit report on the Watchtower Bible and Tract Society of New York, Inc., showed $1.25 billion corporate sales figures for 1991, up from just over $1 billion in 1990.

❧   ❧   ❧

The Toronto Star *of January 20, 1982, reports that "a twenty-six-year-old Meaford woman, a member of the Jehovah's Witnesses, bled to death December 14 [1981] when she refused a blood transfusion shortly after giving birth." The article names her as Carol Sulkye, whose husband, Peter, is quoted as explaining, "It's not just blood. It's a whole way of life."*

❧   ❧   ❧

Since Witness doctrine does not include tithing, much of this income derives from literature sales. Yet, Witnesses in the United States would object vigorously to the thought that they make "sales" or sell their literature. After all, such an admission would make them liable to sales tax in many localities.

If I were to make a regular practice of knocking on doors to sell encyclopedias or other books—even religious books—Massachusetts law would require me to register as a vendor, to collect the state's 5 percent sales tax, and to turn that tax money over to the state. (In actual fact, I am registered as a vendor, because I do sell books as part of my countercult work. Newspapers and magazines are exempt under Massachusetts law, but books are taxable.) Many other states have similar laws. Yet Watchtower factories that crank out thousands of books per day do not collect sales tax on those books. The local Kingdom Hall book rooms (similar to in-house bookstores connected with some churches) receive those shipments of books and act as stocking distributors for the Watchtower factories, but they do not collect sales tax when they sell the books to individual Jehovah's Witnesses. And the individual Witnesses who carry the books from door to door do not collect sales tax when they sell them to the end-user.

Why not? That is a good question. JWs insist they are not selling books. However, their own *Proclaimers* book admits, "For many years they [JWs] referred to their distribution of literature as 'selling.' But this terminology caused some confusion, and so beginning in 1929, it was gradually dropped."[11] Perhaps the terminology was dropped, but the practice of selling literature continued. I know because when I began carrying JW literature from house to house in 1969, the per-copy price was printed on page two of every *Watchtower* and *Awake!* magazine. The Society later adopted the practice of omitting sales information from bound volumes of the year's issues printed after the end of the year, but if you examine any *original* copy of *The Watchtower* or *Awake!* for 1969 (the year I began selling), or an *original* bound volume for that year, you will find the selling price printed on page two: "Five cents a copy," and below that a listing of "Yearly subscription rates for semimonthly editions" with the rate for the U.S. given as "$1." The subscription rate increased as the years went by, and the per-copy price jumped to ten cents in 1978, fifteen cents in 1981, twenty cents in 1984, and twenty-five cents in 1987. Similarly, when I began offering them at the doors the Society's small books were twenty-five cents and the large books fifty cents; those prices, too, rose over the years. The subscription price "$5.00 (U.S.) per year" and the "25 cents (U.S.) a copy" remained in the magazines until the March 15, 1990, *Watchtower* and the March 22, 1990, *Awake!* Then, suddenly, the prices disappeared with the next issue. Why?

On February 25, 1990, a letter from Brooklyn headquarters, dated February 9, was read at Kingdom Halls throughout the United States, announcing a major switch in Watchtower policy. Reversing the practice of more than a hundred years, prices would no longer be set for books, magazines, or subscriptions. In a subsequent letter dated February 21, the Society explained the new policy this way:

By adopting a method of literature distribution based completely on donation, Jehovah's people are able to greatly simplify our Bible education work and separate ourselves from those who commercialize religion.[12]

The real story behind the change goes back to June 22, 1989, when the Watchtower Society filed an *amicus curiae* ("friend of the court") brief with the United States Supreme Court in a legal case involving Jimmy Swaggart Ministries.[13] When California had required the television evangelist to pay approximately $183,000 in sales tax on some $2 million worth of books and tapes sold in the state, he sued for a refund. His appeal eventually found its way to the U.S. Supreme Court, where the Watchtower's New York corporation joined the International Society for Krishna Consciousness of California, the Evangelical Council for Financial Accountability, the Prison Fellowship, the National Council of Churches of Christ, and other religious bodies in filing briefs.

This was strange company for a sect that labels all other religious groups as components of "the great harlot Babylon" and warns its own members not to "share with" them because such groups belong to the devil and will be destroyed by God.[14] Perhaps that is why *The Watchtower* and *Awake!* magazines carried no mention of the Swaggart case or the Society's legal brief, not even in their columns regularly devoted to brief news items. The Society's lawyers were also careful in writing the brief to distance themselves from Jimmy Swaggart and his case. They made it very plain that they were not defending Swaggart or taking his side in the issue. Rather, they were asking the court to avoid making any ruling that would impact negatively on the work of Jehovah's Witnesses.

While Jimmy Swaggart Ministries was selling its materials directly to the consumer, the Watchtower Society was in a different position as an out-of-state manufacturer selling its product to local JW congregations. The Society apparently recognized some of the potential legal problems that individual JWs might face. Its Supreme Court brief stated:

> The California tax at issue on this appeal, if construed to apply to ministers of Jehovah's Witnesses, would clearly impose a burden on their work. Assuming that each of the 132,000 door-to-door ministers of Jehovah's Witnesses in California is a "retailer" involved in the "business" of "sales" under the California tax code, each of them would be obligated to obtain a permit from the State of California for the privilege of "selling" tangible personal property "at retail" and would also be required to file quarterly tax returns on the contributions they receive for religious literature.[15]

By focusing on the individual Witnesses in this manner—and the book-keeping nightmare that would ensue if each were to register as a vendor—the Society diverted attention away from the possibility of requiring each Kingdom Hall to register as a vendor fielding a force of a hundred sales representatives.

In any case, in spite of the support Swaggart received from other religious groups filing briefs, the Supreme Court ruled against him on January 17, 1990, declaring that the sales tax must be paid. The Watchtower Society promptly reacted to this ruling by announcing that literature would no longer be sold to Witnesses at Kingdom Hall, and that no prices would be set when they distributed materials door to door. The letter was read aloud from the pulpit on February 25, 1990, at Sunday meetings of Jehovah's Witnesses across the United States. (The Sunday reading of the February 9 letter was in itself an unusual measure indicating the urgency the Society attached to this matter, since instructions relating to the house-to-house work are generally presented at the Service Meeting held on Thursday or Friday evenings, to a somewhat smaller audience.) The new policy was to go into effect on March 1, 1990, and magazines already printed with the price per issue would be offered without specifying prices. Ironically, the April 1, 1990, *Watchtower*—the first issue printed without the price per copy—featured this statement concerning Jehovah's Witnesses: "They do not dodge taxes or seek to evade inconvenient laws."[16]

In a related development, on March 11, 1990, an announcement was made at Kingdom Halls in the United States that food would henceforth be available at no set cost but on a freewill donation basis at Watchtower conventions. Having done volunteer work myself in the assembly department that counted the money, I know that the convention cafeterias and snack bars were profitable; they covered assembly expenses, paid for new automobiles for circuit and district overseers, and produced surplus money that was sent to Brooklyn headquarters. For decades these cafeterias and snack bars offered hamburgers, hot dogs, ice cream snacks, and complete lunches and dinners at set prices, but ignored laws such as the Massachusetts 5 percent meals tax. Under the new arrangement announced in March 1990, instead of handing money to the food server, convention-goers exiting the food counter had to pass by a contribution box into which they would drop their money. However, that approach, too, must have been challenged by tax authorities, since the December 1994 issue of *Our Kingdom Service* announced that food and drink would no longer be available at all at conventions. Witnesses would have to bring their own—a major inconvenience for families attending for the entire day.

As of this writing, the "complete donation arrangement" remains in place as the method for "placing"—not "selling"!—books, tapes, CDs, and other Watchtower merchandise door to door. Jehovah's Witnesses have told me privately that the Society actually collects double payment for these materials, since JWs are expected to donate when picking up supplies at Kingdom Hall book rooms, and then, when these items have been distributed from door to door, whatever monies are received must also be placed in the contribution box. To guarantee that the organization will not lose money if a householder accepts the offer of a magazine subscription but fails to make a donation, *Our Kingdom Ministry* carries these instructions:

> After accepting a subscription, those who are truly interested will generally show it by a donation. When an interested person cannot give a donation and a subscription is placed, the publisher who obtained the subscription may have an increased responsibility and privilege to honor Jehovah with his valuable things.[17]

In other words, the Witness must cover the subscription cost out of his or her own pocket if the person at the door fails to do so. The individual JW may end up losing money on the transaction, but not the Watchtower Society.

Whether these procedures will actually keep the Watchtower organization free from paying sales tax in all jurisdictions remains to be seen. For some time now, the U.S. Internal Revenue Service (IRS) has been requiring nonprofit organizations to differentiate between outright gifts and donations in exchange for goods or services. Receipts issued to donors show separate amounts for (1) donations for goods received and (2) excess donations over and above the value of goods received by the donor. Only the second amount is considered tax-deductible when the donor itemizes on his federal income tax return. The various states and jurisdictions that levy sales taxes could conceivably apply the same standard. In that case a Jehovah's Witness placing a $1.00 book at the door and receiving a $2.00 donation for it would have to pay sales tax on the first $1.00, with only the excess amount over and above the book's value being tax-free.

Of course, the whole matter of tax-free donations is valid only if Jehovah's Witnesses at the door are actually acting as agents of a qualified nonprofit organization. The Watchtower Society is indeed registered as such an organization, but are the individual JWs serving as its agents when distributing merchandise and receiving monies in the field? One might automatically assume that to be the case, were it not for the fact that the sect's publications have emphatically stated the opposite. The February 1989 issue of *Our Kingdom Ministry* declares that individual Witnesses going from door to door are *not* "agents or representatives of the Watchtower Bible and Tract Society."[18] Apparently eager to avoid financial liability for damages due to accidents that may occur in the course of this door-to-door work, in the context of discussing such accidents, it states firmly:

> Therefore, publishers do well to avoid representing themselves as agents or representatives of the Watchtower Bible and Tract Society of New York, Inc., or any other corporation used by "the faithful and discreet slave" to advance Kingdom interests.—Matt. 24:45–47.[19]

That may free the Society from liability for accidental damage, but it leaves the individual JW in the potentially fraudulent position of soliciting donations for a nonprofit organization that says he does not represent it. Another apparent contradiction is found in the fact that the organization has publicly declared for decades that it does not solicit donations.[20]

Losing his legal appeal before the U.S. Supreme Court, Jimmy Swaggart ended up paying the $183,000 sales tax he owed on some $2 million worth of sales. Those figures look large until placed alongside the Watchtower Society's. According to the January 1, 1990, *Watchtower*, the Society's New York factories alone produced 35,811,000 Bibles, books, and brochures during the previous year.[21] With a conservatively estimated average sale price of $2.00, those publications would account for an annual sales volume of over $71 million. Taxed at the rate Swaggart had to pay, that would give the Society a sales tax liability of some $6.5 million for the New York factories alone for 1989. The Court held Jimmy Swaggart liable for back taxes from 1974 through 1981, all the years covered by his case; a similar eight-year period for the JW literature factories in New York might generate a tax liability in the neighborhood of $50 million. By changing its distribution methods in response to the Swaggart ruling, has the Watchtower Society implied that it recognizes a tax liability for materials distributed for a fixed price prior to March 1, 1990? If so, that would amount to many millions of dollars in taxes owed to several states. How far back a state or jurisdiction could go in attempting to collect delinquent taxes would be determined by the local statute of limitations.

Why aren't the various jurisdictions involved going after the Watchtower Society to collect those taxes? Apparently the organization's most effective ploy has been the pyramid approach to distribution. An active JW ministerial servant secretly in contact with me (he cannot yet leave the sect because the organization controls the minds of family members and would make them shun him if he dissented openly) described how the cash flow works: Local congregations order materials from Brooklyn headquarters. Brooklyn ships whatever is ordered, without issuing an invoice. Individual Witnesses pick up supplies at Kingdom Hall and place money in a box provided for that purpose. (God is watching the amount they put in, JWs are told. The literature servant at each hall is also watching.) The money is then forwarded to Brooklyn headquarters. The taxable retail sale to the consumer thus ends up being made by a private individual, someone who supposedly does not represent the Society. The typical JW devotes ten hours per month to this work and sells one or two books plus a handful of magazines. Registering a million of them in the United States as self-employed salesmen would be a bureaucratic nightmare, and the few cents in revenue collected from each one would hardly offset the expense of collecting it. Yet, do JWs really meet the definition of self-employed salesman? Or has the Watchtower organization employed a tax dodge? Tax authorities, to date, seem to view it as a can of worms they are unwilling to open. So, as matters stand today, this multibillion-dollar corporate empire—one of the world's wealthiest publishing organizations—is distributing its wares without being subject to the sales tax paid by Jimmy Swaggart Ministries, by religious bookstores attached to churches, and by virtually every other distributor of religious literature.

❧   ❧   ❧

A two-year-old Round Lake Park girl "had only five hours to live unless she received" a transfusion that her Jehovah's Witness parents refused to allow, according to a front-page report in the Waukegan, Illinois, News Sun *of June 4–5, 1988. Upon intervention by the Illinois Department of Children and Family Services, Lake County Juvenile Judge Barbara Gilleran Johnson issued an oral order "permitting the transfusion to save the girl's life over the parents' objection."*

❧   ❧   ❧

Ruling over this vast wealth today is the Watchtower Society's president Milton G. Henschel, and a corporate Board of Directors. Outside and above the legal entities is the Governing Body of Jehovah's Witnesses, which supervises the various corporations and includes their corporate boards among its larger membership. The Governing Body has varied in size from as few as seven to as many as eighteen individuals, but most recently has remained just under a dozen. They supposedly receive the same provisions—room and board plus a small cash allowance—as the remaining five thousand volunteers residing at Brooklyn headquarters and nearby facilities. However, unlike the boys who shovel manure on the farms and box literature in the factories, Governing Body members have the wealth and power of the Society at their disposal. They cannot legally transfer any of it to their personal bank accounts, but they can arrange to have themselves sent anywhere in the world on speaking tours and other assignments. Nevertheless, former members of the headquarters staff tell me that Watchtower leaders today, unlike Judge Rutherford, generally do live relatively Spartan lives—occupying small apartments rather than mansions—rather like political leaders in some lands where being identified with "the people" is important.

As it now stands a subcommittee of the Governing Body oversees the sect's Service Department, which in turn issues instructions to a whole hierarchy of functionaries stretching from Brooklyn headquarters to local congregations around the globe. Each congregation is run by a body of elders who conducts worship services; preaches to the congregation; and sits as judge, jury, and prosecutor at "judicial hearings." (I will speak about these later since I experienced them from both sides of the bench.) One of the elders serves as presiding overseer—the closest Kingdom Hall counterpart of a pastor, although all local elders are unpaid and must maintain their families through secular employment. Another serves as secretary, responsible for correspondence with headquarters; a third as service overseer, supervising door-to-door work and studies conducted with potential converts. These three—the presiding overseer, the secretary, and the service overseer—form the Congregation Service Committee, an executive board whose signatures validate official documents. The elders are assisted in more mundane tasks, such as wholesaling books and magazines, by "ministerial servants." Both the elders and the ministerial servants receive their appointments* from New York, with no democratic input from the local congregation.

---

*The existing local elders select nominees, with guidance from the Circuit Overseer.

The elders of sixteen or so congregations report to a Circuit Overseer who travels in a circuit among their cities and towns, usually staying with his wife as houseguests in private JW homes for a week at a time. The work of the Circuit Overseers comes under the scrutiny of District Overseers who travel among the circuits, also staying in private homes or in apartments at nearby Assembly Halls, where the District Overseer runs a weekend convention, or "Circuit Assembly," for a dozen or more congregations at a time. The Circuit and District Overseers, who correspond roughly to bishops and archbishops in the Catholic Church, number roughly four thousand worldwide, some five hundred of these serving in the United States.

Regardless of its size, this vast hierarchy of hundreds of thousands of ministerial servants, elders, and traveling overseers has little input as to the message taught at Kingdom Hall meetings and conventions. Virtually all of the material presented to JW audiences comes from Brooklyn in the form of detailed outlines, manuscript talks to be read verbatim from the pulpit, or books and magazines for question-and-answer discussion. Thus the information is received as "spiritual food" coming from God himself, channeled through "God's organization." Its instructions must be obeyed, even if the message requires the suicidal act of refusing needed medical treatment. For thirteen years I, too, viewed this organization as God's representative on earth. I stood ready to obey its commands, even if it meant sacrificing my life or the life of a child or loved one.

❧   ❧   ❧

According to columnist Joe Dirck, writing in the Cleveland Plain Dealer *of May 9, 1992, JW Doreen Nielson bled to death on September 19, 1991, at a Cleveland clinic after she "refused a blood transfusion that likely would have saved her life." Herself a nurse from Niagara Falls, New York, forty-nine-year-old Nielson had entered the clinic for scheduled surgery to clear clogged arteries, and had signed papers ahead of time refusing blood. Dirck adds that the widower, James Nielson, subsequently filed a $30 million lawsuit alleging that doctors should not have subjected his wife to the risky procedure.*

❧   ❧   ❧

Infighting that spilled over into the courts of the land during the late 1980s afforded outsiders an unusual peek at the Watchtower organization's inner workings and corporate wealth. It all began in the summer of 1985, when the local elder serving as Watchtower Study Conductor at the Bonham, Texas, Kingdom Hall departed from the set study arrangement. Along with the paragraph-by-paragraph study of *The Watchtower* magazine on Sunday mornings, he began teaching the congregation some of his own ideas. Eventually he faced trial before a judicial committee (church court) for questioning the position of the Governing Body as God's spokesmen, but by then others in the congregation had also begun questioning their beliefs—including a majority of the elders.

The Society acted decisively. According to Bonham Witnesses I interviewed personally at the time, when the congregation gathered for the Service Meeting one evening that summer, they found the Kingdom Hall packed with men sent in from outside, some from as far away as California. After the program got underway, one of these outside "brothers" stepped up to the podium and introduced himself as a special representative of the Watchtower Society. He took control of the meeting, and a "special committee" appointed by the Society proceeded to remove the local elders and replace them with hand-picked men.

These high-handed tactics did not sit well, however, with some of the Bonham Witnesses, and a court fight ensued. The majority of the Kingdom Hall Trustees—some of them still "in good standing" in the organization—filed suit, charging the Society's representatives with "forcible entry" and illegally taking possession of the hall. In the words of U.S. District Judge Paul Brown, who eventually ruled on the case, there followed "a series of fast and furious civil actions in the county, state, and federal courts in late 1985 and early 1986."[22]

On February 7, 1986, a local court found the Watchtower Society representatives guilty of forcible entry and granted possession of the Kingdom Hall to the dissident group. An ensuing series of suits and countersuits resulted in new rulings requiring both parties to share the hall equally. Then, according to Judge Brown's later twenty-six-page ruling, the Society's representatives took the case to federal court with the "claim that they were 'forced to abandon' the Kingdom Hall because sharing the Hall" with the dissidents "amounted to a 'desecration' of the Hall." They, "by their own admission, were unwilling to tolerate the defendants' presence in the Hall, even on a temporary basis, as provided in the state district court's order."[23]

On March 21, 1986, the local newspaper featured photographs of the Kingdom Hall doors chained shut and reported that this action was taken by Watchtower representatives in apparent violation of the court order. When the dissident Witnesses "broke into the Hall by removing the padlocks and chains that the plaintiffs had placed on the doors of the building," quoting the judge, the Society's lawyer brought suit against the chief of the Bonham Police Department, and later sued the state district attorney, because they "failed to prosecute defendants for trespass at the Kingdom Hall."[24]

"However," said Judge Brown, "the evidence in the summary judgment record shows that this 'break-in' occurred after the plaintiffs [Watchtower Society representatives] locked out the defendants [dissidents] and after the state district court ordered the two groups to share the Hall."[25]

Witnesses loyal to the Society then abandoned the building and built a new hall elsewhere in town. But the legal maneuvers to oust the dissident group and regain the old hall continued.

"When the Watchtower received several unfavorable rulings in the state court action I was handling," explained David W. Bercot of Henderson, Texas, attorney for the dissidents in the earlier actions, "they [the Watchtower] decided to take the action to federal court. However, they had no legal basis to remove the hearings from state court to federal court. Therefore, they brought a civil rights suit in federal court, saying that there had been a conspiracy between the 'dissidents' and the local officials to deprive the Witnesses of their civil rights."

"It was a pretty far-fetched scheme," Bercot added, "and it didn't work."[26]

According to the federal judge's November 9, 1988, ruling, "Sometime in 1986," one of the elders "installed a microphone in the ceiling of the Kingdom Hall which he apparently used to record his disfellowship or excommunication trial and the trials of the other defendants. The plaintiffs [Watchtower Society representatives] were conducting these trials, and the trials were closed to all non-Jehovah's."[27] The dissident elder first obtained the district attorney's opinion that "it was not illegal for a conversation to be recorded so long as at least one party to the conversation had consented."[28] When Watchtower representatives later discovered the microphone, they demanded that Bonham police take action against the dissidents. The police chief, however, inquired of the district attorney and concluded that no offense had been committed. In response to these events, the Watchtower Society charged the police chief and the district attorney with entering into a conspiracy with the dissidents, but the courts ruled that no laws had been broken.

Perhaps one of the most interesting aspects of the case was that the Watchtower Society argued for possession of the Bonham Kingdom Hall on the grounds that the organization is a "hierarchy" similar to the Roman Catholic Church, and therefore has the authority to control local congregations. According to a February 9, 1986, news story in the *Dallas Times Herald*, a local attorney representing the Watchtower said the Society should control the Bonham congregation because it is a "structured or hierarchical body."[29] The Bonham *Daily Favorite* reported likewise the Watchtower Society's representatives' testifying in court that Kingdom Hall trustees were "just a figurehead, or a puppet" for the Governing Body and that the organization was "hierarchical."[30] These statements made under oath by the Society's legal representatives were especially interesting in view of the fact that the Society says the opposite outside of court. In the past, JW publications frequently attacked the Catholic Church for having a hierarchy that claims authority over believers: "All such claims to apostolic succession and origin are false, and the Hierarchy's structure is grossly contrary to the original Theocratic organization as established by Christ Jesus."[31] Elsewhere hierarchy is given diabolical connotations:

> Satan has erected his gigantic, lawless, Antichrist organization, a masterpiece of deception, iniquity and oppression all guided under the hierarchic priesthood after the order of Nimrod. As the word "hierarchy" means "a body of ecclesiastical rulers," A.D. 325 is, in fact, the founding date of the Catholic Hierarchy.[32]

JW publications declare that the Watchtower Society's "theocratic rule is not exercised through any earthly hierarchy."[33]

The sect repeatedly flew in members of its Brooklyn legal staff in addition to paying an estimated forty thousand dollars for the services of a top Dallas law firm throughout the lengthy series of court appearances. These expenses may have added up to more than the value of the East Texas real estate in dispute. Nevertheless, U.S. District Judge Paul Brown's November 9, 1988, ruling dismissed the Society's suit and left in place the state court rulings. Unwilling to share the Kingdom Hall with dissidents, the Witnesses constructed a new building. The Brooklyn leadership also restructured the organization's arrangements for owning property so that renegade local trustees could not repeat what those in Bonham had done.

NOTES

1. *Knowledge That Leads to Eternal Life* (Brooklyn, N.Y.: Watchtower Society, 1995), p 91.

2. "Looking beyond Brooklyn Heights toward Heaven," *The New York Times*, November 29, 1992, p. 46.

3. *1995 Yearbook of Jehovah's Witnesses* (Brooklyn, N.Y.: Watchtower Society, 1995), pp. 5–6.

4. *Jehovah's Witnesses—Proclaimers of God's Kingdom* (Brooklyn, N.Y.: Watchtower Society, 1993), p. 351.

5. *1995 Yearbook*, p. 5.

6. *Jehovah's Witnesses—Proclaimers of God's Kingdom*, pp. 588–89.

7. Ibid., p. 356.

8. *Sunday Record* (Middletown, N.Y.), October 7, 1990, pp. 8 and 31.

9. *Jehovah's Witnesses—Proclaimers of God's Kingdom*, p. 334.

10. Ibid., p. 331.

11. Ibid., p. 349.

12. "Watchtower 'No Charge' Called a Tax Dodge," *Brooklyn Heights Press*, March 15, 1990, p. 11.

13. No. 88-1374, In The Supreme Court of the United States, October Term, 1988; Jimmy Swaggart Ministries, *Appellant*, v. Board of Equalization of California, *Appellee.*; On Appeal from the California Court of Appeal, Fourth Appellate District; Brief of *Amicus Curiae* Watchtower Bible and Tract Society of New York, Inc.

14. See, for example, *The Watchtower*, May 15, 1980, pp. 16–27.

15. *Swaggart* v. *Board of Equalization of California*, p. 5.

16. *The Watchtower*, April 1, 1990, p. 20.

17. *Our Kingdom Ministry*, April 1990, pp. 1–7.

18. *Our Kingdom Ministry*, February 1989, p. 3.

19. Ibid.

20. See *Zion's Watch Tower*, January/February 1882, p. 2, and *Jehovah's Witnesses in the Divine Purpose* (Brooklyn, N.Y.: Watchtower Society, 1959), p. 24, where this same policy is reiterated as if it were still current.

21. *The Watchtower*, January 1, 1990, p. 24.

22. U.S. District Judge Paul Brown, U.S. District Court, Eastern Division of Texas, Civil Action No. P-86-22-CA, November 9, 1988.

23. Ibid.

24. Ibid.

25. Ibid.

26. Atty. David W. Bercot, December 1, 1988, letter to the author.

27. U.S. District Judge Paul Brown, p. 14.

28. Ibid.

29. Lisa Ellis, "Doubt Tears at Denomination," *Dallas Times Herald*, February 9, 1986, p. 32.

30. "Jehovah's Witnesses to Appeal Ruling," *Bonham Daily Favorite*, February 9, 1986 (page number obscured on available copy).

31. *Theocratic Aid to Kingdom Publishers* (Brooklyn, N.Y.: Watchtower Society, 1945), p. 299.

32. *Qualified to Be Ministers* (Brooklyn, N.Y.: Watchtower Society, 1955), pp. 288, 290.

33. *Life Everlasting—In Freedom of the Sons of God* (Brooklyn, N.Y.: Watchtower Society, 1966), p. 169.

8

Recruitment, Enforcement, and Defection

The JW magazine Awake! *in its issue of September 22, 1972, pp. 17–21, describes the death of two-year-old Irene Walter of Steyr, Upper Austria, who died on November 5, 1970, after her parents refused blood transfusion therapy for her leukemia. Although charged with violating the law in connection with their daughter's death, the parents were acquitted, and* Awake! *uses this acquittal to argue in support of the JW position on blood.*

While world attention was still focused on Waco, people could be heard asking, "Why did all those people stay inside?" "How could mothers with little children choose flames over freedom?" One woman was indeed spotted just outside the burning compound. A federal agent climbed out of the safety of his armored vehicle to help her. But by the time he reached her, she was attempting to go back inside. She fought the agent off as he dragged her to safety.

Why? What powerful force can make men and women face flames rather than flee for their lives, or make a father deny his dying child a blood transfusion? "Brainwashing!" is the answer most often heard. I remember being present on a ballfield when an informal team of Jehovah's Witnesses was about to play an impromptu game of softball against a team of "worldly" people. While the players were warming up, one of the men on the "worldly" team accused a Witness of being brainwashed. The young man shot back an evidently well-rehearsed reply to an accusation he had faced more than once before: "I would rather have my brain washed clean than still have a dirty mind like you do!"

This fellow was just being a smart aleck, of course. Generally, Jehovah's Witnesses will not admit to being brainwashed. Nor will other cult members. And, technically, they are correct. Brainwashing actually refers to a form of indoctrination that is both intensive and coercive, such as the reeducation process brutally forced on captured pilots downed during the Korean War. Technically the indoctrination methods employed by Jehovah's Witnesses and by similar sects are not brainwashing because they are not coercive, at least not in the beginning when the prospective convert is being drawn into the group. Coercion may enter the picture later on, after the believer is fully under Watchtower control. But the Watchtower organization does exercise mind control over its followers, and the results are the same.

To the cult member under mind control, it is no longer difficult to face flames or to refuse a life-saving medical procedure. In fact, the normal course of behavior is what becomes difficult. The Jehovah's Witness refuses blood because the alternative is unthinkable. The normal course of behavior is not even considered an option, because the thinking process has been tampered with.

How does this happen? How is an individual's mind brought under such total control by a cultic organization? The process varies from sect to sect.

"Moonies" (members of Rev. Sun-Myung Moon's Unification Church) are reportedly converted in a matter of days. College students accept the invitation to a weekend seminar or retreat where they are isolated from family and friends at a remote conference center with no transportation home, and are bombarded with information virtually around the clock, both from the speaker's platform and from the members. By the time they go home early Monday morning, their thinking has been altered. They have a new outlook on life. They are Moonies. They are ready to quit school and devote their lives to selling roses on the street corner for Rev. Moon.

Jehovah's Witnesses actually undergo a similar form of indoctrination, but it is much more subtle and takes place gradually over a much longer period of time. Actually, the controlling force is stronger in the case of Jehovah's Witnesses. Rev. Moon's followers have often been "deprogramed"—kidnapped by family members and subjected to a weekend of intense bombardment with information debunking the Unification Church—with the result that the victim is no longer a Moonie. Such weekend deprogramming generally does not work with Jehovah's Witnesses. It takes a person months or years to become a JW, and it usually takes at least as long to reverse or undo the process.

What is that process? How do people come to surrender to the life-and-death authority of a secretive council in Brooklyn? It all starts with a knock on the door.

Before examining the process of controlling someone's mind, however, it should be noted that certain people are predisposed to fall victim to a cult. I was, although I didn't realize it at the time, and, as a result, I spent thirteen years of my life as a Jehovah's Witness. What makes someone predisposed to recruitment? Is it lack of intelligence? No, to the contrary; intelligent people are often drawn to cults, particularly to the Watchtower because JWs spend so much of their time reading and studying, receiving indoctrination and indoctrinating others. Intelligent people excel as Witnesses, and the resulting praise and adoration from fellow Witnesses serves as an emotional reward that tends to keep them in the group, even if their intelligence begins to tell them that something is wrong.

When I speak before an audience and tell my listeners that I carried a card in my wallet for many years, a legal document, instructing doctors not to give me blood even if I were found unconscious and dying, and that I have spaces in my mouth where I had dentists pull teeth rather than do expensive dental work because the world was about to end and I would be restored to perfect health—with no defects—in a paradise earth, I often get the feeling that people in the audience are thinking, "He must have been really stupid to believe those things."

So, that's when I tell them that I was a member of the National Honor Society, graduated from high school at the top of my class, and was majoring in government at Harvard University. I tell them that my wife, also a devoted JW, majored in psychology and sociology at the University of Western Michigan and went on to teach school after graduation. So why didn't our intelligence keep us from falling victim to a cult? Because intelligence or lack thereof is not usually the deciding factor. The factors that predispose someone to falling victim to mind control are primarily emotional rather than intellectual. And they are often determined by time and circumstance.

A common factor that most everyone experiences at one time or another is loneliness. A man's job is transferred, and he moves his family to a new town. Before he and his wife begin to make new friends, two Witness ladies call and the wife, feeling lonely, invites them in for coffee. They, in turn, offer her an hour of instruction. She is not really interested in what they tell her about the earth being restored to paradise, but, since she and her husband have not yet made any social connections in their new neighborhood, she accepts their invitation to come hear a talk on how the Bible can help parents guide adolescents through the difficult years. Her husband decides to go bowling with some of his new workmates instead, but tells his wife to let him know if she hears anything that would help them with their twelve-year-old daughter.

The wife takes their daughter to the meeting, finds it rather confusing and boring, but appreciates the interest people show in wanting to meet her. It seems as though everyone at Kingdom Hall comes up and speaks, and it turns out that one family lives just around the corner, and they have a twelve-year-old girl, too. Before they realize what is happening, the mother and daughter are well on their way toward becoming Jehovah's Witnesses—not because they are attracted by the message, but simply because the warm interest shown by the JWs fills a need in their lives at that time. They continue attending Kingdom Hall for the companionship they find there and don't even notice that their thinking and outlook on life are being reshaped by what they hear from the speakers and from their companions.

Recent bereavement is another predisposing factor. It results not only in sudden loneliness but also in a painful sense of loss. Such heartache may find itself soothed by the loving attention cult members lavish on prospective converts. (This organized activity, expected of all members as a responsibility, is often referred to as "love-bombing" by students of group dynamics. It exerts a powerful emotional pull.) The bereavement factor is not found merely among widows and widowers; it can affect anyone who has lost a close companion through death or separation. Again, the Witnesses come along to fill the need.

Another emotional factor can be the desire for recognition. A person may initially accept the Witnesses' invitation to sit down for a discussion simply to avoid the embarrassment of having to say no. His or her intention may be not to answer the door if they come back again. But in the course of the discussion the Witnesses give plenty of commendation for right answers—and even for wrong ones in the beginning! So, if the person targeted for conversion is encountering a lot of criticism and complaint on the job, at school, or in the home, such praise from the Witnesses may be a welcome change. The visit may prove so pleasurable that the door will be opened the next time, after all.

Kingdom Hall provides the opportunity for every visitor to feel important, but sometimes it goes beyond that. Peter Chadwick, for example, who ended up in my local congregation, had wanted to rise to the top at his place of employment but found the way blocked by racial prejudice. He applied to become a policeman, but found that he had to "know somebody" to get hired. He tried joining a political group, but found that the leadership positions were jealously guarded. Then, when he gave in to a neighbor's persistent invitations and finally agreed to visit the local Kingdom Hall, he quickly saw that the requirements for leadership could easily be met with a little persistence and hard work, and that here he could fulfill the desire that had been blocked elsewhere, to hold an important position. Even if Peter's intellect encountered obstacles in accepting all that he was taught during the indoctrination process, his heart overruled so that he could attain that goal.

Ralph Baxter in a neighboring congregation also appeared to have been drawn by the desire for personal importance. Though a poor speaker who had difficulty organizing his thoughts, and who even found it difficult to speak in complete sentences, he used organizational connections to secure public speaking assignments whenever possible. (Kingdom Hall audiences fidgeted and dozed through Ralph's hour-long talks, but dutifully thanked him for the "fine spiritual food" provided.) Hard work, friendships, and favors in high places got him appointed an elder, for which he was likewise unqualified. Not content with that, though, Ralph secured a position of special authority among the elders, which took priority over all his other interests; I remember one occasion when Ralph continued to man his prominent post at a local JW convention while his wife lay hemorrhaging in a Boston hospital and nearly died. Like other cult leaders, those high in the Watchtower hierarchy love men like Ralph and gladly exploit their craving for importance.

Another factor predisposing some to succumb to mind control is physical infirmity. An individual who suffers from a chronic illness or a handicap may be attracted by the JW message of an earth turned into paradise and the hope of being restored to perfect health in that new earth so close at hand. It is just a matter of months, or a few years at most, the Witness recruiters say, and they appear to be experts on Bible prophecy. Once the potential convert focuses on that hope, obstacles to belief and conversion seem to melt away.

Others are drawn initially by romantic interest in a Witness who makes it clear that marriage to, or even dating someone, outside the faith is not permitted. The saying that "love is blind" has some truth, and in this case it blinds the romantically attracted person to the flaws not just in the person loved but also in the beloved's religious organization.

In all the above situations the person introduced to Watchtower teachings has a strong emotional reason for wanting to accept them, for wanting them to be true. And to the extent that such wishful thinking overshadows clear judgment, the individual is prevented by his or her emotions from making a rational, objective evaluation of the message the JWs present.

But even those not emotionally predisposed can still fall victim to cult recruiters. Why? Because the average person is not on the alert for, or prepared to defend against, such an assault. The Jehovah's Witness recruiter, on the other hand, has his goal in mind from the beginning of the conversation and has been well trained to accomplish that goal. JWs attend five hours of meetings each week that are geared specifically toward teaching them to speak persuasively, to overcome other people's objections, to produce biblical references that appear to support their beliefs, and to win religious arguments and debates. The programs presented at Kingdom Hall even include role-playing demonstrations with some Witnesses acting the part of non-Witnesses and raising objections and counterarguments, followed by other Witnesses showing how to overcome those objections and defeat them.

In addition to these weekly training sessions, Jehovah's Witnesses spend many hours each month actually going door to door, often accompanied by a more experienced partner, trying out the approaches and techniques they see demonstrated at Kingdom Hall, and discovering what works best for them. Through many hours of on-the-job training they learn to perfect their initial presentations and the answers they use as comebacks to objections non-Witnesses commonly raise.

So, when the average person gets into a verbal sparring match with a JW on religious issues, he has about as much chance of winning as he would climbing into a boxing ring to face a professional prize fighter. A lack of training and experience places one at a distinct disadvantage when facing any opponent.

There is more involved in the mind-control procedure, however, than mere persuasive argumentation. Several steps are needed to complete the process—steps that Henry Schenck followed in indoctrinating me, and identical steps that I followed when bringing others under the organization's control. Here is what usually takes place.

First comes one or more informal discussions in which the Witness teacher flips the pages of the Bible from one verse to another, "proving" the Watchtower position on whatever points are brought up for discussion. Such informal sessions establish the Witness (and the organization) as an authority on the Bible and religious matters. The initial discussions also establish that the non-Witness needs to learn something from the Witness—not necessarily how to become a JW, but rather how to "really understand the Bible," or how to "see the hope the Bible gives for a happy future," or how to "use the Bible as a guide to solving today's problems."

A time is then set for a "free home Bible study," usually a one-hour weekly meeting the Witness conducts with an individual or with a whole family. Rather than an examination of the Bible itself, the study actually consists of reading paragraph by paragraph through a JW book produced for that purpose, asking questions found on the bottom of each page, and locating the answers in the paragraphs. Since 1982 the preferred study text for potential converts has been *You Can Live Forever in Paradise on Earth*, a large, colorfully illustrated volume. In 1995 a streamlined pocket-size book titled *Knowledge That Leads to Everlasting Life* was released to replace it, with the announced purpose of speeding up the conversion process. Some Bible verses are quoted in the text, and others simply cited as references. At first the JW teacher may open the Bible and look up many of these verses with the new student, primarily to establish that the teachings in the Watchtower book are actually based on the Bible. But after the student accepts this, the Bible is opened less frequently, and more attention is focused on the Watchtower book.

The new student is given the impression that he or she is studying the Bible, when in fact the study material is the Watchtower Society's publication. Bible verses are quoted or looked up, but they are taken out of context. Not only are the preceding and following verses omitted, but the verse examined is actually placed in a different context, namely, that of the Watchtower book. To grasp how this can change the meaning, think of the entire biblical passage as a cooked turkey breast. Someone cutting into that turkey breast and eating a mouthful of it will know what it tastes like. However, someone else who is given just a thin slice smothered with mustard between layers of pumpernickel rye bread will know what the sandwich tastes like, but will not know the taste of the turkey itself. Similarly, the original flavor or meaning of a Bible verse can be completely lost or changed when placed in what I call a "scripture sandwich"—a lone verse examined in the foreign context of a Watchtower discussion.[1]

The Witness teacher uses questions at the bottom of each page to elicit responses from the student, who may start out giving answers based upon his own ideas but who soon learns that the "correct" answer is that given in the corresponding paragraph. Smiles and commendation reinforce the student's behavior each time he or she gives the answer read directly from the book.

Next, the teacher encourages the student to put the book's answer into his or her own words. This involves actually thinking the thought presented in the book—not just rote recitation—and making that thought one's own. Before going on to the next paragraph the teacher makes sure that the student understands and believes what has been taught.

Each Watchtower textbook typically begins with ideas most everyone would accept: sickness, war, crime, and violence are undesirable; good health, peace, prosperity, and happy family life are desirable goals. Peculiar JW teachings such as abstinence from voting in elections and refusing blood transfusions are reserved for much later in the lessons, when the student has gotten into the habit of accepting everything that is taught.

Very early in the series of lessons the teacher encourages the student to purchase a Watchtower Bible, the *New World Translation of the Holy Scriptures*, and to use this in place of any other Bible owned previously, since this is the version quoted in the book. A quick comparison with other modern-language translations shows this to read essentially the same, but a closer look would reveal that nearly three hundred key verses in the *New World Translation* have been changed to support Watchtower teachings.[2]

Also beginning early in the study, the Witness teacher uses the printed material in the book along with current news items to undermine confidence in all institutions outside the Watchtower organization. Churches, governments, colleges, and various "secular" organizations are all presented as instruments of the Devil. The worst examples are highlighted, such as corrupt television evangelists and Hitler's Nazi regime, and then all churches and governments are tarred with the same brush.

Very early in the study the student is warned that Satan will try to stop the "free home Bible study" by sending a friend or relative with anti-JW propaganda. So, when a concerned loved one does come along to caution the student not to get involved with the cult, this may appear to be a fulfillment of the Witnesses' prophecy, actually adding credibility to their story, and even making it seem likely that the second part of the Witnesses' warning may also be true, namely, that the concerned loved one is, in fact, a tool of the Devil.

If the power of suggestion has succeeded in producing such a fear in the new student, he or she is already well on the way to coming under JW mind control. In any case, a crossroads has been reached. At this point many new students either heed the words of their loved one and break off the study, or else give in to the Witness and begin to view family and friends with suspicion.[3]

Witnesses conducting home Bible studies must turn in monthly reports on these to the Service Overseer in their congregation. If the Service Overseer notes that a particular study has been conducted for several months, yet the student has not begun attending Kingdom Hall meetings, he may recommend that the Witness bring the matter to a head, giving the student an ultimatum to demonstrate progress by commencing meeting attendance, or else the study will be discontinued. Thus the student will lose out on everlasting life, since God will be displeased with this individual who lacked appreciation for the congregation meetings provided by His organization. This is another crossroads. If the student responds to the ultimatum by attending Kingdom Hall, this demonstrates that mind control is truly taking place and that the Watchtower Society has begun to take over his or her decision-making process.

As the student begins to accept Watchtower teachings that Christmas, Easter, Mother's Day, and birthday celebrations are of pagan origin and therefore offensive to God, fellowship with non-JW family and friends on those occasions comes to an abrupt halt, and social interaction with non-Witnesses on other occasions becomes more difficult. Eventually outside friendships cease altogether for the fully committed Jehovah's Witness, and family ties outside the sect cool to the point that relatives feel the JW has become a stranger. This, too, is by design and is a key part of the mind-control process.

The same sort of social isolation from outsiders that David Koresh's Branch Davidians (and certain other mind-control cults) imposed by physically removing members to a communal compound, the Watchtower organization imposes by erecting numerous invisible barriers:

- objections to holidays and other occasions when families traditionally get together

- rejection of tobacco smoking as extremely sinful, not just a health hazard

- complete rejection of the political process so that even casting a ballot for the local dog catcher or high school class president can result in expulsion from the sect

- classification of the flag salute, the pledge of allegiance, and rising for the national anthem as acts of religious idolatry, so that even attendance at sporting events becomes stressful and embarrassing

- rejection of all non-JW religious services as satanic worship, so that Witnesses avoid church weddings and clergy-conducted funerals, even of close friends and relatives.

This social isolation is a key element of mind control because it cuts off the sect member from the free flow of ideas that normally occur among friends or relatives. Once it is in place, only Watchtower ideas are heard and taken into the mind. If other opinions are encountered from outsiders at school or at a JW's place of employment, these are viewed with suspicion and contempt as coming from ungodly, "worldly" people who are no longer regarded as peers.

Five hours of Kingdom Hall meetings each week, formal family sessions at home studying material in preparation for those meetings, personal quiet time spent reading Watchtower publications, fellowship exclusively with other Witnesses who parrot phrases learned at Kingdom Hall—all this adds up to a degree of repetition that is not only the mother of retention but also an effective mind-control tool. Prisoners in concentration camps may mentally resist the brainwashing messages blared at them continually from loudspeakers, but Jehovah's Witnesses gladly accept the repetitive reminders from "God's organization" that they hear at meetings and that they in turn echo to each other.

The final ingredient in the mind-control process is added when the new convert comes under the authority of the Watchtower Society's judicial system and can face trial and punishment for any infraction. But more will be said on that aspect a bit farther on in this chapter.

The end result of this effective and well-designed program of mind control is that a fully committed Jehovah's Witness will readily "avoid independent thinking . . . questioning the counsel that is provided by God's visible organization," and will even "fight against independent thinking."[4]

"Untheocratic" thinking or behavior—i.e., that not approved by the theocratic or God-ruled organization—is abhorrent. If untheocratic thinking is heard from another Witness, it is reported to the elders; and if it arises in one's own mind it is either confessed and corrected with help from the elders, or else it causes internal conflict, stress, and sometimes even mental illness. Elders typically cite scripture—in particular Leviticus 5:1 ("And if a soul sin, and hear the voice of swearing, and is a witness, whether he hath seen or known of it; if he do not utter it, then he shall bear his iniquity")—to remind members that God will punish them if they become aware of sinful acts or speech and fail to report it.

Former Witnesses in the process of recovery often find it helpful to read George Orwell's futuristic novel *Nineteen Eighty-Four*, about a totalitarian state where *thoughtcrime* and *facecrime* (Witnesses may be taken to task for "inappropriate facial expression") are punishable offenses, and where the population practices *doublethink*—a form of mental gymnastics enabling one to believe that white is black or that *yes* means *no* if the ruling authority says so. Former Witnesses who read the novel find themselves drawing parallels with their own Watchtower experience and recognize that they, too, practiced doublethink. This can be illustrated by an incident related in former JW Governing Body member Raymond Franz's book *Crisis of Conscience*. Franz describes a District Overseer, Bart Thompson, who, at a training meeting for elders, held up in his hand a book with a green cover and told the audience, "If the Society told me that this book is black instead of green, I would say, 'Y'know I could have sworn that it was green, but if the Society says it's black, then it's black!' "[5]

Nor is that an isolated example. One personal experience that I frequently relate, because it helps people understand why biblical discussions with JWs can prove so frustrating, involves the visit of two JW ladies to the front door of my new home about a year after I left the sect.

I asked one of them, a woman in her fifties or early sixties, to show me in the Bible the proof for their belief that the "great crowd" of believers will end up living forever on earth instead of going to heaven. She pulled out of context a verse from Revelation, chapter 7, which, if put back into its proper context, actually said the opposite. But, realizing that my explanation was going over her head, I asked her to turn her Bible a few pages to Revelation 19:1 and to read it aloud from her *New World Translation*.

She read, "After these things I heard what was as a loud voice of a great crowd in heaven. They said, 'Praise Jah, YOU people! The salvation and the glory and the power belong to our God. . . .' " Then I asked her where the verse located the great crowd. "On earth," she replied. So, I had her read it again, this time interrupting after she read the words, "great crowd in heaven." Again, I asked her where the verse located the great crowd. And again she answered, "On earth." So, I pointed to the verse in her Bible and asked her, "But what is that word there—the last word you read?" "It says 'heaven,' " she finally acknowledged, immediately adding, "but the great crowd is on earth." Then she explained, "You don't understand. We have men at our headquarters in Brooklyn, New York, who explain the Bible to us. And they can prove that the great crowd is on earth; I just can't explain it that well."

There it is: a real-life example of mind control in full operation. Now, if a Jehovah's Witness can see a green book and declare that it is black if the headquarters organization says so, and if a JW can see the word *heaven* clearly printed on a page but read it in her mind as *earth* because Watchtower leaders tell her to, it should come as no surprise that they can be told that Bible verses about the Jewish diet of kosher meat actually constitute a command from God to refuse the medical procedure of administering plasma or blood platelets in life-threatening emergencies.

✺   ✺   ✺

A nineteen-year-old woman, Minel Koehler, who had just lost her newborn baby, died at St. Luke's Medical Center "after refusing blood transfusions at two Wisconsin hospitals because of her beliefs," an Associated Press dispatch reported in St. Paul's Pioneer Press *of April 29, 1992, on page 2C. She had been traveling to a JW convention when the hemorrhaging began.*

✺   ✺   ✺

In 1972, the year after I married Penni, the Watchtower magazine began teaching "new truths" about smoking: It was not merely a bad habit, harmful to health, but was actually a form of spiritism or demonic worship. Tobacco contained nicotine; nicotine was a drug; and the Greek word *pharmakia* in ancient Bible manuscripts, although commonly translated "spiritism" in the JW *New World Translation*, actually derived from the same root word as pharmacy and therefore meant "druggery." People who used tobacco were using the drug nicotine, hence practicing *pharmakia,* or engaging in demonic worship. Such people could no longer be accepted for baptism and, if already baptized, would be expelled from the organization unless they quit smoking. A grace period of six months would be allowed for this new "law of God" to take effect as regards existing members of JW congregations. After that, Witnesses who still smoked would by summoned before judicial committees and "disfellowshipped."*

We had been taught to see this judicial arrangement as one piece of evidence that we were in God's organization, that Jehovah's Wit-

---

*At the end of 1981, the sect's publications changed the spelling from *disfellowshiped* and *disfellowshiping* to *disfellowshipped* and *disfellowshipping*. Failure of JWs to conform, even in such a minor matter as this, would raise questions about their loyalty and faithfulness to God.

nesses are already living under the Kingdom of God: A kingdom is a government, and God's kingdom is a theocratic government, with Jehovah God himself holding the highest position. But, like any other government, God's kingdom has a judicial branch that judges wrongdoers. When a case comes to the attention of the elders, they appoint three or more of their number to form a judicial committee and summon the sinner to stand trial.

Obedience is thus compelled by two powerful forces: the mind control exercised over individual JWs by the organization, and the threat of punishment through the sect's judicial committee arrangement. Witnesses whose thinking has been brought completely into line willingly obey whatever the Watchtower Society says, rejoicing at the opportunity to do "God's will." Those who have not completely surrendered, or whose ability to think independently has somehow been reawakened, are kept in line through fear of punishment. This punishment results in the victim being totally shunned by JW family and friends. Witnesses will not speak or even say as much as hello on the street, and the offender is no longer welcome in the homes of friends or relatives. He or she is no longer considered a Witness, and faces divine execution at the Battle of Armageddon instead of life in paradise.

Cigarette smoking made my mother and my sister, Barbara, hesitate to become baptized Jehovah's Witnesses. Few Witnesses smoked, and those who did were looked down upon as weak. Mama and Barbara had both tried to quit smoking many times over the years but always failed. They were convinced they couldn't quit. If they became Witnesses they would be guaranteed the disapproval of their new peers, at least in regard to this aspect of their lifestyle. But I persuaded them both to join the sect anyway. As JWs they would survive Armageddon, and then God would take away their bad habit; but if they remained outside God's organization, they would die with the rest of the world.

Because Barbara and Mama failed to quit smoking within the prescribed six-month time period, the elders in our congregation formed a judicial committee, summoned them to appear, and pronounced them unrepentant sinners. An announcement would be made at the next meeting, to the effect that they had been disfellowshipped and should therefore be shunned.

When Penni and I heard the news we were deeply grieved, but we resolved immediately to cease all association with my mother and my sister. They were no longer welcome in our home, and if we went to theirs at all it would be only to see my father or my brothers. It was almost as if Mama and Barbara had died; worse, it was as if they were ghosts, present in the room when we visited their home, but to be ignored as if invisible.

Then, two years later, the August 1, 1974, *Watchtower* magazine surprised us with a new truth: it instructed JWs to greet disfellowshipped persons and to see relatives. So, it was all right for us to visit my mother and my sister again—for the next seven years, that is, until the September 15, 1981, issue of *The Watchtower* reversed the rule once more and required even more severe shunning. This time, however, my wife and I chose not to obey. We were beginning to break free from the control we had been under.

The extent of the organization's power in commanding JWs to shun people can be seen in what happened in November 1988. At that time millions of Jehovah's Witnesses changed their mind again. They all decided to start talking to certain family members and acquaintances they had previously been avoiding. Why did they all change their mind unanimously and simultaneously? Because the November 15, 1988, issue of *The Watchtower,* in yet another reversal, told them to. For many Jehovah's Witnesses the Watchtower Society's back-and-forth changes in disfellowshipping policy have produced an up-and-down sort of existence such as one might experience at the end of a yo-yo string. More than any of the sect's other doctrinal changes, these reversals have wreaked havoc on the lives and emotions of shunned individuals and their families.

When the August 1, 1974, *Watchtower* modified the disfellowshipping arrangement it presented this new position as more Christlike:

> Thus, Jesus' own example protects us against adopting the extreme view of certain rabbinical writers in this matter of dealing with persons as "a man of the nations and as a tax collector." . . . [A]s Jesus' example shows, this does not require our treating such a one as an enemy or refusing to show common courtesy and consideration. . . . There is . . . nothing to show that Jews with a balanced and Scriptural viewpoint would refuse to greet a "man of the nations" or a tax collector. Jesus' counsel about greetings, in connection with his exhortation to imitate God in his undeserved kindness toward "wicked people and good," would seem to rule against such a rigid stand. . . .
> . . . [W]hen sons or daughters render honor to a parent, though disfellowshiped, by calling to see how such a one's physical health is or what needs he or she may have, this act in itself is not a spiritual fellowshipping.[6]

When the November 15, 1988, *Watchtower* once more reversed the policy of 1981, it applied only to unbaptized persons, including children raised in the organization: "Previously, unbaptized ones who unrepentantly sinned were completely avoided."[7] But, now, "The Bible does not require that Witnesses avoid speaking with him, for he is not disfellowshipped."[8]

Wouldn't normal people balk at being jerked around like this? Wouldn't they find ways to get around the prohibitions, to see close relatives anyway and talk with them? Yes, normal people would. But we weren't normal. We were convinced that the organization spoke for God, and that the judgments rendered regarding Mama and Barbara and their smoking were correct.

Some JWs, however—"weak" ones or those who only half believe—do cheat the system and fellowship secretly with expelled relatives or friends. But they risk expulsion themselves in doing so. Obedience to the organization is compelled, not simply by the elders and judicial committees themselves, but also by a network of informers among the Witnesses. JWs see themselves as under obligation to report all infractions of Watchtower rules. I still encounter this myself on a regular basis through the recorded message line I began operating as an outreach to members of the sect soon after my leaving. By dialing a number a JW can hear a brief message exposing Watchtower errors and can leave an address for me to send additional information. Fear of informers forces some who call to go to great lengths to guarantee their secrecy. Some have told me later that they would get up during the middle of the night to place the call so that family members would not observe and report them to the elders. Most are afraid, at first, to leave an address. Those who do often use an assumed name and a post office box, or arrange to receive mail in care of a trusted non-JW neighbor or relative.

Spying and reporting is not limited to family members, however. A Witness secretly accepting a blood transfusion must live with the fear that a JW employed as a clerk or typist at the doctor's office or the hospital might discover this and report it. Wouldn't that violate the employer's rules regarding the confidentiality of patient records? Might it not also violate certain laws designed to protect patients from just this sort of invasion of privacy? Yes, but *The Watchtower* has told its followers that they should violate such rules and laws under these circumstances. The September 1, 1987, issue features an article titled " 'A Time to Speak'—When?" that addresses this very question by citing the case of a "hypothetical person" named Mary who encounters evidence that another Witness has had an abortion:

Mary works as a medical assistant at a hospital. One requirement she has to abide by in her work is confidentiality. She must keep documents and information pertaining to her work from going to unauthorized persons. Law codes in her state also regulate the disclosure of confidential information on patients. . . .

. . . Was this the time for Mary to keep quiet, or was it the time to speak about what she had learned?[9]

The article argues that "there may be times when a Christian is obligated to bring a matter to the attention of the elders," even when doing so is "illegal," because "the law of God" outweighs "the demands of lesser authorities."[10] It goes on to conclude that a Witness would be required "to strain or even breach the requirements of confidentiality because of the superior demands of divine law."[11] Presented with the voice of authority, the magazine's instructions make it clear what JWs must do with confidential records at their place of employment. It also puts on notice the rest of the sect's members that confidential records may be used against them in church courts. Any who think they have an opportunity to break JW taboos and get away with it should think twice. The forbidden conduct might be noted or implied in school records, a lawyer's files, hospital records, or some other confidential document, and if a Witness is employed in the office in any capacity whatsoever, the confidential information is no longer secret from the local elders.

Awareness of this Watchtower policy should also put on notice doctors, lawyers, educators, and other employers who maintain confidential records on individuals. They have a right to know that such information is not safe in the hands of JW secretaries, typists, filing clerks—or even janitors or night watchmen—who might feel obliged to act as the eyes and ears of a congregation judicial committee. Thus, the official *Journal of the American Bar Association* featured in its February 1988 issue an article titled "Confidentiality vs. Doctrine: Jehovah's Witness Lawyers, Workers Face Dilemma." The article discusses legal ramifications of this JW policy. A hospital, law firm, or other institution might find itself caught between the horns of a dilemma: whether to face a lawsuit from a client whose privacy is breached or to face a religious discrimination suit for dismissing a Witness working with sensitive records. Most employers, however, live in blissful ignorance of the problem—unaware that a Jehovah's Witness employee would feel obligated to photocopy or disclose the contents of confidential files for the scrutiny of prying elders.

Seeing themselves as God's special agents working for "a higher authority," these overseers seldom hesitate to invade the jurisdiction of medical or legal professionals. Consider the case of Alex Paisley, for example, a middle-aged Witness associated with a Massachusetts congregation not far from ours. After he was taken to a nearby hospital, doctors discovered that he had inoperable cancer and, in fact, that death was imminent. Alex would not last long enough for his grown children on the West Coast to be brought to his bedside unless he received a blood transfusion. It would not cure him or avert death, but it would extend his life a day or two longer. As a last resort, Alex accepted the transfusion. Within a short time three solemn visitors appeared at his bedside—not his children who were still en route, but a judicial committee of elders from the local congregation of Jehovah's Witnesses. Right there in the hospital, they put Alex on trial for violating the Watchtower Society's ban on blood. Acting as prosecutor, judge, jury, and executioner, the committee found Alex guilty and "disfellowshipped" him, cutting him off from all association with other Witnesses, even relatives. Despite the hospital staff's valiant efforts to save him, Alex died hours later, shortly after his children arrived. The elders monitoring the situation quickly instructed his Witness friends and relatives not to attend his funeral, warning that any who did attend would also be put on trial.

In a different hospital, teenagers Tom and Cindy faced a difficult decision. Married only months before and now well along in her first pregnancy, Cindy was hemorrhaging beyond control. The doctors predicted her death within hours if she were not given blood quickly. Although Jehovah's Witnesses, Tom and Cindy agreed to accept the prescribed treatment. It worked, and her life was spared. But she and Tom were called to stand trial before a judicial committee.

Hundreds of cases tell the same story: Jehovah's Witnesses who fail to obey the Watchtower Society's ban on blood transfusions face severe discipline. *The Watchtower* of January 15, 1961, put it this way:

> . . . the receiver of a blood transfusion must be cut off from God's people by excommunication or disfellowshiping. . . . If the taking of a blood transfusion is the first offense . . . and he sees the error of his action and grieves and repents over it and begs divine forgiveness and forgiveness of God's congregation on earth . . . he need not be disfellowshiped. He needs to be put under surveillance. . . .[12]

In thousands of other cases, however—the vast majority, in fact—Witnesses obey the organization, even when refusing blood leads to their own death or that of a relative or loved one.

But can't a JW simply resign from the organization, and then receive a transfusion? Why didn't my mother and my sister Barbara leave the church during the prescribed six-month period to quit smoking, before the elders could put them on trial? This certainly can be done. But the problem is that a person who resigns is then treated the same as one who is expelled. Instead of announcing that she has been disfellowshipped, the elders announce that she has "disassociated" herself. Either way, she is to be shunned.

"Disassociation" is also announced in many cases that do not involve voluntary separation, primarily when the sect seeks to shield itself from legal liability for having taken action against the offender. This was done often in past years when a young man would accept a call from his draft board, either to enter the military or to perform alternative service in a civilian hospital. Punishing members for obeying the law could put the organization itself in violation of the law. So it was said that the young man, by his course of action, separated himself from the sect; the sect did not expel him. More recently the term "disassociation" has been resorted to, on occasion, when the elders have taken action against a JW who has exercised freedom of speech or some other freedom in a manner not permitted by the organization.

In any case, whether the elders who put a JW on trial pass a sentence of disfellowship or disassociation, the result is the same: the individual is totally cut off from family and friends who are required to shun him or else face the same penalty themselves. A new member discovers, at some point, that a door has slammed shut behind him. He is now obligated to obey the Watchtower Society, or face the consequences. Once a person has joined the Jehovah's Witness organization, there is no honorable way out.

JWs know this full well, but by practicing *doublethink* they are also able to believe that, as their *Proclaimers* book declares, theirs "is not a forced conformity; it results from education . . . they are free to leave the organization."[13] Yes, like a child speaking with fingers crossed, they can honestly say they are free to leave, the same way they are free to take blood transfusions—free to leave and take the consequences, the same way a hostage with a gun to his head is free to leave and take the bullet.

❧   ❧   ❧

The 1975 Yearbook of Jehovah's Witnesses *reports on page 223 that Samuel Muscariello contracted "the kind of strep throat that results in uremic poisoning" in 1947. Doctors gave him "two years at the most to live" after he refused an operation accompanied by blood transfusions. "In exactly two years, Sam was taken back to the hospital, dying." The* Yearbook *quotes a JW relative as saying the family "was strengthened by Sam's clear thinking and integrity to Jehovah even until death."*

❧   ❧   ❧

The February 1981 letter that Circuit Overseer Tom Halloran and the local elders wrote to Brooklyn removing me as a member of the elder body was only tentative. It awaited the Society's confirmation. My letter objecting to their actions would normally have triggered an appeal procedure, with an appeal hearing to be held within a matter of days. Two weeks passed, however, with no reply. March came, and then April, with no action taken by headquarters. The Society did not reply until the end of May. Something was really wrong.

In the meantime, the remaining elders had a field day. They insinuated from the podium at meetings that men in the congregation who wore modern hair styles had homosexual leanings and that the women who wore pantsuits inclined toward lesbianism. In his concluding prayer at the end of the following Thursday night's meeting, one elder expressed his confidence that, "now that the obstacle is out of the way, we will be able to clean up the congregation." A newly baptized woman was sitting in the audience in a pantsuit when another elder delivered a stinging denunciation of that style of dress. The three victorious elders began dangling over my head the threat of being disfellowshipped for apostasy. "It's no longer a case of just cutting the hair; you must wholeheartedly respond to the counsel," one of them told me. He then asked me for the names of any in the congregation who phoned me or approached me at meetings to express their displeasure with what the elders were doing. Many, in fact, objected but were afraid to speak to the elders, so I did not give out their names.

The official letter from Brooklyn finally arrived, dated May 26, 1981. Why did it take so long? "We did not immediately reply because at the time the brother dealing with such matters was away," it stated. Then it added, "Inadvertently the material became misplaced." In actuality, as Penni and I managed to piece together much later, the headquarters organization was still reeling from the removal of President Frederick Franz's nephew Raymond Franz from the Governing

Body, as discussed in chapter 5, and the related purge at headquarters. The conservatives had not yet rooted out all the moderates in the organization's mid-level hierarchy, and issues such as those involved in my case were still up in the air. When the Society's letter finally arrived, amazingly it said that I had *not* been removed as an elder. Rather, the Society was sending District Overseer Sam Goodwin into the congregation to deal with the issues in person.

🌿   🌿   🌿

"Medical officials say a Virginia Tech Airport employee who lost both arms in an accident at the airport might have had one arm saved if he had not refused a blood transfusion," begins an undated newspaper clipping. The Associated Press dispatch datelined Charlottesville identifies the accident victim as Jehovah's Witness Julio Pasada. It adds that his right arm was too mangled to save, and doctors' efforts to reattach his left arm were stymied by the patient's refusal to accept blood.

🌿   🌿   🌿

My wife and I had no knowledge whatsoever of the dramatic events taking place behind the scenes at Watchtower headquarters, even though those events would, to a large extent, determine the outcome of the struggle we faced in our local congregation. The high-level purge that began in 1980 took place behind closed doors, and a detailed account was not available until Raymond Franz published his book *Crisis of Conscience* in 1983. Yet the drama that played out in Brooklyn affected our lives in much the same way that intrigues among the mythical gods and goddesses of Mount Olympus altered the fate of human heroes in ancient Greek tragedies. In our case the "gods" were the Governing Body members and high-ranking hierarchs at headquarters, whose fears and jealousies caused them to see conspiracies in their midst; the thunderbolts they hurled at one another in their private heaven had deadly fallout for those of us down here on earth.

In his book Franz confesses that he was disappointed as soon as he joined the Governing Body in 1971—disappointed because decisions were arrived at not through Bible study and prayer, but back-room politics and majority votes. The late 1970s saw him growing increasingly uncomfortable in his role as a prominent member of the spiritual jet set, flying to countries all over the world to address audiences large and small. He knew that his uncle Fred's prophecies for 1975 had failed miserably and that the entire chronology based on the invisible return of Christ in 1914 was unsound. Moreover, he hesitated to approve some of the *Watchtower* articles the president and others were producing; as a member of the Governing Body's Writing Committee his signature constituted part of the approval procedure leading to publication, but he found himself silently abstaining from this collective imprimatur. On speaking tours, however, Franz repeatedly found himself called upon to explain publicly and privately doctrines that he had no desire to defend. Since *The Watchtower*[14] had declared Christ to be the mediator only for the elite "anointed" Witnesses and not for the remaining millions of JWs, a rank-and-file member would ask a question such as, "Brother Franz, what role does Jesus play in *my* prayers?" and he would find himself giving a carefully worded answer to take the sting out of the exclusionist doctrine without denying the teaching altogether.

Stressed by this internal conflict and fearing ill effects on his health, Franz and his wife left Brooklyn for a planned four-month leave of absence beginning March 24, 1980. Ray and Cynthia found refreshment in the company of friends in Gadsden, Alabama, but they were gone less than a month when the Service Department began interviewing resident volunteer workers at the Bethel complex concerning personal reservations or doubts on doctrinal matters. The interrogations began with low-level staff members and quickly focused on obtaining the names of others who had shared unorthodox thoughts or opinions in private conversation—especially others of higher rank. In less than a week the inquisitors had reached Ed Dunlap, a prominent instructor at the sect's Gilead School for training missionaries and anonymous author of the book *Commentary on the Letter of James* published by the Society in 1979. After Governing Body members Lloyd Barry and Jack Barr interrogated Dunlap for three hours, he phoned his friend Ray Franz in Alabama.

Franz in turn phoned Brooklyn to find out what was going on, but was given evasive answers. His name was coming up in the interrogations, and his fellow Governing Body members pushing the inquisition were apparently more interested in building a case against him than in consulting him. On April 25, they disfellowshipped headquarters workers Cris and Norma Sanchez and Nestor Kuilan, plus three friends of theirs from nearby New York congregations, Franz relates[15]; finally on May 8, 1980, the Governing Body officially summoned him to return to Brooklyn to face trial.

At the May 21 session the president's nephew was questioned primarily on his views regarding who was in line for a heavenly reward (all JW believers or just an elite group?), the significance of the year 1914 in connection with the invisible return of Christ, and the role of "God's organization" and its Governing Body. After the morning's interrogation the members sitting in judgment of their peer deliberated on and off until the afternoon of the following day, some apparently pushing to disfellowship him as an apostate and others arguing for kinder treatment. Finally their verdict was delivered: Raymond Franz was asked to resign from the Governing Body and as a member of the headquarters staff.

The August 1980 issue of *Our Kingdom Service,* an internal publication distributed only to active Witnesses, carried a brief announcement to the general membership on page 2: "This is a notification that Raymond Victor Franz is no longer a member of the Governing Body and of the Brooklyn Bethel family as of May 22, 1980." Page 1 featured an open letter from the Governing Body discussing the plight of JWs among Cuban refugees who had recently flooded into the United States; the letter also declared:

> We are saddened to report at this time that five members of the Bethel family, and a few others in the New York city area have recently been disfellowshiped. There has been some apostasy against the organization and the promoting of sectarian divisions in some of the congregations of God's people.

This signaled the beginning of a long succession of articles in JW magazines warning of the dangers of apostasy and demanding the most intense loyalty to the organization. The campaign reached its peak, I believe, in the early 1980s with such statements as these: "Avoid independent thinking . . . questioning the counsel that is provided by God's visible organization," and "Fight against independent thinking."[16] By that time judicial committees of elders approached even the slightest evidence of dissent with a witch-hunt mentality.

Meanwhile, Raymond Franz, still a Jehovah's Witness in good standing, returned to Alabama. With a ten-thousand-dollar "gift" from the Society—essentially his severance pay—and a five-thousand-dollar loan he purchased a mobile home and parked it on land owned by JW Peter Gregerson, for whom he also went to work cutting grass and trimming shrubbery.[17]

A few months after his arrival, the East Gadsden congregation elders recommended Franz for appointment to their body, but the Society abruptly rejected him. As time went on, the articles warning against apostates began to produce a climate of fear and distrust. Soon a visiting Circuit Overseer began interrogating Franz's landlord and employer, Peter Gregerson, on the basis of rumors that he entertained some apostate ideas. Not wanting to face trial and hoping to spare his many Witness family members and relatives the complications of having a disfellowshipped person to deal with, Gregerson submitted his resignation from the organization on March 18, 1981. Under the moderate arrangements announced in 1974 and still in effect (as discussed earlier in this chapter), JWs would not be required to shun him completely. He had not been disfellowshipped as an apostate, but had merely resigned.

Toward the end of August, however, JWs everywhere began receiving in the mail the September 15, 1981, *Watchtower* with new instructions on "how to treat expelled ones" and "those who disassociate themselves."[18] Shortly after this magazine arrived, the local elders in Gadsden began investigating the former Governing Body member's association with Gregerson, now resigned, who had given Franz shelter when he was asked to leave Bethel headquarters. They insisted that he break off all contact with Gregerson, whereupon Franz wrote to the Governing Body asking for clarification of how the new instructions would apply in such a case as his where he worked for the disassociated person and resided on his property. (JWs of all ranks have traditionally written letters to Brooklyn for rulings on all sorts of questions; Franz was not exploiting his former connections with the Governing Body but was merely following a widespread practice.) Without waiting for him to receive a reply, the Gadsden elders formally summoned Franz to a judicial committee meeting in November.

At the formal hearing two Witnesses—one of them also serving as a member of the judicial committee rendering judgment—accused Franz of sharing a meal with Gregerson. When he asked them to wait for Brooklyn to respond to his letter asking for clarification on the new rules, they responded that they had all the authority they needed to act. They had spoken to the Service Department at headquarters and had been told to proceed with the trial. The committee duly found Raymond Franz guilty and disfellowshipped him.

❧   ❧   ❧

"Woman refuses blood transfusions. Court rules in 'right to die' Jehovah case." So reads a headline in the British Western Morning News *of July 24, 1992, concerning a twenty-year-old JW girl identified only as "T" to protect her identity. A High Court Judge had ruled in favor of the transfusions,* but *the case was being taken to the Court of Appeal.*

❦   ❦   ❦

When the Society's letter regarding the attempt to remove me as an elder arrived at the end of May, 1981, the dust from recent shakeups in the organization was still settling. Ray Franz remained a JW in good standing in Alabama; moderates were still to be found at various levels of the organization. Our District Overseer, Sam Goodwin, was apparently one of them.

He arrived to serve our congregation the second week of June, together with Circuit Overseer Tom Halloran, who had orchestrated the trial that initially removed me as an elder. When both sat down to meet with the elders on Wednesday evening, I was part of the body again, because the Society's letter had left it for the District Overseer to determine my fate in person. The other elders appeared confident, though, that he would remove me permanently. To their surprise, however, his whole approach was one of conciliation. I quickly caught on and offered to trim my hair a bit as a gesture of cooperation with the other elders. They, however—led by Circuit Overseer Halloran—had nothing to offer but harsh words of condemnation for me and my wife. Goodwin let them express themselves but then shot them down, especially the arrogant Circuit Overseer whom he humbled by pulling rank on him. After all, the District Overseer was the Circuit Overseer's immediate superior, and he knew that the solution he decided to impose would have to be accepted by everyone. Like it or not, the other elders had to live with my presence on the body. That was his decision. Moreover, they were to publicly apologize from the podium for the abusive talks they had given aimed at Penni and me.

The following evening District Overseer Goodwin addressed the congregation at the Service Meeting and told everyone that pantsuits and beards were not sinful or immoral, and that people who dressed or groomed in the previously forbidden styles should not be excluded from participation in door-to-door work. Penni and I exulted. We had been completely vindicated! People of our generation would no longer be turned away from the organization by elders demanding that they dress and groom according to the previous generation's norms. The issue had been settled once and for all, or so we thought.

Then came our District Assembly at the end of June, with ten or twenty thousand filling the Civic Center in Providence, Rhode Island. We enjoyed the program until we heard the talk titled "Forward, You Ministers," delivered on June 26 by Governing Body member Jack E.

Barr. He taught that a young man should be "clean-cut" and that we should "stand out as different among worldlings" as to our grooming. I couldn't believe I was hearing this from a Governing Body member. Assuming Barr had ad-libbed those remarks on the basis of his own opinion, I wrote him a respectful letter questioning him along these lines:

> I can understand why a man of your age, having grown up at a time when being "clean-cut" was in vogue, would prefer such a style. But is it Scriptural to advocate it from the platform? I can't think of a single one of the faithful men of old who was "clean-cut." In fact, even Christ Jesus must have followed the command at Leviticus 19:27, "You must *not* cut your side locks *short* around, and you must *not destroy* the extremity of your *beard.*" [*New World Translation*]
>
> . . . As to our "standing out as different among worldlings" by our grooming . . . why didn't our brothers grow beards and longer hair during World War II in order to "stand out as different" from the clean shaven, short-haired soldiers . . . ?
>
> . . . It may seem that I am making much of a small matter. But, as a member of the Governing Body, your word is taken by many of the friends as law. (Emphasis added)

I was surprised to receive a two-page signed response dated July 4, 1981, that Jack Barr had evidently typed himself. Between flowery opening and closing paragraphs he answered me to the point:

> . . . First of all let me assure you that the material was from a manuscript talk which is being presented exactly the same at ALL the District Conventions throughout the world this year. This takes away any personal opinion on one speaker's part. But of course I hasten to add that I wholly agree with what I did present.
>
> . . . This material was all very carefully prepared and agreed upon by the Society. So any difference of feeling you may have is with the Society, not just an individual brother like myself.

This left me wondering whether the Society had indeed changed its position on the matter—or was Jack Barr misleading me as to how closely he had followed the wording of the manuscript for his talk? If Circuit Overseer Tom Halloran and District Overseer Sam Goodwin could be worlds apart on their approach to issues of dress and grooming, could there also be similar differences among Governing Body members? What if personnel changes had led to a shift in the majority viewpoint?

My questions did not wait long for answers. Wesley Daniels, one of the Brockton elders who had been trying to remove me from the body, announced at our next elders meeting that he had spoken with Halloran at the District Assembly and that the Circuit Overseer had received a new letter from the Society with new information that would make it possible for them to remove me now. He added that Tom Halloran had spoken with Jack Barr of the Governing Body at the convention and, "Bro. Barr said, 'We were letting the friends use their conscience—it didn't work well—now we'll have to tell them what to do.'"

Another blow came on August 14, when Penni and I received our copy of the September 15, 1981, *Watchtower.* The "new truths" contained in this magazine left us shaken. How could they possibly have come from God?

I was still puzzling over how to respond to these new instructions on shunning when August 27 brought substitute Circuit Overseer Jared Binghamton to our Kingdom Hall for the scheduled semi-annual visit. (A long-time elder in a nearby congregation, Binghamton had served years earlier in the circuit work. It seemed logical that the Society would not send Halloran back to us so soon after he was humiliated by having his deeds undone.) In his Thursday evening Service Meeting talk Binghamton forcefully denounced what he called "Beatles haircuts" and then went on to preach about the virtues of "unquestioning obedience." How could he denounce what the District Overseer had approved just a month earlier? And where did he get this harsh doctrine of unquestioning obedience? Apparently this represented the Society's new position on these matters. Imagine, then, my horror two days later when I walked into the meeting Binghamton was to conduct with our body of elders, only to discover that he was initiating new proceedings against me on account of my hair style and Penni's pantsuits! How could he and the elders even *think* of doing this, when District Overseer Sam Goodwin had just undone the previous attempt, had put me back on as an elder, and had told the congregation that these styles of dress and grooming were acceptable? What Penni and I didn't know—and what Circuit Overseer Tom Halloran had evidently found out from connections at headquarters and passed on to his substitute Jared Binghamton—was that the remaining moderates at headquarters had totally caved in under pressure from the inquisition. The balance of power at Brooklyn headquarters had now tilted so far toward the archconservatives that there was no one left to restrain them. Not yet knowing this, however, and not realizing the futility of my position, I appealed the elders' decision.

Meanwhile, my younger brother Jonathan, who was a Ministerial

Servant in a congregation at Machias, Maine, had grown a beard. Beards were common up there in the north woods near the Canadian border, but the Machias elders immediately removed him from his position. Letters from the Society first urged him to shave and then officially confirmed his removal. Because the beard remained on his face, even after this discipline was imposed, the elders were infuriated and informally suggested to congregation members that they shun Jonathan and his wife and young daughter—in spite of the fact that wearing facial hair was obviously not a disfellowshipping offense. Treated as an outcast by close friends, Jonathan was about to leave Maine with his small family and all their possessions and return to Brockton.

At this point I had become desperate. It seemed as if everything I had trusted in was crumbling around me. Because the world outside was so evil and cynical, I had taken refuge in the Watchtower organization, which seemed to be built upon truth and high standards of conduct; but now my little Watchtower world was also falling apart. In the hope of making some sense of what was happening, I decided to write a letter to the speaker from Bethel headquarters mentioned in chapter 5, who told the audience at a special one-day assembly that the elders were "driving the young people out of the Truth by enforcing rules on dress and grooming that are not biblical." I felt that if anyone would understand my problem, he would, but I knew that a frank and honest letter on my part could also get me disfellowshipped, if it fell into the wrong hands. Desperation drove me to write anyway.

Because it reflects the doubts, fears, and inner turmoil common to many who are unsure about their status as Jehovah's Witnesses, I will quote large portions of my four-page single-spaced letter. However, for reasons that will become clear from his response, I will omit anything that could betray the identity of the prominent Witness I addressed it to in an enveloped marked "personal and confidential."

September 16, 1981

Dear Brother ———:

There comes a time when each one of us must turn to another for help, counsel, or advice, and that is why I am writing this letter. Although I don't know you personally—I merely heard you speak at ——— on ——— —I feel that you are the only elder I know of that I can approach for advice at this time. Not that I mean to flatter you with the implication that your discernment is superior to that of all others; rather, it is due to the attitude prevailing among the elders that I do know personally.

For example, I know of two congregations in which the elders have used the word "apostasy" in counseling brothers on personal grooming. An elder in still a third congregation raised the question of whether another elder's unwillingness to support the first-Sunday-of-the-month field service program could be considered as "apostasy." And I heard a circuit overseer's talk last month in which the brother commended "unquestioning obedience" on the part of the friends.

So, perhaps you can see why I fear to approach any one of these men to discuss the questions that have been nagging at my mind and heart. Yes, I have prayed to Jehovah many, many times about these matters, but I realize that one of the ways Jehovah answers prayers for guidance can be through the Scriptural advice of experienced, older men.

First, let me give you a few details about myself. [I related briefly my background and how I became a Witness.]

Since coming into the Truth I have always had some minor private disagreements with the Society—(What thinking person hasn't?)—but I've always believed that this is Jehovah's organization, made up of imperfect men sincerely seeking to do His will. I've always rejoiced to see the light grow brighter and have encouraged others to be patient when they had disagreements with the Society—in time, Jehovah would correct either the individual or the Society.

Now, however, I feel that a change is taking place that threatens to produce deep divisions and perhaps splits among Jehovah's people. Since I can't point to one specific evidence of such an impending disaster, please be patient as I enumerate several things that contribute to my having this feeling:

1) The Society seems to be swinging back and forth between opposite views on certain matters. For example: (a) First we were not to speak to disfellowshipped persons. Then we could speak briefly and politely. Now we are to turn our head away from their "Hello!" without answering. (b) First we were all ministers. Then only the servants in the congregation were ministers. Now we are all ministers again. (c) First "righteous Lot" could do no wrong, so even his offering his daughters to the perverted mob must have been good. Then it was admitted that Lot had human weaknesses. Then Lot was right again in offering his daughters.

It almost seems to the reader outside Bethel as if different ones are struggling over control of the typewriter, with the battle going back and forth between this faction and that faction.

It's one thing for the light to grow brighter, but another thing for it to be blinking on and off.

And when the matter involves our actions, such as how we treat disfellowshipped persons, it is difficult for a brother or sister who has come into a relationship with Jehovah to put conscience aside so as to jump when Simon says, "Jump!," sit when Simon says, "Sit!," and jump when Simon says, "Jump!" again.

2) When the Society does change its position, as cited above, usually the new article attacks the old position as if the Society had never held it at all—as if the former position was one that "no reasonable person" would ever support, but only fools or apostates. One wonders if the writer of the earlier article has really changed his mind or if he has been removed and perhaps disciplined. . . .

3) The Society appears to be divided on whether to keep in force the male grooming styles of the 1950s as a permanent standard for Christian men. While the *James** book and the Sept. 1, 1981, *Watchtower* say we shouldn't be judging our brothers on such personal matters, other current information says just the opposite.

For example, at the Divine Loyalty assembly in Providence, Rhode Island, Bro. Jack Barr of the Governing Body, in his talk "Forward You Ministers," spoke approvingly of a "clean-cut" young man, stated that we should "stand out as different among worldlings" in our grooming and suggested we follow the elders' example in grooming. (I wrote him asking if this was his personal opinion or if he had a Scriptural basis for the counsel he gave. His reply did not refer to a single scripture but warned me to "guard against . . . making an issue" of this matter. I wanted to question him further but feared that I would get into trouble if I did.) . . .

In June a hard-working young ministerial servant (my fleshly brother, Jonathan Reed) in the Machias, Maine, congregation grew a neat, trim beard. When he rejected their orders to shave it off, the local elders immediately removed him from his assignments, took away his territory, and taught the congregation not to work with him or his wife in the field. . . .

But the thing that is most disturbing to me is the climate of intolerance—the almost witch-hunt mentality—that seems to be developing. Article after article stresses loyalty, obedience, submission—not so much to Jehovah and Christ Jesus as to the men who are writing the articles. Local elders, in turn, use words such as "disloyal," "rebellious," "apostate" to describe any who disagree with them, even in such inconsequential matters as shaving and combing one's hair. . . .

The situation is most disturbing to me and to many others that I know. I have been praying to Jehovah about these matters day and night for months. And now I am turning to you for whatever counsel or advice you might have to offer as to how I might cope with these things. If you prefer not to put your answer in writing, perhaps you could tell me how to reach you by phone or call me collect . . . some evening soon. It is at considerable risk that I have written you—obtaining a copy of this letter would facilitate the local elders' efforts to

---

*Anonymous, *Commentary on the Letter of James* (Brooklyn: Watchtower Society, 1979).

remove me, or even begin judicial proceedings for "apostasy" if they so desired. But I feel that the need to maintain an honest conscience before Jehovah is more important than keeping a position before men.

A few days later this prominent leader—I'll call him Brother X— phoned me from Watchtower headquarters to say that he would soon be flying out of Brooklyn for a speaking tour abroad but that I could reach him in his office that Saturday morning, when he would have opportunity to speak more privately. I returned his call at the time he specified and learned of his behind-the-scenes leadership role in writing and editing Watchtower Society publications over the years. Some of the articles I cited to him as presenting a moderate, reasonable view turned out to be ones he himself had authored. "They wouldn't get past the censorship today," he added.

Brother X acknowledged that there was, indeed, a sort of struggle over the typewriters going on at headquarters. "They're throwing the best people out of the organization," he lamented. When I asked why, he responded by characterizing the Governing Body as "a bunch of old men off on a kick." This led me to ask Brother X why he remained with the organization. "I've been in full-time service most of my life," he replied. "How could I go back to [digging ditches] at my age?" Now he was past retirement age. He hadn't been in the secular labor force long enough to earn a Social Security retirement check, never mind invest money for his old age. If he left Bethel now he could easily find himself sleeping on a park bench or in a homeless shelter. At Watchtower headquarters he would at least have meals guaranteed and a roof over his head as long as he could keep pushing a pencil, even if it meant working for an organization that had disappointed him.

I can't say that I was encouraged by my conversation with Brother X, but I was definitely relieved. Penni and I had finally found another intelligent human being who, although publicly admiring the emperor's new clothes, admitted privately that the emperor was naked. We weren't imagining all the problems we saw in "God's organization." The problems were really there. In fact, we had seen only the base of the mountain; Brother X was positioned high enough to see the rest of it, and he assured us it was rotten all the way to the top.

When appealing my own removal from the body of elders, I had specifically requested an appeal committee that would be made up of elders from outside our immediate area, since I knew that standard practice was to use men from a neighboring congregation, and these had been among the first to demand my removal. The Society sent in three older men—two of them gray-haired businessmen—from Rhode Island as a Special Committee that would hold hearings each Saturday morning until a decision could be reached. As these solemn sessions commenced on October 3, with the full body of elders from Brockton and the three Rhode Islanders seated in one room and a number of people sitting outside the closed door awaiting their opportunity to testify, I began to wonder about the sanity of "Christians" who would go to such great lengths in a dispute over an inch of hair. Somehow I was able to step back and look at the scene as a whole. Suddenly it hit me: we must be crazy to keep going along with all of this.

At the end of October Jonathan received word that the Machias elders were not satisfied with removing him from his position and driving his family out of the state; now they were filing formal charges of "slander," accusing him of speaking improperly about them and their actions—a charge that could result in his being disfellowshipped. The Special Committee hearing my case finally informed me on November 11 that it was recommending that the elders' action in removing me should be upheld. A week later we learned that a similar body was convening to hear Jonathan's appeal, but that it would be meeting in Maine, and he would have to go back up there if he wanted to be heard—a full day's drive from his new home in Massachusetts.

Not yet officially removed as an elder, I still held a responsible position in the congregation. As Service Overseer I was responsible for visiting the various Tuesday night book study groups—gatherings of fifteen to twenty Witnesses in private homes throughout the city—one group each month, for the purpose of encouraging them in their house-to-house activity. On one of my last such visits Paul Washington approached after the meeting to share a word of encouragement with me. An African-American in his early thirties, Paul was not yet baptized, although his wife was. He wanted to encourage me by telling me how he had recently overcome a problem.

Paul began by saying that he had started reading the Bible some weeks earlier, but the more he read the more confused he had become. Finally, he mentioned this confusion to one of the elders at Kingdom Hall, and this elder, Frank Salluchi, had given him some advice: Quit reading the Bible, and read only the Watchtower Society's publications instead. The advice proved to be good, Paul told me with real conviction in his voice. Since he'd stopped reading the Bible, his confused mental state had cleared right up. So he felt he ought to encourage me by sharing that piece of good news.

My mouth must have hung open as I searched for words. I couldn't believe that an elder would actually advise someone not to read the Bible. To me this was not good news but an atrocity. Although I was furiously indignant, I concealed my fury from Paul, since I realized he was merely the victim of such blasphemous advice, not the perpetrator. My response to Paul was measured and consisted of little more than letting him know that I disagreed with Frank Salluchi and that I felt his advice had been wrong. Paul's confusion should have been dealt with through deeper study, perhaps with Frank's assistance, rather than through abandonment of the Bible.

Yet I realized that the elder's approach was typical, and that I was the peculiar one in reading the Bible myself and in urging other Witnesses to do so. Still, I felt that I was right and that everyone at Kingdom Hall needed to hear that it was better to read the Bible than *The Watchtower*. So I began preparing my Thursday night Instruction Talk with that in mind. The fifteen-minute talk was the most important speaking part of the hour-long weekly Theocratic School meeting, usually assigned to an elder or a capable ministerial servant—always a male viewed as a teacher in the congregation. The assigned subject matter for my talk that week was the Bible book of Zechariah, based on a four-page discussion of it in the Society's book *All Scripture Is Inspired of God and Beneficial*.

I knew ahead of time that virtually no one at Kingdom Hall would have read the book of Zechariah itself in preparation for the meeting. Those who usually did their homework would read the material in the *All Scripture* book instead. So, I decided to set everyone straight.

During the course of delivering my talk to the hundred-odd JWs in attendance, I embellished the assigned material by adding this admonition of my own: "I know that most of us here tonight have read the article on the book of Zechariah in the *All Scripture* book, but that probably no one has sat down and read the book of Zechariah itself. And that is understandable, since we all lead busy lives. But we really ought to be giving priority to the Bible itself, rather than to what the Society has written about the Bible. After all, the Bible is inspired of God and teaches truths that are eternal, whereas Watchtower publications are written by men and have often needed correction as errors have been found in them. If you have only a limited amount of time for reading and study, and you find yourself forced to choose between reading Watchtower publications and reading the Bible itself, the wise choice would be to read the Bible rather than *The Watchtower*."

No one came forward to pull me off the speaker's platform or to unplug my microphone, as I feared might happen, but you could have heard a pin drop on the carpeted floor. Raised eyebrows replaced the ho-hum expressions on faces that normally nodded through Thursday night meetings. Such words had never been heard at Kingdom Hall before. Nor would they be heard again—at least not from the podium.

As I walked back to my seat with every eye in the auditorium still fixed on me in disbelief, I passed one of the attendants and heard him growl in my ear, "Now I know what you're up to!" The elders, too, began to realize what I was up to, and they never gave me another speaking assignment. But I wasn't going to let that stop me from saying things my friends needed to hear. There was still the opportunity to comment from my seat during the question-and-answer study of the *Watchtower* magazine on Sunday mornings.

By the beginning of November the proceedings of the Special Committee had taken an unusual turn. One member of the Brockton congregation after another kept testifying that my wife and I set a good example as JWs, while the other elders who had accused me were in fact the instigators of the problem. Moreover, some were testifying to abuses by these elders in other areas, such as *their* family members dressing immodestly, *their* teaching not lining up with the organization's, *their* misuse of power. The Special Committee announced to all of us at its next-to-last meeting that it was considering whether to remove the other elders, rather than me.

Then at the beginning of its final meeting on November 11, the chairman of the Special Committee announced still another change of course. He had phoned the Service Department in Brooklyn and was told to focus on my qualifications rather than those of the other elders, and to remove me on the basis of the testimony received so far. The remainder of that final meeting would be devoted to determining whether or not I should also be disfellowshipped for apostasy. The committee members began asking me a series of questions from a loyalty test: Did I believe that this was God's organization? Did I believe that God used Watchtower publications to instruct his people? and so on. Although Penni and I were both ready to quit the sect, I chose my words very carefully so as to pass the test and avoid being disfellowshipped. Why? We had begun to see ourselves as residents of an apartment building on fire, and we felt an obligation to bang on doors and rouse the other tenants before fleeing to the street for our own safety— all the more so since twenty or more of those tenants were in the burning building because we had brought them there.

I should mention, however, the last circuit convention we attended on November 7, 1981, at the Assembly Hall in Natick, Massachusetts.

At the Assembly Hall were some two thousand people from our own congregation and neighboring congregations in our circuit, including dozens of elders who had rejected me as a visiting speaker due to my haircut. Attending was not a pleasant experience. Most shocking, though, was not the hostile looks from others in attendance, but rather the teaching that came from the pulpit.

One particular part of the program went under the title "Theocratic Subjection." Under the direction of a male overseer, it featured a dialogue between two women, one of them instructing the other in the proper view. Among other things the "instructor" said that women in the congregation "should not express disagreement with judicial decisions of the elders—not even by their facial expressions."

Penni and I sat stunned. We both held back from applauding with the rest of the audience. An older woman sitting next to Penni in the auditorium must have noticed her intentional failure to clap; she turned to her and said, very pointedly, "We really needed that counsel, didn't we!"

Penni and I questioned whether such a strong statement actually appeared in the Society's outline for that part of the program. We wondered whether the speakers might simply have gotten carried away with their parts and ad-libbed the offensive words. To check it out, I phoned a friendly District Overseer who had served our district at one time but was now stationed elsewhere in the country. He would have been in charge of identical assemblies in his locality, and he would have had in his possession the complete instructions furnished from Brooklyn for all parts of the program. Did the part titled "Theocratic Subjection" really call for the woman to say that women should not express disagreement with the elders, even by their facial expressions? Yes, was his reply. He himself found it as objectionable as we did, he confided, but he presented the information faithfully, nevertheless.

A letter from the Society confirming my removal as an elder arrived on December 14 and was read to the congregation on the seventeenth, but I could still participate in meetings like anyone else in the audience. I remember clearly the last time I was handed a microphone and allowed to answer a question from my seat. It was Sunday, January 17, 1982, and the lesson that morning was found in the December 1, 1981, *Watchtower,* an issue devoted to organizational loyalty. An earlier part of the lesson discussed at a prior meeting had said:

> What is your attitude toward directives from "the faithful and discreet slave"? Loyalty should move you to be "ready to obey." . . . Instead of forging ahead with our own ideas and methods, let us willingly submit to the theocratic arrangement, recognizing the channel through

which Jehovah directs his people.[19]

But that morning the lesson consisted of the third study article, titled "The Path of the Righteous Does Keep Getting Brighter," beginning on page 26. I planned to comment on the paragraph on page 27 that said, "Unless we are in touch with this channel of communication that God is using, we will not progress along the road to life, no matter how much Bible reading we do." To me, that was a blasphemous elevation of man's word above God's, and I wanted to say so. But the study conductor did not call on me for that paragraph.

The lesson went on to discuss helping JWs accept the Society's back-and-forth doctrinal changes over the years. It said:

> However, it may have seemed to some as though that path has not always gone straight forward. At times explanations given by Jehovah's visible organization have shown adjustments, seemingly to previous points of view. But this has not actually been the case. This might be compared to what is known in navigational circles as "tacking." By maneuvering the sails the sailors can cause a ship to go from right to left, back and forth, but all the time making progress toward their destination in spite of contrary winds.[20]

An accompanying drawing showed a sailboat and its zigzag path as it went tacking into the wind. The article glossed over doctrinal reversals on matters such as the prominence of Christ, the identity of the "higher powers" or "superior authorities" of Romans 13, and the application of the word "minister" among Jehovah's Witnesses—issues on which the Society had reversed its teaching, only to revert to the old view a few years later.

Older members of the congregation who raised their hands and received the microphone reminisced about these changes, confessing that they had felt a particular teaching was wrong at the time, but they had stuck loyally with the organization anyway and expressed no disagreement with the teaching they had regarded as error. The Watchtower Study Conductor commended them for their loyalty.

Then a paragraph on page 30 attacked worldly patriots who express their national loyalty by declaring, " 'Our country! . . . may she always be in the right; but our country, right or wrong.' " Yet, to me, that was exactly the way my fellow Witnesses had just been expressing their own organizational loyalty. So, I raised my hand to answer, and when I was given the microphone I said, "How can we condemn the worldly people for saying,

'Our country, right or wrong,' when people here at Kingdom Hall this morning are saying, 'The Watchtower Society, right or wrong!'?"

People gasped. Every head in the hall turned to see who would say such a thing. The Study Conductor disparaged my comment and called on another elder for the "correct" answer. I was never handed the microphone again.

Prevented from giving talks, and now even from commenting from my seat in the audience, I was effectively silenced at Kingdom Hall. But that did not matter, as I had already found another way of speaking out. The organizational boasts and outright falsehoods in that issue of *The Watchtower* had so offended me that I had already typed up and mailed out an answer. I set it up as a two-column newsletter on legal size paper, with the tacking sailboat illustration clipped from the magazine and pasted in, and with the handwritten heading "Comments from the Friends." Not wanting to be disfellowshipped and shunned by family and friends, I wrote that I was a Witness in good standing, but used the pen name "Bill Tyndale, Jr."—explaining that I felt like early Bible translator William Tyndale who hid to avoid being arrested for disagreeing with church authorities in England. (Tyndale was eventually captured, strangled, and burned at the stake.)

With JW relatives living in the same apartment building, Penni and I were careful about mailing out my underground newsletter. After printing a thousand copies and addressing envelopes to local Witnesses and to Kingdom Halls across the country, from addresses listed in out-of-town phone books in the public library, we filled several grocery bags with them and slipped out of the house late at night. Knowing that a local postmark would implicate us, we drove across state lines and mailed hundreds from post offices in Connecticut and Rhode Island. Since it was close to Christmas, I also sent a batch in a large parcel to the postmaster in Bethlehem, Pennsylvania, to be remailed from there with the "Bethlehem" postmark, as many people did with Christmas cards. A similar parcel went to the town of Truth-or-Consequences, New Mexico, for mailing with that meaningful postmark.

Only later did we learn that the Watchtower Society received phone calls from elders all over the country about the mailings. Brooklyn headquarters officials pieced together the postmarks from several states and feared that there was a nationwide underground movement among JWs. When judicial committees questioned members suspected of apostasy, they began asking the suspects if they were part of "the Tyndale group."

By February 1, I had published and mailed a second issue, and had already dropped hints to close friends that I was responsible for the literature that was causing such a stir. They apparently reported their suspicions to the elders and to other Witnesses. We began to feel some heat.

When Penni answered the phone one evening, the caller asked for me. Thinking she recognized the voice as my friend and former student Tim Burgess, Penni passed me the phone with the words, "Here, David! It's Tim, for you."

"This isn't Tim," the anonymous caller began. "And if I get another one of those things in the mail I'm going to come over and take care of you personally." With that he hung up.

At that point we decided to stop attending Kingdom Hall meetings: we could live with verbal harassment, but threats of physical violence were too much. The verbal and emotional gauntlet we had to run at the hall was already taking its toll on Penni. Less sensitive to that sort of thing, I had pushed her to keep attending as long as possible, even after we realized that the organization was not "the Truth" as we had been taught to think. It was our only opportunity to help rescue the twenty-five or so we had brought in, including some of our close relatives. But now, with the threat of physical violence, I gave in to Penni's request for relief.

One dark night, a few days after our final meeting at Kingdom Hall, two elders accosted my wife and me on the street outside our apartment building, where they had been sitting in a parked car waiting for us to return home. They wanted us to face trial before a judicial committee for publishing my newsletter. We told them they would have to try us *in absentia*. After having sat through dozens of hours of trials and appeal hearings concerning half an inch of hair, it seemed pointless to submit to additional trials. On February 24 the elders phoned again to inform us they had met and disfellowshipped us.

I placed small newspaper ads stating that the elders were about to disfellowship us for exposing Watchtower teachings not found in the Bible—small postage stamp-sized ads in the Brockton *Enterprise*, the Boston *Herald American*, and the New York *Daily News*. It was through responses to those ads that my wife and I first made contact with other ex-Witnesses and with counter-cult organizations. Afterward, by placing further ads inviting ex-JWs and other concerned individuals to phone our number for a recorded message available twenty-four hours a day, we were able to start a small support group for people suffering ill effects in one way or another due to the sect. Since then we have linked up with similar support groups across the country, so that we can often direct people to sources of help in their own community. Eventually, in 1986, I wrote *Jehovah's Witnesses Answered Verse by Verse* so that such helpful information could be more widely available. (Besides the more than 100,000 copies distributed by Baker Book House, it has also been published in French, Spanish, Portuguese, and Romanian.) Hundreds of letters of response to that book convinced me of the need to write *How to Rescue Your Loved One from the Watchtower*, which Baker published in 1989. Readers seeking such referrals or help are welcome to write to David A. Reed, P.O. Box 819, Assonet, MA 02702, or e-mail comments @ ultramet.com. All such inquiries are kept strictly confidential.

Virtually all former Witnesses we've spoken with have had a difficult time leaving the organization and re-adapting to life outside. Penni and I quickly began to realize that Watchtower thinking had totally dominated our minds, from the most important matters to the smallest affairs of life. Now all of that had to change.

Some things changed automatically. I remember stopping for traffic and seeing an old woman on the sidewalk lugging a couple of heavy shopping bags. In the past I would have looked down my nose at her, dismissing her and her difficulties; she was a "worldly person," an enemy, whom God would destroy at Armageddon along with the rest of this wicked world. Now I saw her as a fellow human being, and I felt compassion. It was a refreshing feeling.

Other changes in our outlook came with greater difficulty. Without yet calling it such, Penni and I were actually "deprogramming" ourselves: we were examining our beliefs one at a time and re-evaluating each one separately. It was a slow, painstaking process. Actually, it was very much like the study program we had followed to become Jehovah's Witnesses in the first place, only now we were running it in reverse and unlearning the things we had learned. The difference was that the original study was laid out for us in the pages of a book, with one issue following another in predetermined order, while the unlearning process was more random and brought on by necessity. A form letter came in the mail soliciting funds for Red Cross disaster relief: should we contribute? Thanksgiving Day was coming up: should we buy a turkey? Election day was approaching: should we register to vote? All of these are questions a JW would automatically answer with a strong "no!" We lay awake at night talking about theology, too. If Jesus isn't Michael the Archangel, then who is he? Is the Holy Spirit really an impersonal force like electricity, as the Society taught us? Penni and I were fortunate to be going through this together. We were able to help deprogram each other. Things that I was slow to understand she grasped quickly, and vice versa.

What about our JW families and friends? We had been talking to them as much as we dared, trying to prepare them for our departure from the organization. Would they leave, too? Or would they remain Witnesses and shun us as they would be required to do? Penni had been talking to her sister Bonnie and to her parents. I had been talking to my brothers. We had friends, too, at Kingdom Hall who had agreed with the things we were saying and who had testified on our behalf at various judicial hearings. But when it started to become clear that the Society was going to have us expelled, most had immediately begun to distance themselves from us. Had we lost all of them? The Sunday morning following our expulsion, Penni and I decided to hold a meeting in our apartment—a time for Bible reading and prayer as an alternative for family and friends who might want to meet with us instead of going to Kingdom Hall. Our immediate families came; happily, we had not lost them. Eventually others began coming also, with as many as fifteen in attendance at one time.

Our purpose was not to start our own congregation or religious organization. We just wanted to provide a temporary alternative for those who were sick of Kingdom Hall but who were not yet ready to integrate with a local church or other fellowship. After all, we had all been taught that the other churches were lurking places of demons where the worship actually went to Satan the Devil, not to God.

Ex-Witnesses who don't undergo deprogramming, whether on their own or with outside help, never completely leave the organization. They carry Watchtower thinking with them, regardless of where they go physically. And because they are thinking like Witnesses but not doing the things expected of Witnesses, they also carry a lot of guilt. Brenda Derry is a prime example of this. A tall brunette of rather distinguished mien, she came to one of our early support group meetings in our home. Although she had left the organization some time before us, Brenda still believed most of what she had been taught as a JW. The mental residue was giving her emotional problems, she said. Penni encouraged Brenda to keep meeting with us to talk out some of her areas of concern, but we didn't hear from her again. But some years later, after I had written *Jehovah's Witnesses Answered Verse by Verse* and *How to Rescue Your Loved One from the Watchtower,* Brenda phoned me asking for help. She had never gone back to the organization, but her old JW beliefs were still troubling her. She wanted to know whether or not they were true. I told her my books would answer her questions, and I mailed her a gift copy of each. About a year ago Brenda dropped in on another support group session, now being held at the home of my brother Jonathan. I was there, too. She told the roughly ten people present—mostly ex-JWs—that she had a lot of unresolved questions haunting her and that she lived in fear of being destroyed by Jehovah God at Armageddon.

"Brenda, have you read my books?" I inquired, so as to know where to begin.

"No," she stated rather matter-of-factly. "You sent me two of them, but I was afraid, and so I burned them."

Brenda may have been a bit extreme in burning my books, but she is typical of former Jehovah's Witnesses who are still troubled by the sect's teachings five, ten, or even twenty years after leaving, because the indoctrination process has never been run through in reverse. Unless a conscious effort is made to re-examine the whole range of beliefs, reasoning afresh on whether each doctrine is true or false and rejecting those found wanting, the individual never gains real freedom.

People like Penni and me who were zealous JWs, but who objected to the organization's excesses, usually deprogram themselves in the process of leaving and manage to find a comfortable worldview more in conformity with reality; they build stable, happy lives outside the sect. But those who tire of the Watchtower's works program and simply stop going to meetings, or young people who violate the rules on smoking or sexual immorality and find themselves expelled, tend to feel guilty about their course. This guilt often makes them feel that the "brothers at headquarters" are more righteous than they themselves are. They may even find themselves defending the organization that expelled them. Such former Witnesses are doomed either to return to the organization eventually, through a humiliating reinstatement procedure, or to live in the shadow of fear and guilt.

Unfortunately, there are tens of thousands in this condition. It is not unusual for as many as thirty-five thousand members to be disfellowshipped in a single year, most for sexual sins.[21] As an elder, I personally sat on judicial committees involving cases of fornication, adultery, wife-swapping, and homosexuality.

The Witness who is out of the organization but has not been deprogrammed is like a runaway horse that has thrown off its rider but that remains saddled and bridled. It may run across the plains with wild horses, but the saddle binds and chafes. It may eat grass with wild horses, but the bridle interferes. Sooner or later another rider may mount the horse and take control. Or the saddle and bridle may cause sores that infect and lead to the animal's premature death. Real freedom comes only when the saddle and bridle are unbuckled and removed.

While a horse cannot unbuckle its own saddle, a former Witness may prove able to deprogram himself or herself, especially with the aid of books or tapes by others who have gone down the same road. However, help usually has to come from the outside, at least to start the ball rolling. Readjustment is often least painful for those who are able to connect with other ex-Witnesses. Some larger cities have support groups that meet regularly for this purpose. As many as two or three hundred ex-JWs at a time have gotten together for conventions to share experiences and encouragement, the largest of these being an annual gathering in eastern Pennsylvania that has been held for more than fifteen years.

Dissident but still practicing JWs occasionally work up the courage to attend such ex-member conventions or support groups. Usually, however, it is only those who are ready to leave who dare allow their faces to be seen at such gatherings. The secrecy of the Governing Body is exceeded, in fact, by that of the dissident underground movement that continues to function among JWs today. Some of the confidential Watchtower materials used in researching this book came from Witnesses who asked me to use a plain envelope when responding or who requested that correspondence be directed in care of a neighbor or relative or to a post office box rented under an assumed name. Many of the anonymous phone calls to my recorded message number came in during the middle of the night from callers bent on escaping observation by family members who would have reported them to the elders. In most cases it is family—the desire to avoid losing a JW wife and kids or the wish not to be shunned by relatives outside the home—that keeps dissidents inside the organization. Some stay just long enough to help loved ones find their way out, as my wife and I did after seeing the need to leave, while others see no hope of accomplishing such a rescue and instead elect to remain within the confines of the organization.

NOTES

1. For numerous examples, please see my book *Jehovah's Witnesses Answered Verse by Verse* (Grand Rapids, Mich.: Baker Book House, 1986).

2. Most of these are discussed in *The Jehovah's Witnesses' New Testament: A Critical Analysis of the New World Translation of the Christian Greek Scriptures* by Robert H. Countess (Phillipsburg, N.J.: Presbyterian and Reformed Publishing Co., 1987), a scholarly study that assumes a working knowledge of Greek on the part of the reader. Some of

the more important alterations are discussed in layman's terms in my own book *Jehovah's Witnesses Answered Verse by Verse*. Although accepted as authoritative by few except Jehovah's Witnesses themselves, nearly eighty million copies of the *New World Translation* are circulating in a dozen languages.

3. Suggestions for avoiding disaster when trying to intervene to stop a person from studying with the Witnesses are found in my book *How to Rescue Your Loved One from the Watchtower* (Grand Rapids, Mich.: Baker Book House, 1989).

4. *The Watchtower,* January 15, 1983, pp. 22 and 27.

5. Raymond Franz, *Crisis of Conscience,* 2d ed. (Atlanta: Commentary Press, 1991), p. 296.

6. *The Watchtower,* August 1, 1974, pp. 464, 465, 471.

7. *The Watchtower,* November 15, 1988, p. 19.

8. Ibid.

9. *The Watchtower,* September 1, 1987, p. 12.

10. Ibid., p. 13

11. Ibid., p. 15.

12. *The Watchtower,* January 15, 1961, p. 64.

13. *Jehovah's Witnesses—Proclaimers of God's Kingdom* (Brooklyn, N.Y.: Watchtower Society, 1993), p. 232.

14. See *The Watchtower,* April 1, 1979, p. 31, and November 15, 1979, pp. 21–27.

15. Franz, *Crisis of Conscience,* p. 255.

16. *The Watchtower,* January 15, 1983, pp. 22 and 27.

17. Franz, *Crisis of Conscience,* pp. 302–303.

18. *The Watchtower,* September 15, 1981, pp. 16–31.

19. *The Watchtower,* December 1, 1981, p. 14.

20. Ibid., p. 27.

21. *The Watchtower,* September 15, 1987, p. 13.

9

The Kingdom versus the World

Fourteen-year-old Kevin Rattenbury of Chesterfield Township, Michigan, was riding a moped when struck by an automobile on August 6, 1991. He agreed with his parents in refusing a blood transfusion. Kevin died while doctors were trying to obtain a court order to proceed, according to reports in the Cleveland Plain Dealer *and the* Chicago Tribune *of August 14, 1991.*

This statement by the Watchtower Society's second president sums up the Jehovah's Witness worldview: "The clergy, the profiteers, and the politicians are in an alliance to govern the peoples of earth, and their god or invisible ruler is Satan the Devil, the prince of evil."[1] That is, everything that is not part of their organization is part of the Devil's world. Therefore, JWs expect to come into conflict with everyone else in virtually every aspect of life. Unlike the Branch Davidians, they don't retreat into a cult compound to hold off the outside world with heavy weapons; unlike the followers of Rev. Jim Jones, they don't withdraw to the jungles of Guyana to construct an isolated Jonestown; but Jehovah's Witnesses do erect invisible barriers between themselves and the outside world. These barriers and resulting conflicts fall into three general areas: political, social, and doctrinal, although some naturally overlap with others.

POLITICAL BARRIERS

"And in the days of these kings shall the God of heaven set up a kingdom, which shall never be destroyed: and the kingdom shall not be left to other people, but it shall break in pieces and consume all these kingdoms, and it shall stand for ever" (Daniel 2:44 King James version). Jehovah's Witnesses share with other Bible-based fundamentalist groups the belief that the kingdom of God will someday literally replace human governments, with Christ ruling in the place of our present prime ministers, presidents, and kings. One major difference is that Jehovah's Witnesses see God's kingdom as *already* ruling, not just in a spiritual sense over those who look to Christ personally as Lord, but literally through their Brooklyn-based organization (see chapter 7). This transforms the existing secular governments into rivals—enemies—of the Watchtower kingdom to which Witnesses give their allegiance.

JWs are taught that participation in the political process—voting or holding office as an elected official—is off limits. Even casting a ballot for the local dogcatcher or signing a candidate's nomination papers can result in a summons to appear before a judicial committee. The charge? Violating "Christian neutrality." Under the headline "Voting costs man religion, friends," a front-page article in the July 16, 1993, *Butler Eagle* reported that Steven Crawford, a local man in Brady's Bend Township, Pennsylvania, was formally "disassociated" from the organization for participating in the previous year's primary and general elections. Crawford himself must have brought the story to the attention of the small-town newspaper, since such expulsions normally escape notice by the press. (Although disassociation usually refers to voluntary departure from the sect, the word is sometimes used in cases like this, when the "sin" of the offending JW involves exercise of a civic right or duty. The organization would be embarrassed to say it expelled someone for voting, so it declares that the person disassociated himself by his course of action.)

Even though the Bible depicts the Apostle Peter as baptizing Roman army officer Cornelius (Acts 10), Jehovah's Witnesses will not baptize a soldier. He must first resign from the military. They do not claim to be pacifists, however. They would gladly serve in "God's army," as they believe ancient Israel's warrior-kings did, but they insist on remaining neutral in conflicts between modern-day secular governments. If Brooklyn headquarters instructed JWs to fight, they would do so readily.

In fact, during the late 1930s, when physical conflict erupted between Witnesses and supporters of radio priest Father Charles Coughlin who showed up to disrupt their conventions, the organization supplied to each young male usher "a sturdy cane to be used in the event of any interference."[2] When five hundred of the priest's militant supporters filled an upper balcony and took up booing and yelling during Judge Rutherford's lecture at Madison Square Garden on June 25, 1939, large numbers of ushers waded into them, flailing their canes. "A couple of the more obstreperous Coughlinites were rapped on the head with a cane, and all of them were unceremoniously hurled down the ramps and out of the auditorium," testified an eyewitness.[3] New York City tabloids displayed a photo of one of Coughlin's men, his head bandaged like a turban, to accompany their reports on the disturbance. Three Witness ushers were arrested for assault but later acquitted.

Before the end of the draft, young JWs reaching the age of eighteen and facing the prospect of military conscription were encouraged to enter the "pioneer work" as full-time door-to-door preachers and to apply for exemption as ministers. Draft boards that classified them as conscientious objectors—the classification commonly sought by Quakers, Mennonites, Brethren, and members of other pacifist churches—were often surprised to see JWs refuse this as firmly as they refused military service. They would not obey a draft board's assignment to perform civilian alternative service work in a hospital or other public facility.

🌿   🌿   🌿

"My life is dedicated to the service of the Most High," read the press report, "and I cannot serve two masters." Those words from my statement to the British Ministry of Labour and National Service authorities in 1941 presented my reason for refusing their direction to do hospital work during World War II. Shortly thereafter I was convicted and sentenced to three months in prison for my refusal.

Hilda Padgett spoke those words at a time when women in England were subject to the call, and her account of the position she took is quoted in the October 1, 1995, *Watchtower*[4] as an example for others to follow. The sect required potential conscripts to accept only total exemption from service—usually a minister's exemption—which allowed them to continue going door to door full time distributing the Society's literature; if that was not granted, they would have to refuse the draft board's orders and face prosecution as lawbreakers. (Any who compromised by accepting either military service or alternative conscientious objector service were tried *in absentia* by a church court and ordered shunned as disassociated persons—as in the case of the Pennsylvania man who exercised his right to vote.)

Since their allegiance belongs to God's kingdom, as represented on earth by the Watchtower organization, naturally JWs will not salute or pledge their allegiance to any nation or to the flag of any nation. Moreover, they have been taught that flags are objects of worship, idols made of cloth. The *Awake!* magazine of September 8, 1971, calls a flag "an idolatrous symbol" and asserts that "historical works trace national flags back to the standards used by armies of ancient peoples such as the Egyptians, Persians, and Romans."[5] The Society's publications ignore the fact that the ancient Israelites, who were required by the Law of Moses to avoid idols, freely employed standards or flags to mark the encampments of their different families and clans (Num. 1:52; 2:1–2).

A JW member who salutes a flag or who pledges allegiance is put on trial before a judicial committee and punished through forced shunning. Most adults, of course, seldom encounter situations that would put this belief to the test, but Witness parents thoroughly indoctrinate their children on the matter before sending them to public school. This policy gained them considerable notoriety in the United States. On November 6, 1935, schoolchildren William and Lillian Gobitas were expelled from school in Minersville, Pennsylvania, for refusing to salute the flag. Their father went to court to have them readmitted. He won the case, but the school district appealed. Gobitas won the appeal, but then school officials took it to the United States Supreme Court. By then, World War II was raging in Europe and the Far East, American involvement was becoming a certainty, and emotions were swayed by fear and patriotic fervor. Rendering its eight-to-one decision in 1940 in the case of *Minersville School District* v. *Gobitis* (*sic*), the Supreme Court upheld compulsory flag saluting in public schools.[6]

With the explosive atmosphere in the country at the time, the overwhelming decision against the Witnesses triggered a wave of persecution. Swaggering bullies pulled out flags at every opportunity—at places of employment, at the doorstep when Witnesses called, and in public places—with orders for the hapless JWs to salute, *or else!* Like African-Americans handed over to mobs by racist Southern sheriffs during the pre-civil rights era, Witnesses were often treated as if outside the protection of the law. Between 1940 and 1944 there were reportedly 2,500 cases of mob violence against sect members in the United States.[7] Meeting places, homes, and automobiles were trashed and burned, while the victims themselves were assaulted, beaten, viciously abused, jailed, and sometimes even shot. Law enforcement authorities often stood by as observers or actively participated in the abuse.

Even before the flag salute issue unleashed such mob violence, Jehovah's Witnesses had come into conflict with the law over many other issues. Seeing themselves as God's representatives, they refused to apply for door-to-door salesmen's licenses or permits to hold public meetings, and they refused to pay license taxes on the sale of literature from house to house. When they carried picket signs outside churches or through downtown streets, with slogans such as "Religion is a snare and a racket," they refused to apply for parade permits. Moreover, since the Society taught them that paying a fine constituted an admission of guilt (a teaching that was reversed in 1975), they refused to pay and went to jail instead—by the hundreds in some cases. Arrests of JWs in the United States exceeded a thousand in 1936 and totaled more than ten thousand between 1934 and 1949.[8]

Nearly a hundred and forty JW legal cases have gone to the U.S. Supreme Court. Watchtower president J. F. Rutherford resumed his role as an attorney for some of these, but most of them—one hundred eleven cases from 1939 to 1963—were handled by Hayden Covington, who succeeded Rutherford as the Society's counsel. Covington's experience with JWs who refused the draft made him the nation's top defense lawyer against Selective Service prosecutions. On June 14—Flag Day—1943, the Supreme Court announced a six-to-three decision in *West Virginia State Board of Education* v. *Barnette* that overturned the earlier *Gobitas* decision. It barred public schools from imposing compulsory flag saluting. With this decision, and with the end of the war, tempers cooled and Jehovah's Witnesses in the United States resumed a more peaceful life.

In retrospect, the conflict over the flag was not really an instance of outsiders deciding to go after the Witnesses; it was more precisely a case of both parties deciding to step into the arena for the battle. For decades previously, the Witnesses had had no objections to the American flag, and even made patriotic use of it themselves. The *Watch Tower* of May 15, 1917, made this observation about Brooklyn headquarters:

> Since the Bethel Home was established, in one end of the Drawing Room there has been kept a small bust of Abraham Lincoln with two American flags displayed about the bust. This is deemed entirely proper. . . .[9]

That was printed during the early months of Judge Rutherford's presidency; he whipped up the sect's opposition to the flag later, as an afterthought—just in time for others to whip up their opposition to the Witnesses.

Similar conflict has erupted over the years between JWs and various foreign governments. The most serious problems occurred in Nazi Germany, where Hitler's government not only banned dissent but also demanded active support from the entire population. Thousands of Witnesses ended up in concentration camps. The sect has typically encountered problems under totalitarian regimes and in lands where war fever or newly won independence fosters extreme nationalism. Placing "God's law," as expounded from Brooklyn, above the demands of the secular state, Witnesses refuse to abandon their routine of meetings and door-to-door work, or to participate in patriotic ceremonies, regardless of the consequences. Long-term oppression, first by Nazis and then by Communists, resulted in the organization operating underground in Eastern Europe for decades. Such persecution has proved to be a mixed blessing for the sect. While timid folk are discouraged from joining under such circumstances, the illegal operations conducted under cover in totalitarian states draw some converts who are glad to join any sort of a resistance movement; meanwhile, JWs around the globe point to examples of persecution as evidence that they are following in Jesus' footsteps as the only true Christians.

SOCIAL BARRIERS

Jehovah's Witnesses are taught to take Jesus' words about being "not of the world" (John 17:14-16) as a basis for separating themselves from non-Witnesses. They do not go so far as to retreat into a fenced-off cult compound, but they normally avoid sharing a home or apartment with an unbeliever unless compelled by family obligations. Marrying or even dating an unbeliever brings disciplinary action by the elders.

A JW will accept employment from others and, if the Witness owns a farm or business, will hire outsiders, but the sect discourages partnership arrangements with a nonmember. Employment by another church or a political or military organization—even as a clerk, window washer, or cafeteria worker—is prohibited. The same is true of jobs in the tobacco industry or in gambling establishments.

Socializing with nonmembers is frowned upon, unless part of a strategy whose immediate aim is to initiate the conversion process—such as when inviting a Witness and her unbelieving husband to dinner, in the hope of starting a Bible study with him. Some individual discretion is allowed when it comes to unbelieving relatives. Looking after the needs of an elderly parent is always acceptable, but many see the need to do some witnessing to siblings or cousins in order to justify a visit with them.

In practice, the sect's taboo against holiday and birthday celebrations automatically rules out attending most office parties and family gatherings. The chief objection to Christmas, Easter, and Halloween is their alleged pagan origin. Birthday celebrations—whether children's or those of Washington, Lincoln, or Martin Luther King—are improper because they exalt an individual rather than God. Watchtower publications also cite biblical accounts of Pharaoh and King Herod executing prisoners on the monarch's birthday. (Nevertheless, the July 1, 1979, *Watchtower* was a "special issue"[10] celebrating a century of publication, and the Watch Tower corporation celebrated its own hundredth birthday—its "Centennial to Remember"—in 1984.[11]) Mother's Day and Father's Day similarly exalt individuals. The political connotations of Labor Day, Memorial Day, and Independence Day eliminate them from the JW's social calendar. New Year's Day can be traced to a pagan Roman god, and even Thanksgiving Day must be avoided because non-Witnesses give thanks on that day, and sharing with them would constitute interfaith worship which JWs see as spiritual adultery.

Birthdays and holidays are especially difficult times for Witness kids in school. A kindergarten or early elementary class of thirty children finds itself singing "Happy Birthday" to someone nearly every week, or coloring commemorative pictures of Columbus, Washington, Lincoln, or Thanksgiving turkeys—all of which furnish occasions for the child to ask to be excused. Of course, the daily stress of standing silently through a flag ceremony helps toughen the youngsters to standing out as different on other occasions. Parents also inform their child's junior high or high school teacher at the beginning of each year that Johnnie or Susie won't be taking part in extracurricular sports, the chess club, the journalism club, the future-anything club, or going to school dances or outings; even if the activity itself isn't objectionable, the "worldly" association with non-Witness youngsters and the time such activities would take away from more important spiritual pursuits are sufficient reasons for JWs to exclude their kids.

Also off-limits to young Witnesses are the Boy Scouts, Girl Scouts, and Cub Scouts (too militaristic!); the "Y" (originally Young Men's or Young Women's *Christian* Association—another religion!); and any other outside club or pursuit (bad association! and a waste of time!). Yet the Watchtower Society provides neither youth groups nor Sunday school classes as an alternative, just a seat in the audience at adult Kingdom Hall meetings. The youth activities usually found in churches are missing from the JW organization.

Similarly, social welfare programs are another common feature of religious organizations conspicuously absent from this sect. The only exception occurs when temporary efforts are mounted to aid the victims of natural disasters through shipments of food and clothing or through volunteer cleanup and construction crews. In these cases, however, such aid is generally given only to fellow religionists in the affected locality—not to the suffering population in general. As their own *Proclaimers* book admits, "The relief efforts of the Witnesses are not meant to care for the physical needs of everyone in the disaster area. . . . these are intended primarily for 'those related to them in the faith.' "[12] Members are taught that their God-given assignment involves ministering to the spiritual needs of humankind, not to their material needs.

With marriage to a nonmember a punishable offense, religiously divided homes generally come about through conversions, when one mate joins the sect and the other does not. Sometimes the convert is an individual raised by Witness parents but never baptized; when religious interest suddenly revives later in life, a return to Kingdom Hall is the natural route of least resistance. In other cases it is a partner who responds to a knock at the door and hears the JW message for the first time after marriage. In either situation the development injects new tension into the couple's relationship, especially if there arc young children in the home.

As with couples from any two differing belief systems, conflict often centers around the basic issue of whether to raise the child in mom's or dad's religion. When one mate is a Jehovah's Witness, however, the matter isn't that simple. Even if the non-Witness is religiously apathetic and content to let the JW mate handle the children's religious training, the sect's numerous prohibitions can still lead to contention: "What? You won't let our Tommy join the Little League!" "Marie just wants to go to the birthday party next door. How can you object?" The JW parent is constantly blocking activities that the other parent perceives as unobjectionable, even desirable, for the youngster.

Much more serious, of course, are the issues that can arise when there's been a serious accident and a child needs medical treatment. *Our Kingdom Ministry* of September 1992 tells Witnesses to "be firmly resolved before any emergency comes up to refuse blood for yourself and your children."[13] By the time elders from Kingdom Hall arrive at the hospital and start talking directly to the surgeon and the pediatrician about avoiding objectionable procedures, many a non-JW parent is ready for a fight.

Religiously mixed marriages involving Witnesses often end up in divorce court, where the Watchtower Society regularly provides assistance through printed materials and its own legal staff. (As mentioned in chapter 1, CBS's "60 Minutes" devoted a segment to this in their program of December 29, 1992.) A booklet of more than sixty pages, titled *Direct and Cross-Examination Questions in Child Custody Cases*, prepares the JW parent by listing dozens of "cross-examination questions that Witness parent could face" and even offers various, often evasive, responses under the heading "Sample Approach by Witness Parent to Cross-Examination." For example, "Do you believe all Catholics (or others) will be destroyed?" Answer: "Jehovah makes those judgments, not we."

Several pages of questions for the lawyer to ask the non-Witness parent in court are also included. In addition, there are suggestions for elders called to testify, and for Witness young people brought in to show the court "that they are normal." Here the booklet openly suggests that the youngsters be instructed to testify to the exact opposite of what they would say if speaking "at a circuit assembly" to a Witness audience:

> Be careful that they don't get the impression that they are in a demonstration at a circuit assembly, when they would show that the first things in life are service and going to the Kingdom Hall. Show hobbies, crafts, social activity, sports, and especially plans for the future. Be careful they don't all say that they are going to be pioneers. Plans can be trade, getting married and having children, journalism, and all kinds of other things. Maybe you can show an interest in art and the theatre.[14]

JW youngsters are always taught that field service and Kingdom Hall activities should be "the most important thing in their lives."[15] Hobbies, crafts, social activities, and sports are usually presented in a negative light. For example: "Witness parents encourage their children to use after-school hours principally to pursue spiritual interests, rather than to excel in some sport. Participation in organized sports, we believe, would expose Witness youths to unwholesome associations."[16]

By instructing Witness kids called to testify in court to say the opposite of what they are really taught to believe, the Watchtower Society requires them to engage in a form of double-talk that most people would consider lying. And, unless the youngsters are to consciously see themselves as liars, they must also engage in doublethink, the mental gymnastics described in George Orwell's novel *Nineteen Eighty-Four*, where people are forced by a totalitarian society to be conscious of complete truthfulness while telling carefully constructed lies.

Another social barrier that Jehovah's Witnesses have erected between themselves and outsiders sometimes stands right in the middle of the marriage bed. I recall an occasion in late 1971 or early 1972, when my wife, Penni, started a free home Bible study with a shapely young woman whose husband displayed no interest whatsoever in religion. He told her, "You have my permission to become a Jehovah's Witness, as long as it won't interfere with our sex life." I laughed when I heard this, as I thought it rather paranoid on his part even to imagine such a possibility. Some months later, however, I was surprised to learn of the Governing Body's tendency to peer into bedroom intimacies.

The December 1, 1972, *Watchtower* magazine outlawed certain forms of sexual contact between husband and wife, particularly oral and anal intercourse. It instructed that "the elders should act to try to correct the situation" if any of these forbidden practices "are brought to their attention" and authorized them to disfellowship violators.[17] Immediately, thousands of guilt-ridden men and women began approaching their local elders to obtain the Society's stamp of approval for their bedroom conduct or to confess imagined wrongs. JW wives dragged their husbands before committees of elders for touching them improperly during foreplay or intercourse. Serious about their responsibility to enforce "God's law," many of these elders went on to interrogate the couples at length concerning the most intimate details of their loveplay. Then the elders, in turn, phoned or wrote Brooklyn headquarters with their questions about where to draw the line. Raymond Franz relates in his book *Crisis of Conscience* that this issue generated a considerable volume of correspondence and phone calls.[18]

The problem was particularly damaging to marriages with a non-Witness husband. In fact, it was just what the husband of my wife's student feared: that her becoming a JW might interfere with their sex life. When the 1972 ruling first came out, some such men found themselves excluded from the bedroom, while others received an invitation to accompany their wife to the local Kingdom Hall—not to hear a Bible lecture but to face a committee of three men who wanted to discuss his most private moments. Still other men whose Witness wives avoided either of these extremes were nevertheless irritated to learn that their sex practices had been submitted for approval by strangers before whom their wives had bared all the details. From his overview at headquarters Franz testified that marriages actually broke up as a direct result of this organizational policy, not to mention those couples who experienced rough sailing. Subsequent articles in *The Watchtower* have readjusted the organization's position on sexual intimacies within marriage, sometimes loosening the elders' hold and at other times tightening the restrictions.

DOCTRINAL BARRIERS

Jehovah's Witness Lysa Biffle was nine months pregnant when she was hit in the stomach by random bullets in New York City. The New York Post *reported on December 27, 1989, that Lysa underwent emergency surgery and a Caesarean section without blood. The article indicated that Dr. Irving Margolis, Queens General Hospital's head of surgery, had acquainted his patient with her urgent need for blood but quoted him as saying she "has been refusing blood or blood products." She died within hours.*

🌿   🌿   🌿

As illustrated in earlier chapters of this book, the doctrinal barriers separating Watchtower followers from their parent Adventist group—and from other denominations—came to be erected gradually over the course of several decades. Charles T. Russell published *Zion's Watch Tower* for more than a year before taking a stand in its pages against the doctrine of the Trinity. Joseph F. Rutherford held the presidency for nearly eighteen years before consigning subsequent converts to an earthly paradise rather than a heavenly reward. Frederick W. Franz had already served Nathan H. Knorr as his behind-the-scenes theologian for a few years when he banned blood transfusions.

Current doctrine is summarized most succinctly as fourteen "Beliefs of Jehovah's Witnesses" in a box covering pages 144 and 145 of *Jehovah's Witnesses—Proclaimers of God's Kingdom.* I list the "beliefs" here in bold italics, with my explanatory comments:

- ***"The Bible is God's inspired Word."*** Members automatically qualify this statement in their minds with the thought that the scripture must be explained by the Society in order to be properly understood: "the Bible is an organizational book. . . . For this reason the Bible cannot be properly understood without Jehovah's visible organization in mind."[19]

- *"Jehovah is the only true God."* Unlike broad-minded believers who promote religious unity with the thought that the people of Islam, Christendom, and Jewry all worship the same God, Jehovah's Witnesses see the true God as their exclusive possession. The Jews left him millennia ago, while Muslims have never known him. As for Christendom's Trinity, J. F. Rutherford declared, "Never was there a more deceptive doctrine advanced than that of the trinity. It could have originated only in one mind, and that the mind of Satan the Devil."[20] Converts from other churches must reorder their theology so that only the Father is God, while the Son is a created being and the Holy Spirit is an impersonal force.

- *"Jesus Christ is the only-begotten Son of God, the only one created directly by God himself."* JWs see Jesus as the human incarnation of Michael the Archangel. He did not become "Christ" until the time of his baptism at the age of thirty, and he died nailed to an upright pole without a crossbeam. The tomb was empty on Easter morning, not due to a bodily resurrection, but because "God disposed of Jesus' body" by dissolving it "into its constituent elements or atoms." Therefore, "the *man* Jesus is dead, forever dead" and only the spirit-creature Michael remains to rule as God's appointed king.[21]

- *"Satan is the invisible 'ruler of this world.' "* Although a mere angelic creature who rebelled and who will eventually be crushed out of existence—annihilated forever—the Devil is a powerful figure to JWs due to the forces he commands. He directs all of the world's governmental, commercial, and religious organizations, with the sole exception of the Watchtower Society.

- *"God's Kingdom under Christ will replace all human governments and will become the one government over all humankind."* As noted in an earlier chapter, Witnesses see their local Kingdom Hall and the Brooklyn organization as the visible portion of a real government to which they give their full allegiance. Christ is the chief executive officer, aided by a cabinet of a hundred forty-four thousand former humans now in heaven, with the few cabinet members remaining on earth today directing the Watchtower Society before their departure.

- *"We are living now, since 1914, in 'the time of the end' of this wicked world."* In 1969 when I was baptized, we believed that "the time of the end" was a fixed period spanning the years from 1914 to the world's end in 1975; the current belief is that it represents the life span of the final generation—that this wicked world will end and will be replaced by "a peaceful and secure new world before the generation that saw the events of 1914 passes away."[22]

• *"There is only one road to life; not all religions or religious practices are approved by God."* With its front cover featuring the title "Put Faith in a Victorious Organization," the March 1, 1979, *Watchtower* states this more bluntly: "Outside the true Christian congregation, what alternative organization is there? Only Satan's organization consisting of his political 'wild beast' and his Babylonian world empire of false religion."[23]

• *"Death is a result of inheritance of sin from Adam."* No spirit or soul survives the death of the body in Witness theology. Rather, death means annihilation, followed by a future resurrection, which consists of God recreating the individual from his memory.

• *"A 'little flock,' only 144,000, go to heaven."* Christ's twelve apostles were the first selected, and the final number was completed in 1935, with a small number of vacancies opening up since then only as unfaithfulness on the part of a few required that they be replaced.

• *"Others who have God's approval will live forever on earth."* More than 99.9 percent of the twelve million attending Kingdom Halls worldwide see this as their goal.

• *"Secular authorities are to be treated with due respect."* Witnesses look forward to the day when all government officials, soldiers, and policeman will be killed, but they expect heavenly executioners to do the job. Meanwhile, they view the authorities as dignitaries on death row.

• *"Christians must conform to Bible standards regarding blood as well as sexual morality."* Although the JW sexual mores coincide closely with those of other conservative sects, the leadership's authority to interpret Scripture converts Frederick Franz's mid-1940s decree banning blood transfusions into an eternal law of God in the minds of believers.

• *"Personal honesty and faithfulness in caring for marital and family responsibilities are important for Christians."* Statements like this that most people would readily agree with are usually the focus of introductory lessons, with the sect's more esoteric doctrines reserved for later.

• *"Acceptable worship of Jehovah requires that we love him above all else."* In practice, this translates into organizational obedience regardless of the cost. A young person training for a professional career instead of entering full-time door-to-door work would be showing a lack of love for God. Accepting a blood transfusion in a life-or-death situation would represent failure to love God above life itself.

It should be noted that the *Proclaimers* book's list of JW beliefs omits the sect's principal doctrine, namely, that the Watchtower Society is God's "channel of communication," the Deity's spokesman to humankind—as will be discussed in the following chapter.

NOTES

1. J. F. Rutherford, *Government* (Brooklyn, N.Y.: Watchtower Society, 1928), p. 329.

2. *1975 Yearbook of Jehovah's Witnesses* (Brooklyn, N.Y.: Watchtower Society), p. 18.

3. Ibid.

4. *The Watchtower,* October 1, 1995, p. 19.

5. *Awake!* September 8, 1971, p. 12.

6. *Jehovah's Witnesses—Proclaimers of God's Kingdom* (Brooklyn, N.Y.: Watchtower Society, 1993), p. 670.

7. Ibid., p. 671.

8. Ibid., p. 680.

9. *The Watch Tower,* May 15, 1917, p. 150.

10. *The Watchtower,* July 1, 1979, p. 3.

11. *The Watchtower,* January 1, 1985, p. 16.

12. *Jehovah's Witnesses—Proclaimers of God's Kingdom,* p. 315.

13. *Our Kingdom Ministry,* September 1992, p. 3.

14. *Direct and Cross-Examination Questions in Child Custody Cases* (Brooklyn, N.Y.: Watchtower Society), p. 42.

15. *The Watchtower,* April 1, 1979, p. 14.

16. *School and Jehovah's Witnesses* (Brooklyn, N.Y.: Watchtower Society, 1983), p. 23.

17. *The Watchtower,* December 1, 1972, p. 735.

18. Raymond Franz, *Crisis of Conscience* (Atlanta: Commentary Press, 1983), pp. 42–48.

19. *The Watchtower,* October 1, 1967, p. 587.

20. J. F. Rutherford, *Reconciliation* (Brooklyn, N.Y.: Watchtower Society, 1928), p. 101.

21. *The Watchtower,* November 15, 1991, p. 31; September 1, 1953, p. 518; *Studies in the Scriptures* (Brooklyn, N.Y.: Watchtower Society, 1899), vol. 5, p. 454.

22. *Awake!* September 8, 1995, p. 4.

23. *The Watchtower,* March 1, 1979, p. 23.

10

God's Channel of Communication

Jehovah's Witness Brian Hunt, a forty-nine-year-old technician from Bromley, Kent, England, "bled to death for his beliefs, despite hospital doctors' warnings that his life was at stake," according to testimony at a subsequent inquest, as reported in the British Western Morning News *of August 28, 1992. Hunt had signed forms "refusing to have blood under any circumstances."*

What is the chief doctrine of Jehovah's Witnesses? What primary characteristic sets them apart from other sects? What is their most important distinguishing feature? The answer, strangely enough, has nothing to do with their theology, their view of the soul, or their concept of the afterlife. Nor does it involve their refusal to salute the flag, their rejection of blood transfusions, or their insistence that members go out knocking on doors. The central doctrine of Jehovah's Witnesses—the belief on which all of these others depend—is the teaching that the Watchtower organization is God's "channel of communication," "the one and only channel which the Lord has used in dispensing his truth," "God's visible organization" operating "under the immediate direction of Jehovah God himself."[1]

Failure to grasp this point explains why religious opponents—or would-be rescuers of a loved one in the sect—are so often frustrated. They spend hours upon hours debating doctrine, looking up Bible verses, and arguing the merits of blood transfusions, yet they accomplish nothing. Their arguments may hit the mark, but they are aiming at the wrong target, so nothing happens as a result. Taking aim at the JW's view of the

Trinity or hellfire, instead of focusing on the organization's claim to be God's spokesman, is comparable to what happens in a bullfight when the bull charges the cape instead of the matador—what a waste of energy!

Why? Because a Jehovah's Witness's belief that Jesus is an angel is not based on Scripture, and the belief in an earthly reward for those baptized after 1935 is not based on logic; that is why no amount of opposing Scripture or logic will shake these beliefs. Rather, these and all other JW beliefs are based on one thing, namely, the fact that the Watchtower Society has said, *This* is what you must believe. Since the various doctrines are all supported entirely by the organization's authority, the only way to bring them down is to bring down that authority. Taking aim at the doctrines themselves proves as ineffective as swinging an axe at the leaves and twigs of a small tree, when a few choice blows to the trunk will topple the whole thing.

This book is not meant to be a platform for debating Jehovah's Witnesses on their doctrinal differences from mainstream Christian churches. In fact, although JWs and opponents alike tend to stress these differences, there is also a great deal of similarity. Viewed from a distant perch atop a Muslim minaret or beside a Shinto shrine, the similarities prevail. Even a Protestant or Catholic church member reading *Watchtower* magazines would, all prejudice aside, find agreement with most of the material, perhaps 85 to 95 percent of it. JW publications typically devote more space to personal experiences, history, child rearing, geography, family life, and so on, than to theology; and, even when it comes to biblical interpretation, the Scripture verses JWs interpret differently from mainstream Christians amount to only a small fraction of the Bible.

Yet the differences that do exist involve key issues and are insurmountable. When Jehovah's Witnesses and opponents clash head on, the discussion invariably turns to conflicting views of deity and the afterlife. Debate on these issues usually generates more heat than light, and both sides part company with the same cherished beliefs as before, and with nothing more to show for their efforts than heightened blood pressure, a headache, and an upset stomach. Final verification of who was right on the nature of God and the eternal destiny of the dead will have to wait until both die and meet their Maker.

Unlike the great spiritual truths at issue in theological debates, however, it is an easy matter to check out a corporation claiming to speak for God, especially when the organization itself has agreed to the criteria for such an investigation. According to standards set out in JW literature, leaders who present contradictory teachings over a period of time do not speak for God; nor those with a record as false prophets;

nor those who fail to adhere to a high standard of truthfulness. How does the Watchtower Society measure up to its own criteria? The record speaks for itself, as documented in the following pages.

✻   ✻   ✻

"If we were following a man undoubtedly it would be different with us; undoubtedly one human idea would contradict another and that which was light one or two or six years ago would be regarded as darkness now. But with God there is no variableness, neither shadow of turning, and so it is with truth; *any knowledge or light coming from God must be like its author. A new view of truth never can contradict a former truth.* 'New light' *never extinguishes older* 'light,' *but adds to it."*[2]

So, if a new teaching contradicts a former teaching, this proves the teachings are not coming from God. That statement appeared just nineteen months after C. T. Russell began publishing *Zion's Watch Tower*. How do the sect's subsequent teachings measure up?

For some fifty years the Great Pyramid of Egypt was presented as a provision from God, "God's Stone Witness," and then the teaching was reversed to say that it was "Satan's Bible," as detailed in chapter 3. *Zion's Watch Tower* suggested the use of the Society's books as Christmas presents and urged followers to join "in celebrating the grand event on the day which the majority celebrate—Christmas day."[3] Today, a Jehovah's Witness who celebrates the holiday is summoned before a judicial committee and put on trial; I know because when I was a JW elder, I sat in judgment in such cases. So, in regard to both the Pyramid and Christmas the new view of truth directly contradicts the former view. This means, according to the criteria cited in the 1881 *Watch Tower* quoted above, that JW teachings are coming from men, not from God.

"Would God Restore the Jews to Palestine?" Under this heading the *Proclaimers* book attempts to smooth over one of the sect's major doctrinal changes.[4] The discussion indirectly acknowledges that the Watchtower Society advocated "Zionism" until the 1930s, when prophecies about Israel were then reinterpreted as referring to Jehovah's Witnesses in a spiritual sense, not to the Jews. Pastor Russell had been such a strong supporter of the Jewish cause in 1946 that the Philosophical Library in New York published a book by David Horowitz titled *Pastor Charles Taze Russell: An Early American Christian Zionist*. Judge Rutherford maintained essentially the same position as his predecessor in his 1925 book *Comfort for the Jews*, but then he abandoned Zionism and reinterpreted the prophecies regarding Israel in his 1932 book *Vindication*, volume two. Here, Rutherford goes so far as to characterize Jews in terms that could be seen as anti-Semitic: "Among the powerful men who control the commerce of the sea are many Jews, so called, yet who are against God and against Christ and against the kingdom of God."[5] A few pages farther on he continues: "It is noted that Judah and the land of Israel had commercial intercourse with Tyre, and doubtless from Tyre the Jews learned how to cheat their fellow man."[6]

Another example of doctrinal reversal is the revision of the date when Christ is alleged to have returned invisibly. The Society proclaimed for decades that this occurred in 1874, with the Lord invisibly present thereafter. Then, as documented in chapter 5, the teaching was revised to say Christ's invisible return took place in 1914. This meant that even the very subtitle of *Zion's Watch Tower* magazine—*and Herald of Christ's Presence*—was erroneous from the publication's founding in 1879 onward.

As discussed earlier, the organization maintained for nearly two decades after his death that the departed spirit of Pastor Russell was still running the organization—until 1934, when Judge Rutherford labeled as "foolish" that belief formerly held to be truth.

Also considered earlier was the teaching, under the presidencies of both Russell and Rutherford, that God's throne and place of residence was located on the star Alcyone in the Pleiades star cluster. It was not until 1953 that the organization finally rejected this old light by declaring that "it would be unwise for us to try to fix God's throne as being at a particular spot in the universe."[7]

Doctrinal reversals by the Witness organization have even involved such fundamental matters as the identity of Jesus Christ. Nowadays it teaches that "Jesus is the archangel Michael." In the past, however, it stated firmly that "Michael is not the Son of God." At one point in time the Society's official teaching was that Michael is "the pope" of the Roman Catholic Church.[8]

Confronted with such doctrinal changes, Witnesses will often respond that the old "light" was just a mistaken notion the sect started out with, which God had not yet corrected, and that only the "new light" was from God. Hence, there was no contradiction. They will even quote Proverbs 4:18 which reads, "But the path of the righteous ones is like the bright light that is getting lighter and lighter until the day is firmly established" (*New World Translation*), as evidence that the Watchtower Society *is* God's organization. Doctrinal changes, according to this way of thinking, are proof that God leads the Witnesses to better understandings of truth.

Well, then, what if someone were to present a certain teaching as truth, then replace it with a contradictory new truth, and later return to the original teaching that had been rejected? Such vacillation could hardly mark the teacher as God's spokesperson. *The Watchtower* of May 15, 1976, expressed it this way:

> It is a serious matter to represent God and Christ in one way, then find that our understanding of the major teachings and fundamental doctrines of the Scriptures was in error, and then after that, to go back to the very doctrines that, by years of study, we had thoroughly determined to be in error. Christians cannot be vacillating—"wishy-washy"—about such fundamental teachings. What confidence can one put in the sincerity or judgment of such persons?[9]

In 1981, the Society denied ever having returned to a teaching that had earlier been rejected in favor of new truth: "At times explanations given by Jehovah's organization have shown adjustments, seemingly to previous points of view. But this has not actually been the case."[10] Appearances notwithstanding, JWs have never gone back to previous points of view, the leadership declares. However, numerous instances of this very thing can be documented.

For example, consider the identity of the "higher powers" (King James version) or "superior authorities" (*New World Translation*) that Romans 13:1 says everyone must obey.* Who are these higher powers? They are the secular rulers—human governments—according to the Watchtower Society's answer around the turn of the century.[11] Then this teaching was "cleaned out" of the organization as a "false doctrine" according to the Society's 1959 publication *Jehovah's Witnesses in the Divine Purpose*. The new teaching was that the higher powers are God and Christ. Later, however, the original teaching was reintroduced as new truth:

> For many years the Bible Students had taught that 'the higher powers' (KJV) were Jehovah God and Jesus Christ. . . .
> Years later, a careful reanalysis of the scripture was made. . . . As a result, in 1962 it was acknowledged that "the superior authorities" are the secular rulers. . . .[12]

This constituted a return to the previously rejected teaching. The *Proclaimers* book goes on to imply that the 1962 teaching included an un-

---

*Prior to the *New World Translation*'s release in 1950, JWs referred to the King James version.

derstanding of the principle of "relative subjection" for the first time, but it can be documented that this, too, was taught around the turn of the century. For example, *Zion's Watch Tower* of September 1, 1892, outlines the same principle of relative subjection taught today,[13] and the January 15, 1916, *Watch Tower* similarly says, "But while seeking to be thus law-abiding in every respect, Christians are to recognize that there is a still higher law . . . and are to be subject to the worldly powers only in the absence of a contrary admonition" from God.[14]

Another such back-and-forth doctrinal flip flop occurred on the question of whether the men of Sodom would be resurrected. The Society first said they would be,[15] then they would not be,[16] then they would be,[17] and then again they would not be.[18] The last change in 1988 apparently occurred in the midst of printing two books for release that summer, so that one of them[19] says the men of Sodom will be resurrected and the other, released at the same conventions,[20] says they will not. In the case of this doctrine and that of the higher powers, the sect's "light" is not getting brighter—it is blinking on and off.

Back-and-forth doctrinal reversals have occurred even in the very question of precisely who it is that serves as God's channel of communication. Watchtower publications identify the channel as the "faithful and wise servant" (King James version) or "faithful and discreet slave" (*New World Translation*) of Matthew 24:45–47. First they taught that this "servant" was "the whole body of Christ," that is, the church collectively.[21] Later the publications endorsed the view that it was not the church collectively, but rather C. T. Russell as an individual: "*The Watch Tower* unhesitatingly proclaims brother Russell as 'that faithful and wise servant.' "[22] Still later, however, the earlier rejected teaching was reinstated: "In February 1927 this erroneous thought that Russell himself was the 'faithful and wise servant' was cleared up."[23] So, the Society today teaches a composite "servant" made up of the body of Christ or the church collectively.

These many doctrinal changes and even reversals—and there are others—are all examples of new truth contradicting former views of truth, or one human idea contradicting another, which the 1881 *Watch Tower*, quoted above, indicates would constitute proof that an organization's teachings do not come from God. How, then, could the organization teaching all these contradictory ideas pretend to be God's "channel of communication"?

❧   ❧   ❧

"Of course, it is easy to say that this group acts as a 'prophet' of God. It is another thing to prove it. The only way that this can be done is to review the record."[24]

What does the record show? Earlier chapters in this book document prophetic statements the Watchtower leadership made predicting the world's end in 1914, the resurrection of Old Testament characters in 1925, and the world's end in 1975. Each of these prophecies proved false—a poor record, indeed.

Yet, the sect's leaders were so confident of their own special role in God's plan that they prophesied that the Almighty would wipe out all other churches in 1918, forcing surviving church members to turn to Watchtower publications for their religious answers. Released in 1917, *The Finished Mystery** offers this prophecy under the heading "The Churches Cease To Be":

> Also, in the year 1918, when God destroys the churches wholesale and the church members by millions, it shall be that any that escape shall come to the works of Pastor Russell to learn the meaning of the downfall of "Christianity."[25]

Obviously, this prophecy proved false as well.

C. J. Woodworth, one of the leaders who helped promote the 1914 prediction, later wrote, "Probably I look ridiculous to you because I did not go to Heaven, October 1st, 1914."[26] And as you will recall, after his own prophecy about 1925 failed to come true, Judge Rutherford confessed, "I made an ass of myself."[27] The sect's present leaders, however, have been less candid. They insist they "should not be viewed as false prophets."[28] In this respect *one* prophetic statement in a 1972 JW publication *did* come true, although not in the way the author intended: "False prophets will try to hide their reason for feeling shame by denying who they really are."[29] Watchtower leaders now try to escape responsibility for the sect's failed prophecies.

❧   ❧   ❧

"Any group or individuals that speak in the name of Jehovah put themselves under obligation to convey his word truthfully."[30]

---

*For more on *The Finished Mystery*, see pp. 73–77.

How does the Watchtower organization measure up in the matter of truthfulness?

In certain contexts the sect has admitted that its teachings have changed over the years, but in other contexts an entirely different picture is presented. For example, *The Watchtower* of August 15, 1993, states, "Jehovah's Witnesses have consistently shown from the Scriptures that the year 1914 marked the beginning of this world's time of the end and that 'the day of judgment and of destruction of the ungodly men' has drawn near."[31] Is that statement true? No. Actually, the sect long taught that the "time of the end" began in 1798 or 1799:

> The papal dominion over both Church and State crippled every energy and prevented Bible searching. The overthrow of that dominion in 1798 by the French Revolution marked the beginning of the "time of the end." . . .[32]

> The year 1799 marked the beginning of the "time of the end," when various events were to occur.[33]

> [The year] 1799 A.D. beginning time of the end.[34]

> Twelve hundred and sixty years* from A.D. 539 brings us to 1799, which is another proof that 1799 definitely marks the beginning of "the time of the end."[35]

In another matter the organization's 1959 history book *Jehovah's Witnesses in the Divine Purpose* alleges that the sect "never published a biography of Pastor Russell."[36] Perhaps for emphasis, it repeats those words, "never published a biography of Pastor Russell," on the same page and implies that to have published one would have been improper, as it would amount to giving Rutherford "honor and credit" that rightfully belong to God. Some readers might find those sentiments admirable, while others would question them; but all readers are left with the supposed fact that the sect "never published a biography of Pastor Russell." However, as a collector of old JW books, I happen to have on my shelf an antique set of the Society's *Watch Tower* reprints, and I notice that the December 1, 1916, *Watch Tower* features a biography of Charles Taze Russell exceeding two thousand words in length.[37] I also own a copy of the 1925 edition of *The Divine Plan of the Ages*, volume one of Russell's *Studies in the Scriptures* series, and I notice that a

---

*Compare the discussion of the Great Pyramid in chapter 2. A digression into the various dates and calculations would be exhausting and serve no useful purpose here. The point at issue is that the sect has falsely claimed consistency on "the time of the end."

thirty-page "Biography of Pastor Russell" is found at the front of that book. Could the 1959 statement have been a simple error? Might the anonymous author of the Witnesses' history book merely have been unaware of the existence of these two biographies that belie his claim? One might think so, if it were not for the fact that one footnote on page 62 of that same book refers to "biographical reports" in the 1916 *Watch Tower* and another on page 17 references the "Biography" in the 1926 edition of *The Divine Plan of the Ages*. Readers must draw their own conclusions as to why the history book's main text denies their existence.

Opponents have charged Jehovah's Witnesses with being false prophets of the ilk described in the Bible at Deuteronomy 18:20–22:

> But the prophet, which shall presume to speak a word in my name, which I have not commanded him to speak, or that shall speak in the name of other gods, even that prophet shall die. And if thou say in thine heart, How shall we know the word which the LORD hath not spoken? When a prophet speaketh in the name of the LORD, if the thing follow not, nor come to pass, that is the thing which the LORD hath not spoken, but the prophet hath spoken it presumptuously: thou shalt not be afraid of him. (King James version)

One of the defenses the organization has used recently in answering such charges is the argument that the various predictions that failed were not spoken in God's name. The March 22, 1993, *Awake!* magazine puts it this way:

> Jehovah's Witnesses, in their eagerness for Jesus' second coming, have suggested dates that turned out to be incorrect. Because of this, some have called them false prophets. Never in these instances, however, did they presume to originate predictions "in the name of Jehovah." Never did they say, "These are the words of Jehovah."[38]

Many, however, would see the claim that prophetic dates are "God's dates, not ours" as equivalent to prophesying in God's name, and this is precisely what was said in connection with predicting the world's end in 1914: "They are, we believe, God's dates, not ours. But bear in mind that the end of 1914 is not the date for the beginning, but for the end of the time of trouble."[39] Whether making prophecies or not, Jehovah's Witnesses present themselves as a "group or individuals that speak in the name of Jehovah."[40] Elsewhere, the sect has specifically ruled out the possibility that the prophecies it publishes might be the mere "opinion or expression of a man," claiming instead that God uses *The Watchtower* to publish "his" prophecies:

> Those who are convinced that *The Watchtower* is publishing the opinion or expression of a man should not waste time in looking at it at all. . . . Those who believe that God uses *The Watchtower* as a means of communicating to his people, or of calling attention to his prophecies, should study *The Watchtower.* . . .[41]

Could it be that the *Awake!* writers and editors claiming that JWs "never" made their predictions in God's name were simply unaware of such instances where this was done? One might think so, if it were not for the fact that prophecies and disclaimers of prophecies have appeared on the same page. Directly below the footnote in the March 22, 1993, *Awake!* already cited, there appears in the magazine's masthead the prediction of "a peaceful and secure new world before the generation that saw the events of 1914 passes away," and this prophetic statement is introduced as "the Creator's promise."

The Watchtower organization's most recent history book (1993) describes itself in its foreword as "objective" and "candid." However, instead of reporting matters in chronological order, *Jehovah's Witnesses—Proclaimers of God's Kingdom* covers JW history topically. The result of this format is that the accounts of embarrassing episodes, when not omitted entirely, can be fragmented into less embarrassing bits and pieces, related in different parts of the book. These bite-size fragments are easier to swallow than the whole truth presented clearly in one place. Discussion of the Society's failed prophecy for 1925, for example, is broken up into separate accounts on pages 78, 425, and 632—each with a different excuse or euphemism to help JWs dismiss the episode as unimportant, or at least excusable.

Moreover, the topical arrangement allows the book to pull critical issues out of the context of surrounding events and thus to mask inconsistencies and historical errors. For example, discussion of Charles Taze Russell's religious affiliation during the decade following 1870 is broken up into separate discussions on pages 43–48, 120–22, 132–35, and 204. So, when the book says on page 204 that "The operation of the organization of Jehovah's Witnesses has undergone significant changes since Charles Taze Russell and his associates first began to study the Bible together in 1870," readers may have forgotten that Russell was still part of an Adventist organization until 1879, as revealed in the earlier material, and that therefore a separate "organization of Jehovah's Witnesses" was not operating at all in 1870.

Similarly, page 147 of the book presents a 1962 doctrinal change (on the interpretation of Romans 13:1) as "progressive understanding." But information presented separately on page 190 shows that the "new" view was already being taught by C. T. Russell in 1904. The 1962 teaching was not really new at all, but actually a doctrinal reversal; however, the book hides this fact by separating the different parts of the story.

Concerning the Beth-Sarim mansion in San Diego, the *1975 Yearbook of Jehovah's Witnesses* states simply that "a direct contribution was made for the purpose of constructing a house in San Diego for Brother Rutherford's use. It was not built at the expense of the Watch Tower Society."[42] The *Proclaimers* book indicates similarly that it was built for the judge.[43] Next it quotes from his 1939 book *Salvation* to the effect that "the purpose of acquiring that property and building the house was that there might be some tangible proof that there are those on earth today . . . who believe that the faithful men of old will soon be resurrected by the Lord, be back on earth, and take charge of the visible affairs of earth."[44] *Proclaimers* adds in a footnote that "At the time, it was believed that faithful men of old times, such as Abraham, Joseph, and David, would be resurrected before the end of this system of things, and would serve as 'princes in all the earth,' in fulfillment of Psalm 45:16. This view was adjusted in 1950."[45] Still, the book leaves the reader puzzled. What was the connection between the mansion and the princes? As discussed in chapter 4 on Rutherford, the answer is found in the Society's 1942 book *The New World*, which says, ". . . [T]hose faithful men of old may be expected back from the dead any day now. . . . In this expectation the house at San Diego, California . . . was built, in 1930, and named 'Beth-Sarim,' meaning 'House of the Princes.' It is now held in trust for the occupancy of those princes on their return."[46] As time passed, the mansion outlived its usefulness. Rutherford was dead, and his successor Nathan Knorr was not one for such sumptuous living. Meanwhile, it had become abundantly clear that the princes were not about to be resurrected to live there, and Beth-Sarim was sold quietly in 1948. Due to the murky accounts in the publications available to them today, most Jehovah's Witnesses have an incomplete understanding of its true role in Watchtower history.*

*An interesting footnote to Beth-Sarim: At a Yankee Stadium convention in 1950, when Vice President Fred Franz announced over the sound system that the "princes of the new earth" had arrived and were present at the stadium, the assembled Witnesses leapt to their feet with sustained applause, all the while glancing about to catch a glimpse of Abraham or King David or one of the others. Eventually, when he was finally able to silence the wild clapping, theologian Franz explained what he really meant—namely, that new light on the Scriptures allowed for the interpretation that many of the "princes" would be appointed from among the modern-day believers there assembled, not that the ancient patriarchs had been resurrected as the audience assumed.

Largely ignoring the role of the Great Pyramid in Watchtower history as discussed in chapter 3, the 750-page *Proclaimers* book devotes only a single small paragraph to the subject:

> For some thirty-five years, Pastor Russell thought that the Great Pyramid of Gizeh [*sic*] was God's stone Witness, corroborating Biblical time periods. (Isa. 19:19) But Jehovah's Witnesses have abandoned the idea that an Egyptian pyramid has anything to do with true worship (see "Watchtower" issues of November 15 and December 1, 1928).[47]

A less misleading account would have admitted that the second president, Joseph F. Rutherford, perpetuated the same teaching for another twelve years. For obvious reasons the *Proclaimers* book conceals the extent to which the Society used pyramidology to predict future events, something JWs today would view with horror as a demonic manifestation of occult spiritism. Moreover, although the passage quoted above is accompanied by a postage-stamp sized photo of an Egyptian pyramid and a larger diagram of its internal passageways (the paragraph actually serves as the only caption for these), and page 64 displays a small photo of Pastor Russell's grave marker, the colorful and abundantly illustrated *Proclaimers* book conspicuously omits any picture or mention of the mammoth stone pyramid dominating the Watch Tower burial lots north of Pittsburgh, also discussed in chapter 3.

Something as simple and straightforward as a periodical's name change can also involve intentional omissions and distortions in *Jehovah's Witnesses—Proclaimers of God's Kingdom*. I happened to notice the omission because the missing pieces were the very ones that had played a part in confirming my decision to leave the sect back in 1982. The Society must have left them out of the book so that they would not have the same effect on others who learned about the matter. It involves one of the doctrinal flip flops that happened to flip in 1976 and to flop back again in 1982—all within the span of my personal involvement with the sect—a doctrinal reversal on the application of the term "minister."

First, all of us who were active Witnesses were considered ministers, because we all shared in the preaching work on the doorstep. (This usage also helped young men secure the coveted "4-D" ministerial exemption from their draft boards, a classification that did not require the alternative service work associated with the more easily obtainable conscientious objector status.) Then, in 1976 the Society redefined the word "minister" to conform more closely to the way non-

Witnesses used the term. Henceforth, it would apply only to appointed elders, ministerial servants, and so on. Women, teenagers, children, and rank-and-file JW men were *not* considered ministers any longer. Early in 1982, however, after the expulsion of influential presidential nephew Raymond Franz, who had apparently been responsible for pushing through the 1976 change, the new conservative majority on the Governing Body rolled back the teaching to where it was originally.

The whole back-and-forth maneuver was reflected in name changes to the monthly newsletter that directed our activity in the door-to-door work. Originally titled *Bulletin* (1919–35), then *Director* (1935–36), and later *Informant* (1936–56), this internal publication was renamed *Kingdom Ministry* in 1956. Twenty years later, however, it was renamed again *Our Kingdom Service*, as we were suddenly no longer "ministers" doing a "ministry" from house to house. Then in 1982, when we became ministers once more, the periodical's name was also changed back, except that the added word "Our" remained part of the title, so that it now became *Our Kingdom Ministry*. The whole embarrassing episode is expunged from the *Proclaimers* book, with both the discussion on page 247 and the accompanying illustrations omitting any reference to the two titles the publication bore from 1956 to 1982. The story and the sample issues photographed to accompany it, both skip directly from *Informant* to *Our Kingdom Ministry*, the present title—unlike the complete coverage the *Proclaimers* book gives to the sect's other periodicals—as if the doctrinal reversal over "ministers" had never happened.

Some additional examples of dishonesty involve alcoholic beverages. One common thread that runs through the stories of many Watchtower headquarters workers I've known is the use of alcohol. Like Texans boasting that everything is bigger in Texas, Bethelites boast about their booze. While I was a Witness I heard it from those still at Brooklyn Bethel and from those returning home to serve in local congregations. Since leaving the organization I've heard the same story from former Witnesses who once lived at headquarters. They all tell of prodigious amounts of beer, wine, and whisky consumed during off hours in the Society's residence buildings.

JWs correctly point out that biblical injunctions speak against drunkenness, not against drinking per se. After all, before the invention of refrigeration, alcoholic beverages were among the few that could be stored safely without spoiling. Jesus turned water into wine at the wedding feast at Cana, and he served wine at the last supper. Judge Rutherford, however, went far beyond this. Known for his personal devotion to spirits of the bottled variety, Rutherford saw Prohibition as a Satanic plot. He went on the air on the Watchtower's radio network to attack Prohibition, and he had the Society publish his speech in booklet form for mass distribution. (*Prohibition and the League of Nations*, 1930). According to Canadian historian M. James Penton, in his book *Apocalypse Delayed: The Story of Jehovah's Witnesses*,[48] high officials in the organization's Brooklyn headquarters sponsored their own rum-running operation, breaking the law by having officials at the Canadian branch headquarters in Toronto smuggle liquor across the international border into New York.

Although never nabbed by the authorities during Prohibition, the organization was caught red-handed in 1982 in another case of misusing whisky—or, rather, a whisky ad. In this case I myself was the whistle blower, after a strange set of circumstances brought the Society's violation to my attention. It was a late-summer weekend just months after Penni and I had been disfellowshipped. She suggested we take advantage of the nice weather to leave our third-floor apartment and relax for a while in Brockton's D. W. Field Park, a beautiful spot of greenery left to the city by one of its early shoe manufacturers. We drove to the park and settled into a cozy spot to read. Penni had brought a few magazines, while I carried along some heavier reading material. After a while, Penni insisted I put down my book to take a personality test she came across in her September *Reader's Digest*. Accidentally losing the page, however, and flipping back to find it, my eyes fell upon a Johnnie Walker Red scotch whisky ad that shocked me—not because anything was wrong with it, but because I was sure I had just seen the same illustration on the front of the September 15, 1982, *Watchtower* magazine.

As soon as I got home, I held the two up side by side: the whisky ad and the *Watchtower* cover were nearly identical. A red sunset in both pictures silhouetted the same building and elevated porch. A couple stood on the porch in the liquor ad, but the *Watchtower* cover showed the man only. Otherwise, the pictures were the same. Only the words were changed: "The most beautiful summer evenings start with red. Johnnie Walker Red. So smooth it's the world's best-selling scotch," in the *Reader's Digest*, and "God's Name, What Is It?—Why It Concerns You," in *The Watchtower*. But who had copied from whom? A little investigation revealed that the copyrighted whisky ad had been running in major U.S. magazines since the summer of 1981, more than a year before the JW artist appropriated the illustration.

Through the pages of my *Comments from the Friends*, then still a typewritten newsletter with tiny circulation, I called attention to what the Watchtower Society had done. A reader passed the information on to Somerset Importers, Ltd., the U.S. distributor of Johnnie Walker Red. Somerset's attorney contacted Watchtower headquarters, and the Society agreed to stop using the illustration. This posed a problem, however, since foreign-language translations of that issue had not yet been printed.

Without offering any explanation the foreign-language editions of that *Watchtower* issue, printed some time after the English edition, appeared with a totally different illustration on the cover. Bound volumes of the English-language magazine printed at the end of the year also featured the new cover instead of the liquor ad illustration. Readers writing Brooklyn to ask about the change received the Watchtower Society's official reply, to the effect that "adjustments" were made in the artwork "to produce a more appropriate and suitable illustration"— an evasive answer concealing what had actually taken place. Apparently, the corporation claiming to be "God's organization" preferred a coverup to a confession.

A similar situation developed around an ongoing problem the sect has had with headquarters workers inserting hidden faces, occult symbols, and other inappropriate matter in Watchtower illustrations. For years, conversations like this have taken place among Jehovah's Witnesses:

"Look! A hidden face in the February 1, 1983, *Watchtower* magazine!"

"Where? Show me!"

"Here it is on page 17, at the bottom of the lady's dress. See it?"

"Yes! It looks like a man with a bushy white mustache and beard."

"How strange!"

Countless numbers of Jehovah's Witnesses and other Watchtower readers noticed the tiny face, just three-sixteenths of an inch tall and barely an eighth of an inch wide. What was it doing there? they wondered. Many wrote to the Society in Brooklyn, asking about this face. Some received official letters from headquarters stating that "A face of a man was not purposely placed on the woman's dress in this illustration." Other hidden faces and symbols continued to appear in other publications, and Witnesses continued to write to headquarters. (For example, two are found in the 1988 book *Revelation: Its Grand Climax at Hand*. An impish human face appears when a horse's snout is covered on page 91, and there is a grotesque face in an angel's hand on page 159.) Eventually the Society addressed this issue in *The Watchtower* of September 1, 1984:

Even the Watchtower Society's publications have been the subject of rumors—for example, that one of the artists had secretly been introducing pictures of demons into the illustrations, and was subsequently found out and disfellowshipped!

Did you share in spreading any such stories? If so, you were—perhaps unwittingly—spreading an untruth, since they were all false.[49]

However, Witnesses still found it difficult to deny what they saw with their own eyes, and the lack of a clear explanation from Brooklyn left a vacuum that produced further rumors and speculation. The Society responded again with this assurance in the March 1, 1987, *Watchtower* magazine:

Each article in both *The Watchtower* and *Awake!* and every page, including the artwork, is scrutinized by selected members of the Governing Body before it is printed.[50]

Still, Darek Barefoot, a Witness in Colorado, knew what he saw. He collected clippings of dozens of illustrations from the Society's publications that contained hidden faces and, perhaps even more frightening, hidden symbols and messages commonly used in Satanic worship. When Barefoot showed them to his local elders, they, too, were puzzled and suggested he write to Brooklyn headquarters. Later, though, after the elders received a response on the matter, those who had seen the pictures with their own eyes now said, "We've talked to the Society. The pictures aren't there." In his book *Jehovah's Witnesses and the Hour of Darkness*,[51] Barefoot tells how he wrestled with the issues involved. Why would occult symbols and subliminal messages keep appearing in publications of God's organization? Before his case was closed, Barefoot discovered how costly truth can be in human terms. He tells in his book how a mini-inquisition interrogated and disfellowshipped him and others close to him who refused to deny what they saw. Lives were shattered to help an organization save face. If the existence of the hidden faces were acknowledged, it would reveal Watchtower leaders as unable to prevent pranksters at headquarters from tampering with the artwork—hence unable to control the content of the material supposedly channeled from God.

The situation is reminiscent of the old fable "The Emperor's New Clothes" where, in order to keep their jobs, people were required to see something that wasn't there. In this case Witnesses were required not to see something that was. It again calls to mind Orwell's character

Winston Smith in *Nineteen Eighty-Four*, who is tortured brutally until he can look at four fingers and honestly say that he sees five—because the party says so.

Charles Taze Russell founded the Watchtower organization and personally led it for decades. Moreover, it was his personal magnetism that drew the sect's initial converts. Yet, Jehovah's Witnesses today look back at his legacy with mixed feelings. The May 1, 1989, *Watchtower* puts it this way:

> In the early part of our twentieth century prior to 1919, the Bible Students, as Jehovah's Witnesses were then known, had to be released from a form of spiritual captivity to the ideas and practices of false religion. . . . Some were exalting creatures, indulging in a personality cult that focused on Charles T. Russell, the first president of the Watch Tower Bible and Tract Society.[52]

The Watchtower Society here blames this "cult" on "some" within its ranks—which Jehovah's Witnesses generally understand to mean apostates or fringe elements. But who actually promoted the cult? The evidence points to Russell himself and those associated with him in running the Society. After all, a few "apostates" in their midst could not have been responsible for statements in the Society's publications exalting Russell over a period of many years. For example, the November 1, 1917, *Watch Tower* carried an article titled "A Tribute to the Seventh Messenger" in which it said: "The two most prominent messengers, however, are the first and the last—St. Paul and Pastor Russell. . . . 'That wise and faithful servant' . . . now many more are recognizing, that Pastor Russell is that servant."[53] So, it was the Society itself that was promoting this personality cult, not just "some" among the rank-and-file membership.

Ancient Hebrew writers who penned the scrolls later incorporated in what we call the Books of Moses and the Prophets wrote freely about Noah's drunkenness after the Deluge and Lot's drunkenness after the loss of his wife, about David's sin with Bathsheba and his foolishness over Absalom, his son; the New Testament described Thomas's faithless doubting, and about Peter's betrayal of Christ and later prejudice toward Gentiles in the Church. One would have hoped for at least as much candor on the part of Jehovah's Witnesses today. Sadly, however, the organization has often sacrificed truthfulness in order to save face.

So, in these three areas that JW publications themselves set forth as criteria for condemning any so-called godly organization—contradictory teachings, failed prophecies, and the matter of truthfulness—the Watchtower Society disqualifies itself as God's "channel of communication."

❧   ❧   ❧

Bill Korinek, a Witness "pioneer" (full-time door-to-door worker), was a passenger in a car that crashed into a bridge in Utah on July 31, 1957, according to the story related by his close friend and fellow passenger, Walter Davis, in We Left Jehovah's Witnesses—a Non-Prophet Organization *by Edmond C. Gruss. Although growing weaker from loss of blood, Korinek steadfastly refused to accept a transfusion. Davis relates that the Mormon doctor pleaded with the young man's mother to authorize the treatment, but she replied, "I would rather see my boy dead and in the grave than see him violate Jehovah God's commandment against blood!" Korinek died shortly afterward.*

❧   ❧   ❧

Of course, pretending to be the divine spokesman is serious enough when the things spoken in God's name are shaky and often contradictory theological theories, absurd ideas about pyramids and the Pleiades, or petty rules on haircuts and pantsuits; but when a self-appointed "channel of communication" from God starts dictating on life-and-death decisions, the consequences are disastrous.

Jehovah's Witnesses themselves will admit that the Bible does not specifically mention blood transfusion, since such a medical technique did not exist when the Bible was written. The Watchtower Society bases its instructions to members on its own interpretation of Scripture. However, in interpreting certain verses to rule out blood transfusions, could the Watchtower Society be following the pattern of the Pharisees? When it came to the application of God's laws in life-threatening emergencies and situations involving human suffering, the Pharisees put their interpretations ahead of human needs: no healing on the Sabbath was their rule. Jesus rebuked the Pharisees by showing that "the Sabbath was made to benefit man, and not man to benefit the Sabbath" (Mark 2:27 Living Bible). If a person, or even an animal, fell into a hole on the Sabbath, God would want people to break the Pharisees' interpretation of the Sabbath law and work to pull him out, Jesus indicated (Luke 14:5). He also noted with approval how King David, in an emergency, "entered into the house of God, and did eat the shewbread, which was not lawful for him to eat, neither for them which were with him, but only for the priests" (Matt. 12:4 King James version).

Even when it came to the use of blood, Jesus again shocked his audience by telling them, "Truly, truly, I say to you, unless you eat the flesh of the Son of man and drink his blood, you have no life in you; he who eats my flesh and drinks my blood has eternal life . . ." (John 6:53,54 Revised Standard). Whether he was referring to faith in the atoning power of his blood poured out on the cross, or to demonstrating that faith by partaking of the communion cup, he was nevertheless using the concept of drinking human blood in a positive, favorable sense.

So, a decision to ban blood transfusions based on the Bible would be entirely a matter of extrapolation beyond what Scripture actually says. Bible readers of other faiths have not found there a ban on blood transfusions—not even strict Jews who bleed slaughtered animals and who then kosher the meat before eating it. Why did I myself believe the interpretation from Brooklyn Bethel to be the correct one? Largely because of the weight of authority: I believed the organization spoke for God. I had not had opportunity to review its track record on doctrinal flip flops, failed prophecies, and truth-hiding coverups.

In fact, like most other Jehovah's Witnesses, I was totally unaware that the Watchtower Society has a medical track record, too—a long history of commenting on medical issues and instructing its followers on medical procedures, recommending some and banning others.

Throughout the 1930s and 1940s Watchtower publications frequently denounced vaccination as a procedure that was not only worthless but actually harmful from a medical standpoint, and that was morally wrong from a religious or biblical standpoint. The latter, of course, was the deciding factor for Witnesses. The organization had made clear to them that "Vaccination is a direct violation of the everlasting covenant that God made with Noah after the flood."[54]* So Jehovah's Witnesses routinely refused vaccinations for themselves and their children. If the inoculation against smallpox was required for admission to public school, some Witnesses would have a friendly doctor burn a mark on the child's arm with acid to make it look as if the youngster had been vaccinated. (Some who grew up during that time told me this personally.) Others went so far as to have papers made out, falsely certifying that the child had been vaccinated.

No figures are available on deaths that may have resulted from the JW refusal to be vaccinated. Since smallpox was under control through

---

*Actually, this covenant says, "But flesh with the life thereof, which is the blood thereof, shall ye not eat" (Gen. 9:4). It does not mention vaccination.

vaccination of the non-Witness population as a whole, there was little likelihood of a JW encountering the highly contagious disease. The refusal to be vaccinated was therefore more of a nuisance problem than a life-threatening one. Without apology or explanation, Watchtower publications dropped the ban on vaccinations in the early 1950s, and today they recommend the procedure and credit it with curbing disease.

"Should a Christian Consult a Psychiatrist?" asks an article in the March 8, 1960, *Awake!* magazine. No is the answer given, except in certain "serious cases of mental unbalance or breakdown of nerves." The article says Jehovah's Witnesses "have the least need for psychiatrists," because they are "the best-oriented, happiest and most contented group of people on the face of the earth. They get along better with each other than do people of any other religion, tribe or social group."[55] This is, in fact, the carefully constructed image JWs often manage to project to outside observers, and even to their own rank-and-file members, who are willing to believe what they are told more readily than what they see with their own eyes.

However, my eyes were fully opened to the very real presence of psychological problems among Jehovah's Witnesses when I was appointed an elder and had to share in dealing with such matters in my local congregation. There, in a small group of fewer than two hundred people, I recall that we elders had to counsel and sometimes even physically restrain five individuals committing acts of violence toward other JWs or toward outsiders (some actually using knives and other weapons); three couples in emotional turmoil after wife-swapping; one individual caught selling drugs at Kingdom Hall; and various other cases of domestic violence, sexual abuse, compulsive theft, and so on. But, if asked, even the Witnesses involved in these ongoing problems would give the programmed response that JWs were indeed the happiest, most problem-free people on the face of the earth.

My own observations are confirmed in the book *Jehovah's Witnesses and the Problem of Mental Illness* by Dr. Jerry Bergman.[56] It reviews the results of several studies and concludes that JWs have a significantly higher rate of mental illness than the population as a whole. Yet, warnings against the psychiatric profession have been repeated often in Watchtower publications. *Awake!* in its issue of August 22, 1975, says, for example, "instead of turning to psychiatrists and psychologists who likewise, for the most part, are without such faith, let lovers of righteousness turn to the Bible for wisdom. . . ."[57]

The 1960 *Awake!* article cited above accuses psychiatrists of seeing "nothing wrong in adultery, fornication, sodomy and suchlike so long as one can get away with it."[58] But perhaps the real reason for the warnings against this branch of medicine is found in a surprising admission in the same article: "Often, when a witness of Jehovah goes to a psychiatrist, the psychiatrist will try to persuade him that his troubles are caused by his religion. . . ."[59]

Jehovah's Witnesses have read various pronouncements in their publications over the years on a number of other medical matters related to treatment of disease, alleged racial superiority, human anatomy, and so on. For example, *The Watch Tower* of July 1, 1913, said under the heading "A CURE FOR SURFACE CANCER":

> We have recently learned of a very effective and simple remedy for cancers which show themselves on the surface of the body. We are informed that a physician, after testing this remedy, paid $1000 for the information, and that he has established a Cancer Hospital which is doing good work. The recipe has come to us free and we are willing to communicate the formula, but only to those who are troubled with surface cancers and who will write to us directly, stating particulars. No fee will be charged, but in order to protect the sufferers, we require a promise that they will not sell the formula to others, nor receive pay for the use of it, nor communicate the formula to anybody. Anyone known to be a sufferer can be informed of the terms on which the prescription is available through us.[60]

No records are available on the numbers of *Watchtower* readers who may have died as a result of using this "prescription" from Brooklyn instead of seeking professional medical help. The magazine no longer, of course, offers this supposed "cure" for cancer.

Elsewhere, when discussing racial differences among humankind, *The Watch Tower* said

> We are not to forget, either, that Africa is inhabited by various tribes or nations of negroes—some more and some less degraded than the average. . . . While it is true that the white race exhibits some qualities of superiority over any other, we are to remember that there are wide differences in the same Caucasian (Semitic and Aryan) family. . . . The secret of the greater intelligence and aptitude of the Caucasian undoubtedly in great measure is to be attributed to the commingling of blood amongst its various branches. . . .[61]

Speaking of people in general without regard to race, it commented on another occasion concerning the shape of the human brain: "Some have a strong desire to worship God, others have a weak desire, and others have no desire at all. This difference is due to the shape of the brain."[62]

The above quotes are intended neither to be humorous nor to ridicule Jehovah's Witnesses. Rather, they are presented here to provide the context for the sect's prohibition on blood transfusions—a prohibition taken quite seriously by millions of people who are unfamiliar with the sect's earlier medical pronouncements. The Bible verses interpreted by the Watchtower Society as banning blood transfusions are the very same verses the Society used earlier in banning vaccinations and organ transplants—bans it no longer adheres to. Most Bible readers conclude that the Watchtower organization has gone "beyond the things that are written" (1 Cor. 4:6 *New World Translation*) in its interpretation of those verses as prohibiting blood transfusions even in life-threatening emergencies.

With around twelve million people attending JW Kingdom Halls worldwide, some observers had hoped that the broader membership would result in a softening of the sect's stand on blood. However, the anti-blood rule does not originate with the membership; it comes from the top, and the Brooklyn leadership has actually been tightening its enforcement. Witnesses now sign papers in advance giving another loyal member legal power of attorney to block the objectionable treatment in the event that the first Witness is unconscious or incapacitated. *Our Kingdom Ministry* of January 1993 instructs, "Baptized publishers should never leave home without their Advance Medical Directive/Release card," and it further requires, "Unbaptized minor children with a Witness parent should always carry an Identity Card."[63] These provisions were expanded beyond the simple card I had carried while in the sect. There were also no cards specially designed for children at that time. Current instructions call for active intervention at the hospital:

> When there is a crisis, elders may consider it advisable to arrange a 24-hour watch at the hospital, preferably by an elder with the patient's parent or another close family member. Blood transfusions often are given when all relatives and friends have gone home for the night.[64]

Special efforts are now made to prepare JWs to go before a judge to prevent hospitals from obtaining court orders to treat their children with blood products. "What will you do if an attorney or a judge asks you why you are refusing a 'lifesaving' transfusion for your child?" asks *Our Kingdom Ministry* of September 1992, which then proceeds to tell the Witness how to respond so as to avoid the appearance of being a "religious fanatic":

> Although your first inclination might be to explain your belief in the resurrection and express your strong faith that God will bring your child back if he dies, such an answer by itself may do no more than convince the judge, whose paramount concern is the physical welfare of the child, that you are a religious fanatic and that he must step in to protect your child.[65]

So, parents are encouraged to side-step the religious motive to focus instead on requesting alternative forms of treatment—even if blood is the only sound medical treatment for the problem. Trained elders on the local Hospital Liaison Committee first try to persuade doctors not to seek a court order. If unsuccessful, they then accompany the Witness parent to court in the hope of influencing the judge.

Many Jehovah's Witness parents over the years have secretly breathed a sigh of relief when hospital officials obtained a court order to give their sick or injured child a blood transfusion. In this way the child's life would be saved, yet the parents would escape the congregation judicial committee hearing and the punishment of shunning that Watchtower rules mandate for those who accept transfusions for themselves or their children. But now the latest pronouncement requires Jehovah's Witnesses even to "resist a blood transfusion that has been ordered or authorized by a court."[66]

This article suggests that a JW patient should "avoid being accessible" for such a court-ordered transfusion by fleeing the scene, or else follow the example of the twelve-year-old girl mentioned earlier who had been taught to "fight any court-authorized transfusion with all the strength she could muster, that she would scream and struggle, that she would pull the injecting device out of her arm and would attempt to destroy the blood in the bag over her bed."[67] This course is to be followed even if such action might make the Jehovah's Witness "a lawbreaker or make him liable to prosecution" by the authorities. Some JW parents have indeed made headlines as lawbreakers by kidnapping their ailing children from hospital custody.

So, instead of mellowing over the years to become more mainstream as its following has grown into the millions, the Jehovah's Witness organization has grown more militantly cultic, placing its followers' and their children's blood on the altar.

NOTES

1. *The Watchtower,* January 15, 1969, p. 51; December 1, 1981, p. 27; April 1, 1919 Society Reprints, p. 6414; January 15, 1983, p. 22; and June 1, 1965, p. 352.

2. *Zion's Watch Tower,* February 1881, p. 3.

3. *Zion's Watch Tower,* November 15, 1907, p. 4094 Society Reprints; December 1, 1904, p. 3468 Society Reprints.

4. *Jehovah's Witnesses—Proclaimers of God's Kingdom* (Brooklyn, N.Y.: Watchtower Society, 1993), p. 141.

5. J. F. Rutherford, *Vindication* (Brooklyn, N.Y.: Watchtower Society, 1932), vol. 2, p. 55.

6. Ibid., p. 70.

7. *The Watchtower,* November 15, 1953, p. 703.

8. *The Watchtower,* April 15, 1991, p. 28; *Zion's Watch Tower,* November 1879, p. 48; *The Finished Mystery* (Brooklyn, N.Y.: Watchtower Society, 1917), p. 188.

9. *The Watchtower,* May 15, 1976, p. 298.

10. *The Watchtower,* December 1, 1981, p. 27.

11. *Jehovah's Witnesses—Proclaimers of God's Kingdom,* p. 190.

12. Ibid., p. 147.

13. *Zion's Watch Tower,* September 1, 1882, p. 1440 Society Reprints.

14. *The Watch Tower,* January 15, 1915, p. 5840 Society Reprints.

15. *Zion's Watch Tower,* July 15, 1879, p. 8.

16. *The Watchtower,* June 1, 1952, p. 338.

17. *The Watchtower,* August 1, 1965, p. 479.

18. *The Watchtower,* June 1, 1988, p. 31.

19. *Insight on the Scriptures* (Brooklyn, N.Y.: Watchtower Society, 1988), p. 985.

20. *Revelation—Its Grand Climax at Hand* (Brooklyn, N.Y.: Watchtower Society, 1988), p. 273.

21. *Zion's Watch Tower,* November 1881, p. 271 Society Reprints.

22. *The Watch Tower,* March 1, 1917, p. 6049 Society Reprints.

23. *1975 Yearbook of Jehovah's Witnesses* (Brooklyn, N.Y.: Watchtower Society, 1975), p. 88.

24. *The Watchtower,* April 15, 1972, p. 197.

25. *The Finished Mystery,* pp. 484–85.

26. *Jehovah's Witnesses—Proclaimers of God's Kingdom,* p. 634.

27. *The Watchtower,* October 1, 1984, p. 24.

28. *Awake!* March 27, 1993, p. 4

29. *Paradise Restored to Mankind—By Theocracy!* (Brooklyn, N.Y.: Watchtower Society, 1979), p. 354.

30. *Jehovah's Witnesses—Proclaimers of God's Kingdom,* p. 157.

31. *The Watchtower,* August 15, 1993, p. 9.

32. *Zion's Watch Tower,* August 1879, p. 24 Society Reprints.

33. *The Watch Tower,* November 1, 1914, p. 5565 Society Reprints.

34. *The Watch Tower,* "Topical Index," 1919, p. 6542 Society Reprints.

35. J. F. Rutherford, *Creation,* 1st ed. (Brooklyn, N.Y.: Watchtower Society, 1927), p. 315.

36. *Jehovah's Witnesses in the Divine Purpose* (Brooklyn, N.Y.: Watchtower Society, 1959), p. 63.

37. *The Watch Tower,* December 1, 1916, pp. 5997–98 Society Reprints.
38. *Awake!* March 22, 1993, p. 4 note.
39. *Zion's Watch Tower,* July 15, 1894, p. 1677 Society Reprints.
40. *Jehovah's Witnesses—Proclaimers of God's Kingdom,* p. 157.
41. *The Watchtower,* January 1, 1942, p. 5.
42. *1975 Yearbook of Jehovah's Witnesses,* p. 194.
43. *Jehovah's Witnesses—Proclaimers of God's Kingdom,* p. 76.
44. J. F. Rutherford, *Salvation* (Brooklyn, N.Y.: Watchtower Society, 1939).
45. *Jehovah's Witnesses—Proclaimers of God's Kingdom.*
46. *The New World* (Brooklyn, N.Y.: Watchtower Society, 1942), p. 104.
47. *Jehovah's Witnesses—Proclaimers of God's Kingdom,* p. 201.
48. M. James Penton, *Apocalypse Delayed: The Story of Jehovah's Witnesses* (Toronto: University of Toronto Press, 1985), p. 225.
49. *The Watchtower,* September 1, 1984, p. 20.
50. *The Watchtower,* March 1, 1987, p. 15.
51. Darek Barefoot, *Jehovah's Witnesses and the Hour of Darkness* (Grand Junction, Colo.: Grand Valley Press, 1992).
52. *The Watchtower,* May 1, 1989, p. 4.
53. *The Watch Tower,* November 1, 1917, p. 6159 Society Reprints.
54. *Golden Age,* February 4, 1931, p. 293.
55. *Awake!* March 8, 1960.
56. Jerry Bergman, *Jehovah's Witnesses and the Problem of Mental Illness* (Clayton, Calif.: Witness Inc., 1992).
57. *Awake!* August 22, 1975, p. 26.
58. *Awake!* March 8, 1960.
59. Ibid.
60. *The Watch Tower,* July 1, 1913, p. 200.
61. *Zion's Watch Tower,* July 15, 1902 Society Reprints.
62. *The Watch Tower,* March 15, 1913, p. 63 Society Reprints.
63. *Our Kingdom Ministry,* January 1993, p. 63.
64. *Our Kingdom Ministry,* September 1992, p. 4.
65. Ibid., p. 5.
66. *The Watchtower,* June 15, 1991, p. 31.
67. Ibid.

Appendix A

Ten Billion Pieces of Literature:
A Bibliography

Watchtower founder Charles T. Russell authored works totaling some fifty thousand printed pages, and nearly twenty million copies of his books and booklets had been sold by the time of his death. During Joseph F. Rutherford's presidency the Watch Tower Society produced twenty-four books, eighty-six booklets, and annual Yearbooks, as well as scores of tracts, besides periodical literature. Since 1942, under the presidencies of Nathan H. Knorr, Frederick W. Franz, and Milton G. Henschel, nearly all Jehovah's Witness literature has been published without a byline. The sect published its ten-billionth (10,000,000,000th) piece of literature at some point during the late 1980s. At the current rate of production the twenty-billionth piece will be printed around the year 2000.

All titles in the following bibliography are listed in chronological order. Most post-1970 items are available through local Jehovah's Witness congregations. Older material is out of print and obtainable only through antiquarian book dealers who specialize in Watchtower publications.

For more information, see David A. Reed, *Jehovah's Witness Literature: A Critical Guide to Watchtower Publications* (Grand Rapids, Mich.: Baker Book House, 1993).

CHARLES T. RUSSELL (1879–1916)

Periodicals:

Zion's Watch Tower and Herald of Christ's Presence, renamed in 1909 *The Watch Tower and Herald of Christ's Presence*.

Books:

Barbour, Nelson H., and Charles T. Russell. *Three Worlds, or Plan of Redemption*, 1877.

Songs of the Bride, 1879.

Paton, J. H. *Day Dawn*, 1881.

Russell, Charles T. *Millennial Dawn*, 1886–1904. *Millennial Dawn* is the original title of a series of six books by Pastor Russell: *The Divine Plan of the Ages* (volume 1, 1886*); The Time Is at Hand* (volume 2, 1889); *Thy Kingdom Come* (volume 3, 1891); *The Day of Vengeance* (later retitled *The Battle of Armageddon*) (volume 4, 1897); *The At-one-ment between God and Man* (volume 5, 1899); and *The New Creation* (volume 6, 1904). The series was renamed *Studies in the Scriptures* shortly after the turn of the century. (See *Studies in the Scriptures* and individual titles.) And in 1917, the year following Russell's death, the Watchtower Society under the new presidency of Joseph F. ("Judge") Rutherford published a controversial seventh volume titled *The Finished Mystery*. (*See* individual titles.)

———. *The Divine Plan of the Ages*, 1886 (originally titled *The Plan of the Ages*).

———. *The Time Is at Hand*, 1889.

Poems and Hymns of Millennial Dawn, 1890.

Russell, Charles T. *Thy Kingdom Come*, 1891.

Joseph B. Rotherham's New Testament (12th ed., rev.) 1896. Printing rights were obtained from British translator, Joseph B. Rotherham, to publish in the United States the twelfth edition, revised, of his New Testament.

Russell, Charles T. *The Day of Vengeance or The Battle of Armageddon*, 1897.

———. *The At-one-ment between God and Man*, 1899.

Zion's Glad Songs, 1900.

Holman Linear Bible, 1901.

Wilson, Benjamin. *The Emphatic Diaglott*, 1902. In 1902 the Watch Tower Society became copyright owner and sole publisher and distributor of the interlinear translation.

Russell, Charles T. *The New Creation,* 1904.
Souvenir. (Notes from) *Watch Tower Bible and Tract Society's Conventions,* 1905.
Hymns of the Millennial Dawn, 1905–1906. Dated and copyrighted in 1905, but not actually released until April 1906.
Seibert, Gertrude W. *Daily Heavenly Manna for the Household of Faith,* 1907.
Berean Bible, 1907.
Woodworth, Clayton J. *Bible Student's Manual,* 1909.
Poems of Dawn, 1912.
Russell, Charles T. *Scenario of the Photo-Drama of Creation,* 1914.
Pastor Russell's Sermons, 1917.

Booklets:

Russell, Charles T. *The Object and Manner of Our Lord's Return,* 1877.
———. *Food for Thinking Christians,* 1881.
———. *The Tabernacle and Its Teachings,* 1881.
———. *Tabernacle Shadows of the "Better Sacrifices,"* 1881.
———. *Outlines of Sermons,* 1882.
———. *The Wonderful Story,* 1891.
———. *The Divine Plan of the Ages for Human Salvation (An Epitomized Statement of the Divine Plan of the Ages),* 1892.
———, *"Thy Word Is Truth"—An Answer to Robert Ingersoll's Charges Against Christianity,* 1892.
———. *Zion's Watch Tower and Herald of Christ's Presence (Extra Edition)—A Conspiracy Exposed; Harvest Siftings,* 1894.
———. *What Say the Scriptures About Hell?* 1895.
———. *Outlines of the Divine Plan of the Ages,* 1896.
———. *What Say the Scriptures about Spiritualism (Spiritism)?* 1897.
———. *The Bible versus the Evolution Theory,* 1898.
———. *What Say the Scriptures about Our Lord's Return?* 1898.
———. *Tabernacle Shadows,* 1899.
Instructor's Guide and Berean Index, 1907.
Russell, Charles T. *The Sin-Offering and the Covenants,* 1909.
Berean Studies on The At-one-ment between God and Man, 1910.
Russell, Charles T. *Jewish Hopes,* 1910.
Berean Studies on The Divine Plan of The Ages, 1911.
Questions on "Tabernacle Studies," 1911.
Berean Studies on The Battle of Armageddon, 1912.
Berean Studies on The Time Is At Hand, 1912.

Berean Studies on Thy Kingdom Come, 1912.
Berean Studies on The New Creation, 1914.
Rutherford, Joseph F. *A Great Battle in the Ecclesiastical Heavens*, 1915.
An Index to the Towers From January 1st, 1908 to October 15, 1915, 1916.

J. F. RUTHERFORD (1917–1942)

Books:

Woodworth, Clayton J., and George H. Fisher. *The Finished Mystery*, purportedly the "posthumous work of Pastor Russell," 1917.
Rutherford, J. F. *The Harp of God*, 1921. Early editions are subtitled *Proof Conclusive that Millions Now Living Will Never Die.*
Van Amburgh, W. E. *The Way to Paradise*, 1924. The Watchtower Society's corporate secretary and treasurer from the days of Charles Taze Russell until 1947, the year of his own death.
Kingdom Hymns, 1924–1926. Dated 1924, but not copyrighted until 1925, and not actually released until 1926.
Rutherford, J. F. *Comfort for the Jews*, 1925.
———. *Deliverance*, 1926.
———. *Creation*, 1927.
Year Book, 1927.
Rutherford, J. F. *Government*, 1928.
———. *Reconciliation*, 1928.
Songs of Praise to Jehovah, 1928.
Rutherford, J. F. *Life*, 1929.
———. *Prophecy*, 1929.
———. *Light* (Book One), 1930.
———. *Light* (Book Two), 1930.
———. *Vindication* (Book One), 1931.
———. *Preservation*, 1932.
———. *Vindication* (Book Two), 1932.
———. *Vindication* (Book Three), 1932.
———. *Preparation*, 1933.
———. *Jehovah*, 1934.
———. *Riches*, 1936.
———. *Enemies*, 1937.
———. *Salvation*, 1939.
———. *Religion*, 1940.
———. *Children*, 1941.

Periodicals:

The Watch Tower and Herald of Christ's Presence, 1909; renamed *The Watch-tower and Herald of Christ's Presence* in 1931; *The Watchtower and Herald of Christ's Kingdom* on January 1, 1939; and *The Watchtower Announcing Jehovah's Kingdom* on March 1, 1939, the title and subtitle as of this writing.

The Golden Age, first published on October 1, 1919; renamed *Consolation* in 1937 (now *Awake!*).

Bulletin, first published in 1917; renamed *Director* in 1935 and *Informant* in 1936; later renamed *Kingdom Ministry* (1956), *Our Kingdom Service* (1976), and *Our Kingdom Ministry* (1982).

Booklets:

[Rutherford, Joseph F. *A Great Battle in the Ecclesiastical Heavens*, 1915.]

Berean Studies on The Finished Mystery, 1917.

Harvest Siftings (Parts I and II), 1917.

Rutherford, J. F. *The Revelation of Jesus Christ*, 1918.

Berean Studies on Tabernacle Shadows of the "Better Sacrifices," 1918.

Rutherford, J. F. *Can the Living Talk With the Dead? (Talking With the Dead?)*, 1920.

———. *Millions Now Living Will Never Die*, 1920.

———. *The Bible on Our Lord's Return*, 1922.

———. *World Distress—Why? The Remedy*, 1923.

———. *A Desirable Government*, 1924.

———. *Hell*, 1924.

———. *Comfort for the People*, 1925.

———. *Our Lord's Return*, 1925.

Year Book, 1925.

Rutherford, J. F. *The Standard for the People*, 1926.

———. *Freedom for the Peoples*, 1927.

———. *Questions on Deliverance*, 1927.

———. *Restoration*, 1927.

———. *Where Are the Dead?* 1927.

———. *The Last Days*, 1928.

———. *The Peoples Friend*, 1928.

———. *Prosperity Sure*, 1928.

———. *Judgment*, 1929.

———. *Oppression, When Will It End?* 1929.

Rutherford, J. F. *Crimes and Calamities. The Cause. The Remedy,* 1930.
———. *Prohibition and the League of Nations,* 1930.
———. *War or Peace, Which?* 1930.
———. *Heaven and Purgatory,* 1931.
———. *The Kingdom, the Hope of the World,* 1931.
———. *Cause of Death,* 1932.
———. *The Final War,* 1932.
———. *Good News,* 1932.
———. *Health and Life,* 1932.
———. *Hereafter,* 1932.
———. *Home and Happiness,* 1932.
———. *Keys of Heaven,* 1932.
———. *Liberty,* 1932.
———. *What Is Truth?* 1932.
———. *What You Need,* 1932.
———. *Where Are the Dead?* 1932.
———. *Who Is God?* 1932.
———. *The Crisis,* 1933.
———. *Dividing the People,* 1933.
———. *Escape to the Kingdom,* 1933.
———. *Intolerance,* 1933.
———. *Angels,* 1934.
———. *Beyond the Grave,* 1934.
———. *Favored People,* 1934.
———. *His Vengeance,* 1934.
———. *His Works,* 1934.
———. *Righteous Ruler,* 1934.
———. *Supremacy,* 1934.
———. *Truth—Shall It Be Suppressed?* 1934.
———. *Why Pray for Prosperity?* 1934.
———. *World Recovery,* 1934.
———. *Government—Hiding the Truth, Why?* 1935.
———. *Loyalty,* 1935.
———. *Universal War Near,* 1935.
———. *Who Shall Rule the World?* 1935.
———. *Choosing, Riches or Ruin?* 1936.
———. *Protection,* 1936.
———. *Armageddon,* 1937.
———. *Model Study No. 1,* 1937.
———. *Safety,* 1937.
———. *Uncovered,* 1937.

Rutherford, J. F. *Cure*, 1938.
———. *Face the Facts*, 1938.
———. *Warning*, 1938.
———. *Advice for Kingdom Publishers*, 1939.
———. *Government and Peace*, 1939.
———. *Liberty to Preach*, 1939.
———. *Model Study No. 2*, 1939.
———. *Neutrality*, 1939.
Order of Trial, 1939.
Rutherford, J. F. *Conspiracy Against Democracy*, 1940.
———. *End of Nazism*, 1940.
———. *Judge Rutherford Uncovers Fifth Column*, 1940.
———. *Refugees*, 1940.
———. *Satisfied*, 1940.
———. *Comfort All That Mourn*, 1941.
———. *God and the State*, 1941.
———. *Jehovah's Servants Defended*, 1941.
———. *Model Study No. 3*, 1941.
———. *Theocracy*, 1941.

NATHAN H. KNORR (1942–1977)

Books:

Bible, King James version, 1942.
The New World, 1942.
"The Truth Shall Make You Free," 1943.
Bible, American Standard Version, 1944.
"The Kingdom Is at Hand," 1944.
Kingdom Service Song Book, 1944.
Theocratic Aid to Kingdom Publishers, 1945.
"Equipped for Every Good Work," 1946.
"Let God Be True," 1946.
New World Translation of the Christian Greek Scriptures, 1950.
Songs to Jehovah's Praise, 1950.
"This Means Everlasting Life," 1950.
What Has Religion Done for Mankind? 1951.
"Let God Be True" (rev. ed.), 1952.
"Make Sure of All Things," 1953.
"New Heavens and a New Earth," 1953.

New World Translation of the Hebrew Scriptures, Vol. I, 1953.
New World Translation of the Hebrew Scriptures, Vol. II, 1955.
Qualified to Be Ministers, 1955.
You May Survive Armageddon Into God's New World, 1955.
Macmillan, A. H. *Faith on the March* (Englewood Cliffs, N.J.: Prentice-Hall, Inc.), 1957.
New World Translation of the Hebrew Scriptures, Vol. III, 1957.
Branch Office Procedure of the Watch Tower Bible and Tract Society of Pennsylvania, 1958.
From Paradise Lost to Paradise Regained, 1958.
New World Translation of the Hebrew Scriptures, Vol. IV, 1958.
"Your Will Be Done on Earth," 1958.
Jehovah's Witnesses in the Divine Purpose, 1959.
Kingdom Ministry School Course, 1960.
New World Translation of the Hebrew Scriptures, Vol. V, 1960.
"Let Your Name Be Sanctified," 1961.
New World Translation of the Holy Scriptures, 1961.
Watch Tower Publications Index (1930-1960), 1961.
"All Scripture Is Inspired of God and Beneficial," 1963.
"Babylon the Great Has Fallen," God's Kingdom Rules! 1963.
"Make Sure of All Things; Hold Fast to What Is Fine," 1965.
"Things in Which It Is Impossible for God to Lie," 1965.
Life Everlasting—In Freedom of the Sons of God, 1966.
"Singing and Accompanying Yourselves With Music in Your Hearts," 1966.
Did Man Get Here by Evolution or by Creation? 1967.
Qualified to be Ministers (revised), 1967.
"Your Word Is a Lamp to My Foot," 1967.
The Truth That Leads to Eternal Life, 1968.
Aid to Bible Understanding (A-Exodus), 1969.
Is the Bible Really the Word of God? 1969.
The Kingdom Interlinear Translation of the Greek Scriptures, 1969.
"Then Is Finished the Mystery of God," 1969.
New World Translation of the Holy Scriptures (revised), 1970.
Aid to Bible Understanding, (complete), 1971.
Listening to the Great Teacher, 1971.
"The Nations Shall Know That I Am Jehovah"—How? 1971.
New World Translation of the Holy Scriptures (revised), 1971.
Theocratic Ministry School Guidebook, 1971.
Byington, Steven T. *The Bible in Living English*, 1972.
Organization for Kingdom-Preaching and Disciple-Making, 1972.
Paradise Restored to Mankind—By Theocracy! 1972.

Comprehensive Concordance of the New World Translation of the Holy Scriptures, 1973.
God's Kingdom of a Thousand Years Has Approached, 1973.
True Peace and Security—From What Source? 1973.
God's "Eternal Purpose" Now Triumphing for Man's Good, 1974.
Is This Life All There Is? 1974.
1975 Yearbook of Jehovah's Witnesses, 1974.
Man's Salvation out of World Distress at Hand, 1975.
Good News—To Make You Happy, 1976.
Holy Spirit—The Force behind the Coming New Order, 1976.
Your Youth—Getting the Best out of It, 1976.
Life Does Have a Purpose, 1977.
Our Incoming World Government—God's Kingdom, 1977.
Shining as Illuminators in the World, 1977.

Periodicals:

The Watchtower Announcing Jehovah's Kingdom.
Consolation, renamed *Awake!* in 1946.
Informant, renamed *Kingdom Ministry* in 1956, *Our Kingdom Service* in 1976, and later *Our Kingdom Ministry* (1982).

Booklets:

Children Study Questions, 1942.
Hope, 1942.
Jehovah's Witnesses: Who Are They? What Is Their Work? 1942.
"The New World" Study Questions, 1942.
Organization Instructions, 1942.
Peace—Can It Last? 1942.
Course in Theocratic Ministry, 1943.
Fighting for Liberty on the Home Front, 1943.
Freedom in the New World, 1943.
Freedom of Worship, 1943.
"The Truth Shall Make You Free" Study Questions, 1943.
The Coming World Regeneration, 1944.
"The Kingdom Is at Hand" Study Questions, 1944.
"The Kingdom of God Is Nigh," 1944.
One World, One Government, 1944.
Religion Reaps the Whirlwind, 1944.
"The Commander to the Peoples," 1945.

"The Meek Inherit the Earth," 1945.
"Be Glad, Ye Nations," 1946.
"The Prince of Peace," 1946.
The Joy of All the People, 1947.
The Permanent Governor of All Nations, 1948.
The Watchtower Story, 1948.
Counsel on Theocratic Organization for Jehovah's Witnesses, 1949.
The Kingdom Hope of All Mankind, 1949.
Can You Live Forever in Happiness on Earth? 1950.
Defending and Legally Establishing the Good News, 1950.
Evolution versus the New World, 1950.
Will Religion Meet the World Crisis? 1951.
Dwelling Together in Unity, 1952.
Excerpts From Selective Service Regulations, 1952.
God's Way Is Love, 1952.
After Armageddon—God's New World, 1953.
Basis for Belief in a New World, 1953.
"Preach the Word," 1953.
Working Together in Unity, 1953.
Counsel to Watch Tower Missionaries, 1954.
"This Good News of the Kingdom," 1954.
Unassigned Territory in the United States, 1954.
Christendom or Christianity—Which One Is "the Light of the World"? 1955.
Preaching Together in Unity, 1955.
What Do the Scriptures Say about "Survival After Death"? 1955.
World Conquest Soon—By God's Kingdom, 1955.
Manual of Theocratic News Service Information, 1956.
Healing of the Nations Has Drawn Near, 1957.
God's Kingdom Rules—Is the World's End Near? 1958.
"Look! I Am Making All Things New," 1959.
Preaching and Teaching in Peace and Unity, 1960.
Security during "War of the Great Day of God the Almighty," 1960.
Blood, Medicine and the Law of God, 1961.
Sermon Outlines, 1961.
Watch Tower Publications Index (1961), 1961.
When All Nations Unite under God's Kingdom, 1961.
Take Courage—God's Kingdom Is at Hand! 1962.
"The Word"—Who Is He? According to John, 1962.
Living in Hope of a Righteous New World, 1963.
Report on "Everlasting Good News" Assembly of Jehovah's Witnesses, 1963.
When God Is King over All the Earth, 1963.

"Peace among Men of Good Will" or Armageddon—Which? 1964.
Questions on the Book "Babylon the Great Has Fallen!" God's Kingdom Rules! 1964.
"This Good News of the Kingdom" (revised), 1965.
World Government on the Shoulder of the Prince of Peace, 1965.
Jehovah's Witnesses, 1966.
What Has God's Kingdom Been Doing Since 1914? 1966.
Rescuing a Great Crowd of Mankind out of Armageddon, 1967.
Learn to Read And Write, 1967.
Man's Rule About to Give Way to God's Rule, 1968.
The Approaching Peace of a Thousand Years, 1969.
Questions on the Book "Then Is Finished the Mystery of God," 1969.
Study Questions for the Book Is the Bible Really the Word of God? 1969.
Saving the Human Race—In the Kingdom Way, 1970.
Convention Organization, 1971.
When All Nations Collide, Head On, with God, 1971.
Divine Rulership—The Only Hope of All Mankind, 1972.
Divine Victory—Its Meaning for Distressed Humanity, 1973.
Human Plans Failing as God's Purpose Succeeds, 1974.
A Secure Future—How You Can Find It, 1975.
Is There a God Who Cares? 1975.
One World, One Government, under God's Sovereignty, 1975.
There Is Much More to Life! 1975.
Bible Topics for Discussion, 1977.
Jehovah's Witnesses and the Question of Blood, 1977.
"Pay Attention to Yourselves and to All the Flock" (first booklet), 1977.

FREDERICK W. FRANZ (1977–1992)

Books:

Making Your Family Life Happy, 1978.
My Book of Bible Stories, 1978.
Choosing the Best Way of Life, 1979.
Commentary on the Letter of James, 1979.
Happiness—How to Find It, 1980.
"Let Your Kingdom Come," 1981.
New World Translation of the Holy Scriptures, 1981.
You Can Live Forever in Paradise on Earth, 1982.
Organized to Accomplish Our Ministry, 1983.

United in Worship of the Only True God, 1983.
New World Translation of the Holy Scriptures (revised), 1984.
New World Translation of the Holy Scriptures—With References, 1984.
Survival Into a New Earth, 1984.
Sing Praises to Jehovah, 1984.
The Kingdom Interlinear Translation of the Greek Scriptures (revised), 1985.
Life—How Did It Get Here? By Evolution or by Creation? 1985.
Reasoning From the Scriptures, 1985.
True Peace and Security—How Can You Find It? 1986.
Worldwide Security under the "Prince of Peace," 1986.
Yearbook (without daily texts), 1986.
Watch Tower Publications Index 1930–1985, 1986.
Insight on the Scriptures, 1988.
Revelation—Its Grand Climax at Hand! 1988.
The Bible—God's Word or Man's? 1989.
Questions Young People Ask; Answers That Work, 1989.
"All Scripture Is Inspired of God and Beneficial," 1990.
Mankind's Search for God, 1990.
The Greatest Man Who Ever Lived, 1991.

Periodicals:

Awake!
Our Kingdom Service, renamed *Our Kingdom Ministry* in 1982.
The Watchtower Announcing Jehovah's Kingdom.

Booklets:

Jehovah's Witnesses in the Twentieth Century, 1978.
Unseen Spirits—Do They Help Us? Or Do They Harm Us? 1978.
"Pay Attention to Yourselves and to All the Flock" (second booklet), 1979.
The Path of Divine Truth Leading to Liberation, 1980.
"Pay Attention to Yourselves and to All the Flock" (third booklet), 1981.
Dwelling Together in Unity (revised), 1982.
Enjoy Life on Earth Forever! 1982.
From Kurukshetra to Armageddon, 1983.
Good News for All Nations, 1983.
In Search of a Father, 1983.
School and Jehovah's Witnesses, 1983.
The Time for True Submission to God, 1983.
Centennial of the Watch Tower Bible and Tract Society of Pennsylvania, 1984.

The Divine Name That Will Endure Forever, 1984.
The Government That Will Bring Paradise, 1985.
Examining the Scriptures Daily, 1986.
Jehovah's Witnesses—Unitedly Doing God's Will Worldwide, 1986.
"Look! I Am Making All Things New," 1986.
Should You Believe in the Trinity? 1989.
How Can Blood Save Your Life? 1990.
Pay Attention to Yourselves and to All the Flock, 1991.

MILTON G. HENSCHEL (1992–PRESENT)

Books:

Jehovah's Witnesses—Proclaimers of God's Kingdom, 1993.
Knowledge That Leads to Everlasting Life, 1995.

Periodicals:

Awake!
Our Kingdom Ministry.
The Watchtower.

Booklets:

Jehovah's Witnesses and Education, 1995.

Appendix B

Chronology of Growth and Changes

1844   William Miller's predicted return of Christ fails to occur

1852   Charles T. Russell is born

1869   Russell joins Adventists

1874   Christ returns invisibly, according to N. H. Barbour and C. T. Russell

1876   Russell becomes assistant editor of Barbour's *Herald of the Morning*

1877   Barbour publishes *Three Worlds* with Russell's help

1878   The Rapture predicted by Barbour fails to occur. Russell later teaches that a resurrection of believers occurred invisibly.

1879   Russell resigns from *Herald of the Morning* editorial staff; begins publishing his own magazine titled *Zion's Watch Tower and Herald of Christ's Presence*

1881   The "high calling" to a heavenly hope closed, according to Russell

1881   Zion's Watch Tower Tract Society formed

1884   Zion's Watch Tower Tract Society incorporated in Pennsylvania

1885   300 colporteurs distribute the Society's literature

1886   Russell publishes *The Divine Plan of the Ages*

1889   Bible House built in Allegheny, Pennsylvania, as Watchtower headquarters

1909   Watchtower headquarters moved to Brooklyn, New York

1914   Christ returned invisibly, according to current teaching

1914   The world fails to end in October as predicted

1916   Charles T. Russell dies October 31

1917   Joseph F. Rutherford becomes second president of the Watch-tower Society; removes majority of board of directors

1918   Rutherford and associates sentenced to federal prison

1918   Dead anointed Witnesses raised to life invisibly, in current teaching

1919   Watchtower leaders released from federal prison

1919   *The Golden Age* magazine published

1920   Watchtower printing operations begin in Brooklyn

1920   *Millions Now Living Will Never Die* prophesies patriarchs will be resurrected in 1925

1920   Watchtower literature distributed by 8,402 volunteers

1924   Radio station WBBR begins broadcasts

1925   Resurrection of the patriarchs fails to occur as prophesied

1927   Society builds factory in Brooklyn, New York

1928   Sect rejects Christmas

1930   Beth-Sarim mansion built in San Diego

1931   Rutherford's Bible Students renamed Jehovah's Witnesses

1935   Rutherford declares "great crowd" an earthly class

1935   The heavenly calling closed, according to current teaching

1935   Sect announces Christ died on an upright stake, not a cross

1937   JWs begin playing portable phonographs door to door

1938   Democratic church government replaced by theocratic rule — all local congregation officials appointed by Brooklyn

1941   More than one hundred thousand JWs now preaching house to house

1942   Joseph F. Rutherford dies; Nathan H. Knorr becomes president

1943   Knorr sets up training programs for JWs and missionaries

1944   Sect bans blood transfusions

1950   *New World Translation* of New Testament published

1958   More than a quarter million fill Yankee Stadium and Polo Grounds for a convention

1963   More than one million JWs now preaching house to house

1967   Sect bans organ transplants

1968   The author begins studying with JWs

1968   *Watchtower* article "Why Are You Looking Forward to 1975?" predicts the world's end for that year

1969   The author is formally baptized a JW

1971   Governing Body expanded beyond board of directors

1974   More than two million JWs now preaching house to house
1975   The world fails to end in October as predicted
1977   Nathan H. Knorr dies; Frederick W. Franz becomes president
1980   President's nephew Raymond Franz and other moderates purged from Watchtower leadership
1980   Sect allows organ transplants once again
1982   The author is formally expelled from JWs
1985   More than three million JWs now preaching house to house
1990   More than four million JWs now preaching house to house
1992   Frederick W. Franz dies; Milton G. Henschel becomes president
1995   Sect drops prediction of the world's end within the lifetime of the generation that saw the events of 1914
1996   More than five million JWs now preaching house to house; meeting attendance exceeds thirteen million

Appendix C

Glossary of Organizational Names

Adventists. The broad Adventist movement and specific Adventist denominations developed from the following which Baptist lay preacher William Miller left behind after the failure of his predictions for 1844. C. T. Russell began associating with Adventists in 1869, and he and his followers remained Adventists until 1879, when he resigned as assistant editor of the Adventist magazine *Herald of the Morning*.

Bible Students. C. T. Russell's followers apparently took their name "Bible Students" from the *Bible Students' Tracts* he began producing in 1880, the year following publication of his first *Watch Tower* magazine. By 1931, when Judge Rutherford renamed his followers Jehovah's Witnesses, various independent groups of Russellites not adhering to the Watchtower Society were using the name Bible Students.

International Bible Students Association. This is the name of the legal corporation of Jehovah's Witnesses in Britain, which C. T. Russell set up in 1914 to own property and transact business there. Prior to that, in *The Watch Tower* of April 1, 1910, Russell had told his followers worldwide to use this name when advertising their public meetings.

Jehovah's Witnesses (also, Jehovah's witnesses). Watchtower followers took this name for themselves in 1931 by adopting a resolution to that effect. The purpose was to distinguish them from the independent Bible Students who had broken from the Watchtower organization.

People's Pulpit Association. C. T. Russell formed this legal corporation in 1909 to purchase property and transact business in New York State. In 1939 it was renamed Watchtower Bible and Tract Society, Inc., and Watchtower Bible and Tract Society of New York, Inc., in 1956.

Tower Publishing Company. C. T. Russell owned this private firm which he used to produce the first four volumes of *Studies in the Scriptures* and to publish his *Watch Tower* magazine from 1887 to 1898. In that year he donated the company's real estate and other assets to the Watch Tower Bible and Tract Society.

Watch Tower Bible and Tract Society of Pennsylvania. This organization was set up by C. T. Russell as Zion's Watch Tower Tract Society on February 16, 1881, and then legally incorporated under that name in 1884. Its name was changed to Watch Tower Bible and Tract Society in 1896, and to the present form in 1955. It is the parent corporation for the various legal entities established to own property in other jurisdictions.

Watchtower Bible and Tract Society of New York, Inc. This is the present name of the sect's branch organization directing its operations in the United States. Originally formed in 1909 as the People's Pulpit Association, it functions as an arm of the Pennsylvania corporation.

Watch Tower Society or *Watchtower Society.* These terms are commonly used to denote the JW leadership organization as a whole, without distinguishing the various corporate legal entities with their overlapping boards of directors.

Index